FREEDOM LIES ACROSS THE RIVER

Manumission, the Macedonia Church, and the Development
of the Underground Railroad,
Lawrence County, Ohio.

CARRIE ELDRIDGE

ISBN: 9781928979432

Chesapeake, OH 45619

eldridge1@zoomnet.net

Contents

Illustrations

Abbreviations and Locations

Abbreviations

a = acres
B = Black – m =Mulatto
b = born
bur. = buried
cem. = cemetery
Co. = county
'37' = Twyman manumission
d = died
m = married
s/ = son of – dau/ = daughter of
rd. = road
wh = white
twp. = township

CW = Civil War
OH = Ohio (state)
PA = Pennsylvania
TN = Tennessee
VA = Virginia
US = United States highway
Rev. = Reverend
UGRR = underground railroad
S = south   - E = East
N = north   - W = West
SE/SW – NE/NW etc.
Bryant/Briant/Bryan = use Bryant
Craddock/Cradic/Cradwick/Crandolph
Rosanna/Roseanna/Rosannah/Rose = use Rosanna

Locations

Burlington, Ohio
Gallipolis, Ohio
Ironton, Ohio
Poke Patch, Ohio
Proctorville, Ohio
Quakers Bottom, Ohio
Unionville/Russell's Place/Getaway

Kanawha County, VA/WV
Mason Co. VA/WV
Cabell Co. VA/WV
Washington County, OH
Gallia County, OH
Lawrence Co. OH
Adams Co./Scioto Co. OH

Dedication

This is the story of Lawrence County, Ohio, before the Civil War. It was a time between isolated Indian attacks, struggling frontier existence, and the beginnings of the massive iron ore industry that began, developed, and flourished in the region.

It is also the story of the beginnings of Black freedom in the Northwest Territory and the struggling support system which developed to aid fleeing runaways who searched for freedom: a system that would become known as the Underground Railroad - UGRR.

Finally, it is the story of a dedicated church and a community that was willing to jeopardize safety to ensure other people would have a chance for freedom.

This book is dedicated to the founders and descendants of the Macedonia Church congregation of Burlington, Ohio, and to their total commitment to the Antislavery Baptist Movement of the early Nineteenth Century.

Carrie Eldridge

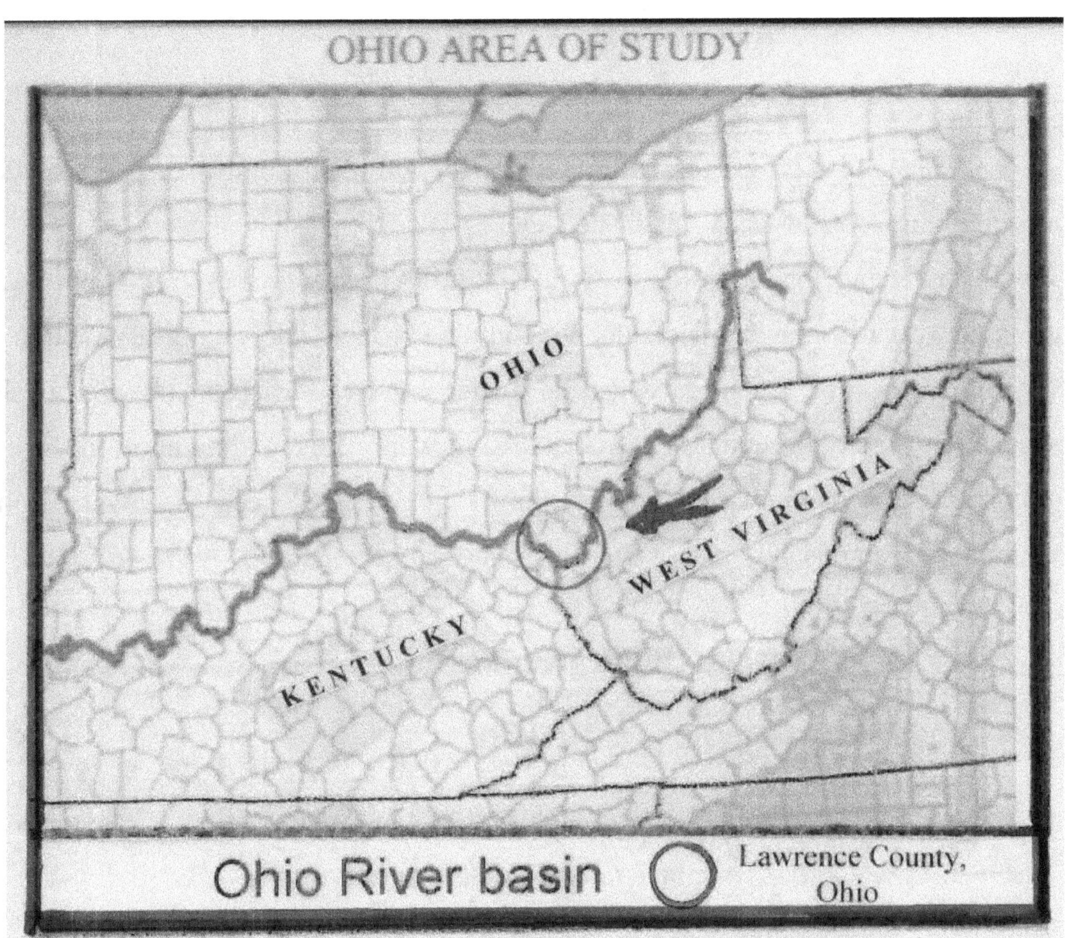

Figure 1 – Ohio Area of Study

Lawrence County, Ohio, is the southernmost county in Ohio. It is located where southern flowing Ohio River makes a sharp turn due west. Part of Virginia in 1790, today, it is the area where the states of West Virginia, Ohio, and Kentucky join the Ohio River.

The county's principal stream (Symmes Creek) is also the most southern stream in Ohio. It is crooked with the many meanders of a mature river which does not offer an easy path for anyone seeking freedom. Runaways were more likely to follow the ridges that headed northwest which ran parallel to the creek.

Manumission

To free by legal means as per a deed or will,

or by removing the slave to a free state.

1. Deeds of manumission were usually used to free a limited number of people, often only one, claiming good service or advanced age.
2. A will conferring manumission - often named all slaves to be freed. It protected the deceased owner from public ridicule, but could be broken unless carefully written.
3. 'Freeing by location' occurred when the owner moved to a free state with his slaves or purchased property to send slaves to that area to work. This method allowed the owner to ignore a state's manumission and freedom requirements, freed the owner from bond requirements, and usually placed the slaves beyond persecution.

The Underground Railroad

UGRR

A secret, hidden group of people who risked their lives

to give assistance to anyone fleeing from slavery.

1. Only limited information exists because the nature of the work required secrecy, protected even at death.
2. Wilburt Siebert's study of the UGRR took place forty years after the period of UGRR activity. The study was mostly volunteer information taken only from selected areas and acquired from student questionnaires. (Students were threatened for asking questions.)

This study will prove the existence of a Black operated UGRR with:

1. Location of hidden trails
2. Knowledge kept and Opportunity provided by local ministers.
3. Personnel and Planning
4. Commitment from an entire community.

Figure 2 – Genealogy of Lawrence County, Ohio

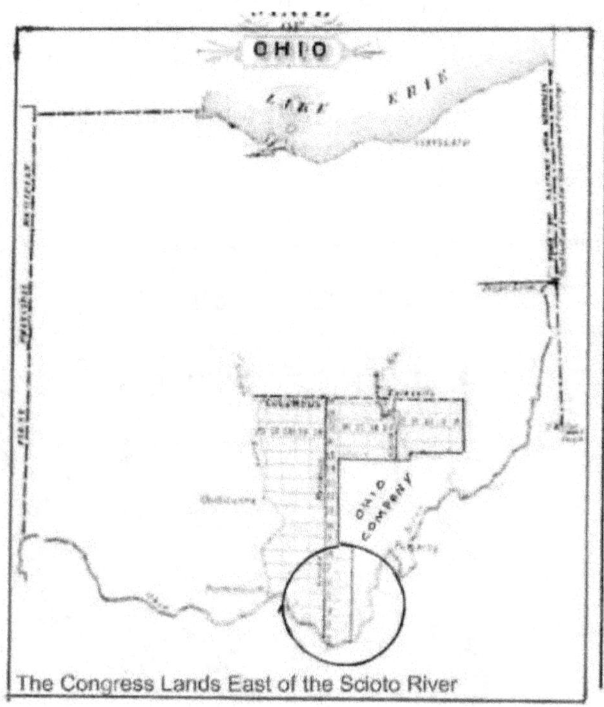

Ohio 1803 Map when Ohio was admitted to the Union
Base Map " OHIO LANDS – A Short History"
Carrie Eldridge 2021

Political areas were created from larger units, and it is useful for you to know where records may be found. Lawrence County was a third-generation division created from two major regions. First, Washington County was created in 1788 on the east side of the Northwest Territory. Second, Adams County was organized in 1797 in the southern section of the territory. Gallia County was created from both in 1803. Lawrence was created from Gallia in 1816-7.

(See *Ohio Lands* for more details.)

Figure 3 – Gallia County 1800

Figure 4 - Gallia County/Lawrence County 1788-1817

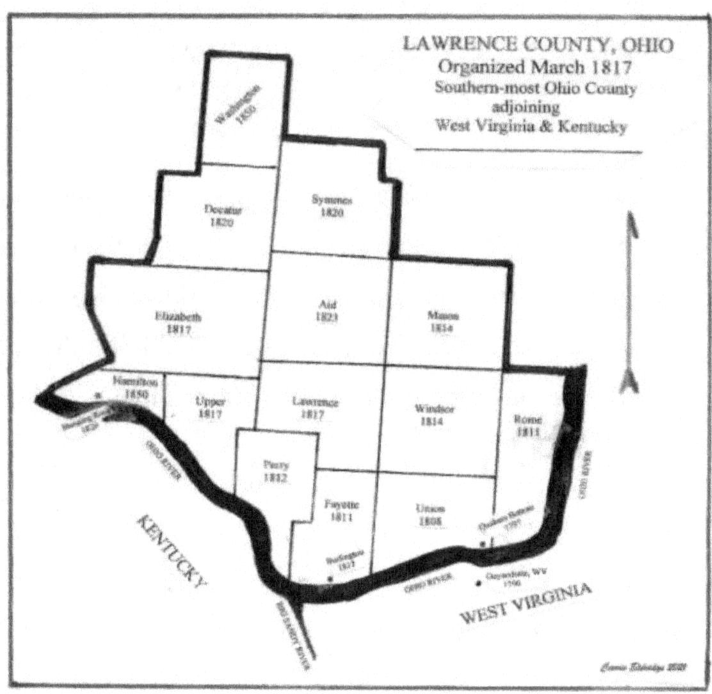

Figure 5 - Lawrence County 1817

Figure 6

This church is considered the oldest Black Baptist Church in the Northwest Territory and the first Black Baptist Church west of the Appalachians. Founding dates between 1809 and 1813, when members met in their homes. This building dates from 1849. From this church, other churches were created across a three-state area. This fellowship developed a community to aid others who were fleeing slavery and oppression with the true meaning of 'love thy neighbor.'

Ohio Black Codes of 1804 (abstract – Library of Congress)

Section 1. No Black or mulatto person shall be permitted to reside in the state unless he or she can produce a certificate from a court within the United States of his or her actual freedom with clerk's seal attached.

Section 2. By the fifth day of June 1804, every Black or mulatto person shall enter his or her name and the names of their children at the clerk's office where they reside with evidence of their freedom. Every entry shall be accompanied by a 12 1/2 cent fee.

Section 3. No person is permitted to hire or employ any Black or mulatto without a certificate under pain of fee from $10 to $50 at the court's discretion and for each offense. One-half of the fee for the informer and one-half for the state.

Section 4. Any person who shall harbor any Black or mulatto, the property of any person whatever, or who hinders the rightful owner retaking his possessions shall upon conviction be fined $10 to $50 per person. The same use of fine as above.

Section 5. Any Black or mulatto must record documents required in Section 1 within two years.

Section 6. Any person claiming property (Black or mulatto) may apply to any judge or justice of the peace with proof of satisfactory claim. The court may order said person arrested by the sheriff and delivered to the owner of said property. The sheriff is allowed compensation for similar services.

Section 7. Any person trying to remove any person from the state contrary to the provisions of this act, upon conviction, is subject to a fine of $1,000.

Most of the Black Registration Books from this period of Ohio's history have been destroyed. The Polley Case in Lawrence County, which concerned abducted children, cited Section 7, but that case was not completed until 2018, many years after the event.

Fugitive Slaves Laws of 1793 and 1850

The wording of the two fugitive slave laws was similar. The main differences were between state and federal enforcement and financial fines.

The Fugitive Slave Law of 1850 passed in September of 1850.

The Law gave the Federal Government the right to track down and apprehend all fugitive slaves.

1. A fine of $1,000 was imposed against any official who did not arrest the alleged runaway.
2. Officials were required to arrest any suspect on 'only' a sworn statement of ownership.
3. Runaways were denied a jury trial.
4. Runaways were not allowed to testify on their own behalf.
5. Anyone providing food or shelter was subject to a $1,000 fine and a 6-month prison term.
6. Created federal commissioners to pursue and return.
7. Empowered commissioners the right to issue warrants and depose witnesses.
8. Allowed federal agents to arrest and imprison within any state or territory.
9. Commissioners received $10 per slave returned, $5 for each set free. (80% were returned)
10. Federal agents could deputize and force citizens to aid in pursuit and arrest.

Northerners and abolitionists opposed: 1) harsh penalties, 2) impinged personal freedom, 3) circumvented state laws, and 4) increased federal authority. In reality, it created sympathy for slaves – hatred for owners.

Introduction

FREEDOM! Many stories were whispered in the dark of night about crossing a great river called the 'River Jordan' to a land of freedom. (Ohio River reference.)

Could the stories really be true?

At the beginning of the Nineteenth Century, the new American nation began to expand westward rapidly. Not only did the pioneers look for new lands, but they sought freedom from fear and bondage, whether it was physical, mental, or political. The "Ohio Country" attracted people from every part of the new nation. These individuals brought ideas and concepts that created a new type of American in the "Northwest Territory." The American Revolution had instilled an idea in the mind of every American…… a man had the "right" to be free.

The westward trek carried that idea like a flag. All men could become free by going west. This life without slavery was a new idea in the world, but most Americans wanted it to include everyone in the new United States of America. Thus, when America expanded north of the Ohio River into the "Northwest Territory," documents included laws for inexpensive land, free education, religious freedom, and abolishment of any type of slavery within the territory.

How It Began in Lawrence County

There must be a group of people willing to take risks before any task can be undertaken.

Between 1790 and 1810, slaves crossed the Ohio River with their masters. These slave owners freed them simply by crossing the river. Some settled in Gallia County of southeast Ohio, where Lawrence County would be created. The first recorded information about Blacks in the area was found in the Gallia County Tax information. In 1811, Henry and Washington Murphy were taxed for their horses and cattle in Union Township (the southern part of Gallia County.) Both Henry and Washington also appeared in the Court Records (along with Washington's wife Polly) involved in various lawsuits. Later records indicate that Washington was from South Carolina and that Henry was probably his brother. There are no records that indicate the men were slaves; instead, they were Black men of property living within the area, which became Lawrence County.

Another Black person of interest was Rosanna Bryant. Apparently, she had been a slave, but her former owner freed her by location (when he moved them across the Ohio River) and registered a piece of property in her name. Few women owned property in America's early history, so Rosanna's sale of one-half of Section 33 Township 2 Range 17 in Lawrence County in 1818 may have been one of the first deeds recorded in Ohio by a Black woman.

Although these people had probably known slavery, they also realized their former master had given them the opportunity to make a difference. 'Someone' met their surety, paid their bonds, and in the case of Rosanna, deeded a quarter section of land to her. The 1820 census enumerated only twenty-three Black people in Lawrence County, but from that small group, a community began, and with it, a church and an idea. These people were determined to do everything in their power to assist anyone trying to escape the institution of slavery.

First, people met in their homes, then they joined together in a religious community and founded the Macedonia Church in the hills overlooking the Ohio River by 1813. Other small groups formed, and by 1819 the first association of Black churches was organized. Next, the members looked for ways to assist freedom seekers. Rosanna may have sold one-half of her property so her family could purchase other property or supply money for better jobs where they could gather information. Finally, the church members created a system of communication to share their knowledge, locate runaways and provide help in escape. As the church membership grew with additional manumitted families, the young people and the ministers of the Macedonia Church developed a system of escape. An underground railroad – UGRR – was created and run by the local Black community connecting west and northwest across Ohio to many sites, including Cass County, Michigan, and Canada.

Figure 7 – Northwest Territory 1787 – Land north of the Ohio River

Chapter 1: Freedom Lies Across the River

The Northwest Territory
and
The Northwest Ordinances

The Northwest Territory was all the land north and west of the Ohio River to the Mississippi River. The Northwest Ordinance was a series of ordinances (or laws) issued over several years to settle colonial land claims released to the Federal Government. At one time, several colonies claimed part of the region, but most was claimed and controlled by Virginia as part of her original grant from the King of England. Since some original colonies had no western claims, a compromise was reached where western colonial claims were released to the Federal Government. The government expected to sell these western lands to pay soldiers and to reduce the debt from the Revolutionary War.

In 1785, the first ordinance determined how the territory would be surveyed, while another ordinance in 1787 declared there would be no slavery in territory that was the land north and west of the Ohio River. Known as the "OHIO COUNTRY", tentative settlements were made in 1788, but the rush to settle the "Ohio Country" did not begin until after 1795, when the Treaty of Greenville forced various Indian tribes to relinquish all claims to most of the area soon to be the state of Ohio.

New lands, new ideas, and new hopes caused many Americans to head west after the Revolution. These pioneers included slave masters and slaves as well as free Blacks looking for a new life. Land in eastern America was not as productive as it had been. War ravages, poor farming methods, and increasing families pushed eastern landowners and immigrants to look for better, cheaper lands. The "Ohio Country" was named the new Promised Land.

Although slavery was an accepted institution at the beginning of the Nineteenth Century, many Americans were opposed to the idea, including some slave owners. These people often inherited slaves they did not want, or they discovered the increasing number of slaves was beyond their use or ability to provide care. These individuals set about to manumit (free) a few or all their "property" even though laws existed to discourage freeing slaves.

Virginia held extensive land during America's Colonial Period, but she released her claims beyond the Ohio River to the Federal Government. Additionally, western Virginia was not plantation land, and although Virginia bordered the Ohio River, few plantations were developed along its shores. Virginias who settled on the southern side of the Ohio River were some of the earliest people to migrate across the Ohio River into the Northwest Territory. These settlers were looking for land to raise their families. They cleared the land to claim small farms in the wooded hills that bordered the river. At the same time, former soldiers from New England raised money with plans to create towns and get rich selling land. Neither group was interested in slavery, but eastern politics would change that attitude. The Ordinance of 1788 guaranteed freedom from slavery in the region north and west of the Ohio River. At the same time Congress soon passed the Fugitive Slave Law, which created many problems for all Black citizens.

Chapter 2: The Ohio River and Its Valley

The Ohio River was a major highway for the Indian tribes and, once discovered, white settlers rapidly made it America's first super-highway. Rivers that flowed into the Ohio River drained almost the entire early American frontier, and all those rivers led the pioneer west. Americans were introduced to the Ohio River during the French and Indian War around 1750. The major powers in North America (England and France) decided only one country would control the continent. The most important location on the frontier was the junction of the Ohio River (now Pittsburgh, PA.), where the Allegheny River from the north joined the Monongalia River flowing from the South. The Ohio River flowed from western Pennsylvania, along the border of Virginia and Kentucky, and joined the Mississippi River six hundred miles to the west.

Both the French and Indian War and then the Revolutionary War introduced many frontiersmen to the wonders of the Ohio Valley and the fertile lands across the Ohio. Between 1750 and 1795, numerous settlers entered the valley only to be repulsed or killed by the Indians who ruled the region. Slowly, America's western migration pushed the Indians west across the Appalachian Mountains and northwest across the Ohio River.

During the American Revolution, settlers pushed across Kentucky to the Ohio River, while others left Pittsburgh and floated down Ohio to settle in the northern part of the Kentucky region. Stories of the level fertile lands to the north but controlled by the Indians were almost more than the farming pioneer could stand. The Battle of Fallen Timbers in western Ohio and the Treaty of Greenville defeated the Indian tribes and forced them to leave Ohio lands. Once the Treaty of Greenville was signed in 1795, it seemed that the entire western movement changed directions. Once headed to the Carolinas, most pioneers soon trekked toward the Ohio River.

The pioneer had to travel by foot or horse for a long distance to reach the Ohio River from any settlement in eastern America. The river began at Pittsburgh in western Pennsylvania. Once there, the pioneer had to build his own raft and float down the turbulent river as it raged in flood or endangered the raft in shallow rapids where Indians still hid in the bushes.

Virginia soon opened its James River and Kanawha Turnpike which became the major wagon road across western Virginia. Also known as the Virginia State Road, it connected Tidewater Virginia on the Atlantic Ocean to her holdings along the Ohio River. That road, which later became US 60, was projected to reach the Ohio River near Guyandotte (an Ohio River port) in 1792. The trail was expanded to Lexington and Louisville, Kentucky. It was a rugged trail which reached the river, but required several decades before it could be called a 'wagon road'. Some travelers followed US 460 across southwestern Virginia and eastern Kentucky to the Lexington area, then turned north to the Ohio River, where Virginia and Kentucky met. (All the early frontier trails were Indian trails.)

Carolina settlers followed the old Indian routes northwest across southern Virginia, which became US 52 and US 23. Both these routes also reached the Ohio River near the James River Turnpike, at the mouth of the Big Sandy River, where West Virginia, Kentucky, and Ohio now meet. Crossing the Ohio River was not a major problem for many streams flowing into the Ohio built sand bars that extended far across Ohio. Other river locations were shallow enough to ford, and most of Ohio River averaged three to five feet deep at the summer pool. (low water in summer) Pioneers raced for the Ohio Territory, and in doing so, they bypassed much of western Virginia and eastern Kentucky in their need to settle the lands north of the Ohio River.

The first state in the Northwest Territory was Ohio, and in 1803 it became the sixteenth state of the Union. Today, it seems strange that the land along the banks of the Ohio River was not settled quickly. Remember, it was a primeval forest with trees fifteen feet across; the rivers and streams were subject to frequent flood water besides being marshy and packed with driftwood and brush. All the land had to be cleared. Stream bottoms were ignored unless a small settlement was built as a riverboat landing near one of the streams flowing into Ohio River.

The Ohio River was bordered on each side by a high ridge. The land on both sides of the river continued the 'ridge and valley region' of western Virginia. The early pioneers moved twenty-five or fifty miles beyond the river, where the hills were lower and the valleys wider. Central Ohio's 'level' glaciated lands were not near the Ohio River.

Although the tri-state area where this story takes place was known to Long Hunters (early frontiersmen who spent months on a hunt) about the time of the American Revolution, the region was slow to attract settlers. Even after the Indians were defeated, the stream valleys of the region remained important Indian trails through the eastern mountains. Gallia County, Ohio, was created in 1803, but Cabell County, Virginia (south across the Ohio River) was not formed until 1809. Greenup County, Kentucky, was laid out in 1810, and finally, Lawrence County, Ohio, was separated from Gallia County, Ohio, in 1817. The largest communities in any of these counties were the county seats with a few hundred people. The settlers wanted farms, not towns.

Primitive trails and roads lead away from the river. Usually connecting the various county seats, these trails allowed the settlers to send their farm produce to the Ohio River, where it was rafted down the river to faraway ports. The tri-state region where Ohio met (West) Virginia and Kentucky was isolated and far away from both eastern settlement and the growing state of Ohio, but three major trails reached the area from the slave states to the east and south.

Virginia completed the James River and Kanawha Turnpike, which connected Richmond to the Ohio River by 1790 (later US 60). The old Indian trails, (US 52 and US 23), also reached the Ohio River across from Ohio's most southern county, Lawrence. Being part of the Northwest Territory meant Lawrence County was free of slavery, but it was adjacent to two slave holding areas, less than one mile away across the Ohio River. Lawrence County was accessible by known trails. It was only natural that slave masters would first consider sending manumitted slaves to the nearest free territory.

By 1800 Blacks who wanted to be free and slave owners who wanted to set their servants free began to arrive in the Ohio Territory. The land was forest-covered, and the settlements were far apart, but all Black persons were legally free. They could register their freedom papers to prove to the local court they had been manumitted. "No papers" meant no work, possible capture by slave hunters and a dreaded return to slavery.

This book is a study of several groups of manumitted Blacks who settled in Lawrence County in the southeast corner of Ohio. These people decided they had to help to escape slaves to make their way to freedom. They ignored the dangers to themselves and created a secret route, "an underground railroad" run by Blacks. It started at the Ohio River and ran northwest through parts of Ohio, Indiana, Michigan, and finally to Canada, where fugitive slaves were safe.

In recent years, several writers have tried to show the Underground Railroad (UGRR) existed across the South, but that was not true. Most slaves who made it to the Ohio River arrived without help and expected nothing. To be caught was severe punishment for all involved. North of the river were Quakers, abolitionists, and free and manumitted Blacks were all willing to help a runaway, but there was limited help for unknown people moving in secret.

The information in this book shows how a core community was built on a foundation of several groups of free persons and slaves manumitted to southeast Ohio. These groups founded a church and created organized assistance to help any runaways who reached their area. They risked their lives and their freedom to help others along trails leading north beyond the reaches of the Fugitive Slave Act. Please draw your own conclusions from the many pieces of information included in the appendixes.

Figure 8a – Hills Along the Mid – Ohio River

Figure 8b Burlington Location

Macedonia Road is the white arrow of settlement north of the highway and Sam's complex

(white area right side).

Chapter 3: Virginia's Claims

Before the Revolutionary War, Virginia claimed the region north of the Ohio River that would become the Northwest Territory. She sent military expeditions into the area to control Indian problems, and some of the people in the armies were manservants and slaves. After the war, some of these attendants were given freedom for service, but most continued to serve in slavery. One thing all men learned during the war – the way west was not as far as they thought.

Virginia recognized the importance of the Ohio River Valley very early and, by 1790, had surveyed and established the James River and Kanawha Turnpike connecting Richmond to the Ohio River and into central Kentucky. After the Treaty of Greenville in 1795 forced most of the Indian tribes out of the Ohio region, there was a mass migration to new lands called the "Ohio Country." Pioneers, immigrants, speculators, landowners, and masters with slaves and free men headed west across imposing mountains and spectacular hills in search of wonderful farmlands that would make everyone rich. Instead, they found an extension of the largest hardwood forest in the world. A forest that had to be cleared before anyone made a profit. The lands along the Ohio River were a continuation of the Appalachian Plateau with rugged hills and deep valleys. Most land claims were small operations which just one family had hacked out of the forest.

Eventually, a few large plantation-type farms were carved from the wilderness in both the Kanawha and Ohio river valleys, but there was little need for slave labor without the cotton and tobacco crops of the east. (By 1840, Cabell County, Virginia had only two farms with more than twenty slaves.) "Everyone" flocked west after the 1795 treaty moved the Indians, but they wanted small farms, and in less than ten years Ohio had become a state and was making a profit from agriculture.

Much of Ohio's settlement passed through Virginia, which had several hundred miles of the Ohio River as her western boundary. The rush to Ohio was so fast that western Virginia was passed by as settlers claimed and purchased Ohio lands. The land along the Ohio River was boggy, easily flooded with massive trash piles of timber. It was unfit for farming for the first twenty years of the century. Settlers already living on the Virginia shores of the Ohio River were some of the first pioneers to cross into Ohio, and many residents of Virginia counties had relatives living on both sides of the Ohio River.

One group of settlers who headed for the Ohio River Valley was the slaveholders looking for more land, although some wished to manumit their slaves. One of the problems Virginia slave owners faced was the necessity to inform the county court before they manumitted any slaves. Some slave owners adopted a new method for freeing their people; they took them west. Many people on the frontier moved from one location to another until local courts lost them, then they crossed the Ohio River. This, 'escaping from the law', applied to the common taxpayer, a slave owner, a debtor, or a criminal.

By 1790, it was accepted practice to lease slaves for certain work projects. One of these projects was the salt industry in the Kanawha Valley of western Virginia. Some owners leased their slaves, collected the slaves' wages, and left them to work or die. Other masters took their slaves to the western lands with the same supposed idea, but with the purpose of removing them from the home county's jurisdiction and restrictions. These masters continued west until they crossed the Ohio River, thus 'manumitting their slaves by location.' By freeing them by location (moving across the Ohio River), the owner avoided many Virginia expenses required for manumission. Once on Ohio soil, the owner could meet the Ohio laws by paying bonds or assisting his former slaves in getting work permits or even land in their own names, but then his responsibility ended.

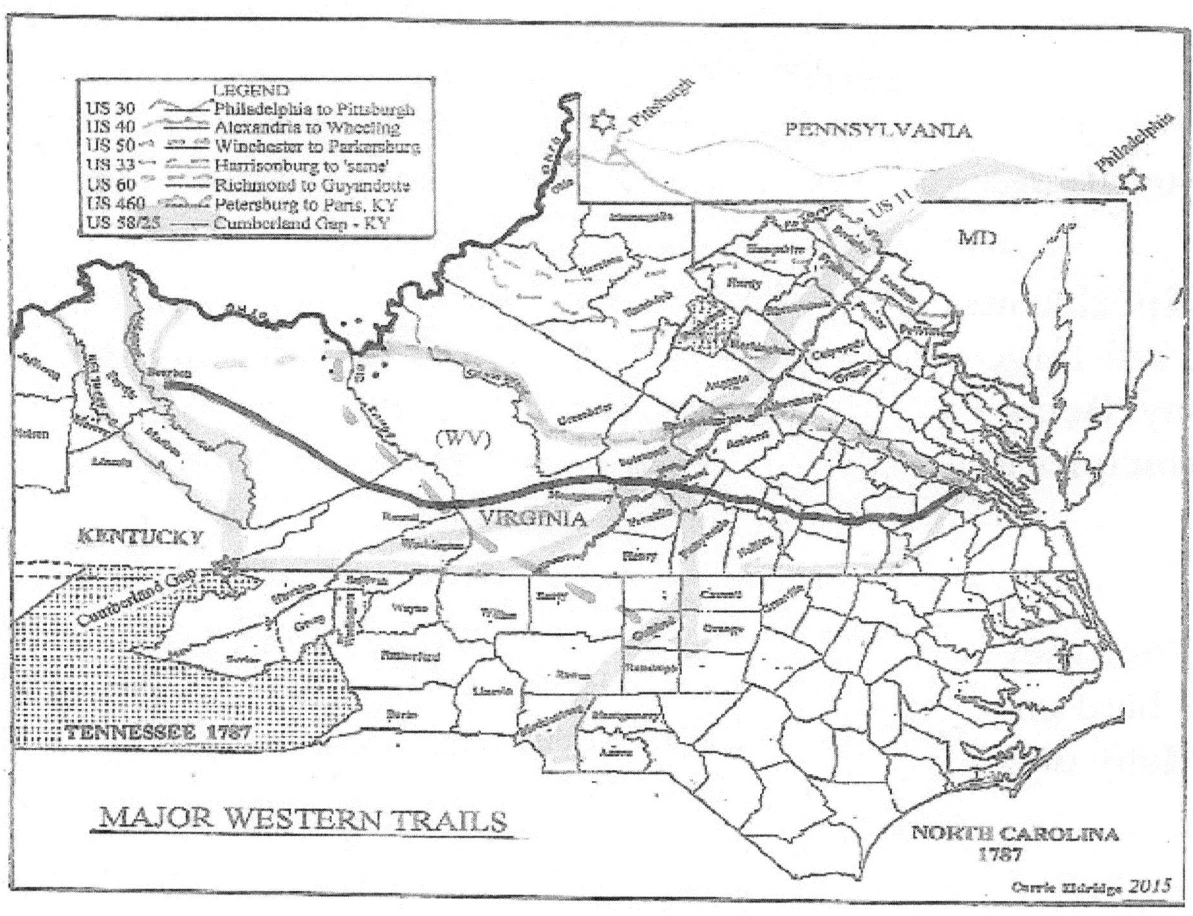

The American Frontier had several major trails and there were junctions where trails crossed. The trails were primitive, following along streams and across mountains by buffalo paths, but all of them lead west or southwest. After the settlers crossed the Blue Ridge between 1820 and 1850, the major trail lead southwest down the Valley of Virginia into North Carolina and then Kentucky. As settlers claimed the lands, the trails moved westward searching for new territory. About 1790, The James River and Kanawha Turnpike from the Atlantic shore to the Ohio River became the favored route. That trail crossed the Great Wagon Road and further south, the trail that became the Kentucky State Road. Settlers stopped wherever they were in 1795 and turned to the Ohio Valley which was suddenly free of Indians.

All these trails lead through rugged mountains and hills and were far from the great plantations of the Eastern Seaboard, but once the Northwest Ordinance guaranteed freedom from slavery many free black and slaves began to make their way west. There were semi-hidden tracks through the forest known only to animals and Indians which snaked along the north flowing rivers of southwest Virginia and Kentucky. The few settlers in the area ignored most of those who passed the lonely homesteads searching for the Ohio River. Lawrence County, Ohio lay across the Ohio at the mouth of both the Guyandotte River of Virginia and the Big Sandy River of Kentucky. It meant freedom.

Chapter 4: Lawrence County, Ohio

Note: Cabell County, Virginia, became Cabell County, West Virginia in 1863.

Lawrence County has several unique features. Its eastern and southern boundaries are the Ohio River, but it does not own the river. It is also Ohio's most southern county, almost fifty miles south of Cincinnati on the western corner of the state. Created in 1817, the county lies across the Ohio River from Cabell County, West Virginia, on the east, and Boyd County, Kentucky, on the south. Today, still a rural area, it has only one city with more than 20,000 people, while the whole county had a population of only 61,781 in 2020.

In 1820, the county had a population of 3,499, and its county seat, Burlington, was located on the eastern side of the county across the Ohio River from Cabell County, Virginia, and near the river port of Guyandotte. The Lawrence County seat was moved downriver to Ironton in 1852 after the iron ore industry developed in that area. Ironton was on the southern side of the county across the Ohio River from Ashland, Kentucky. (Pogue's Landing for many years.)

From 1817 to 1852, Burlington was a river port as well as the county seat of Lawrence County. The economy was mostly agriculture with small farms or orchards, and the main highway was the Ohio River. Each community had a riverboat landing, but roads to connect the villages were mere horse paths. An old road engineer of the Nineteenth Century wrote that no farmer wanted a road over good land, and most insisted that the roads go up and down the many hills at 40% grades. (Reminiscences of Road Building – Ironton Register 1901.)

One road of importance was named the Old Jackson Road. Surveyed in June of 1817, it was established in July of the same year and connected the county seats of Lawrence County (Burlington) and Jackson County (Jackson). (Lawrence County Common Pleas, Vol. 1 – 1817-1825) This trail allowed the pioneers to disembark their rafts at Burlington and trek north to the better lands of Jackson County. At the same time, the Old Road allowed the farmers from Jackson County and the interior area of Lawrence to have an outlet to the Ohio River. They could load their farm products onto rafts or riverboats and send them to large cities such as Cincinnati and Louisville were ready markets paid higher prices.

In its heyday, the Old Jackson Road left the Ohio River and ran out Macedonia Road and past the Macedonia Church on the hill. This was probably an early route for escaped slaves. The area was isolated, and the road continued north to the free Black community called Poke Patch.

A strange thing happened to Old Jackson Road. After the county seat moved from Burlington to Ironton in 1852, it was almost forgotten. A new road was laid out from Ironton to Jackson that connected all the Iron Furnaces along the Iron Railroad. This eventually became Ohio Route 93, the region's main highway. The Old Jackson Road disappeared into the past.

Today, most of the old road can still be located by township roads and private drives, but it can no longer be followed from the Ohio River to Poke Patch. There are two sections through private lands now closed, while the Wayne National Forest has created a horse trail along a section at the head of Aaron's Creek in Aid and Decatur townships. Although these three sections are each just about a mile long, the detours around the closed areas can be daunting.

One fact about the road remains, this was a route of the local Underground Railroad. After much of the county population moved to Ironton, the old road was reasonably safe, and it led directly North from the Ohio River to Poke Patch. If the runaway could reach the area near Rock Camp, about ten miles from the river, he could make the rest of the trip to Poke Patch in one night. Few slave catchers would have traveled the thirty-five miles to Poke Patch, nor would they have confronted the serious people who lived there.

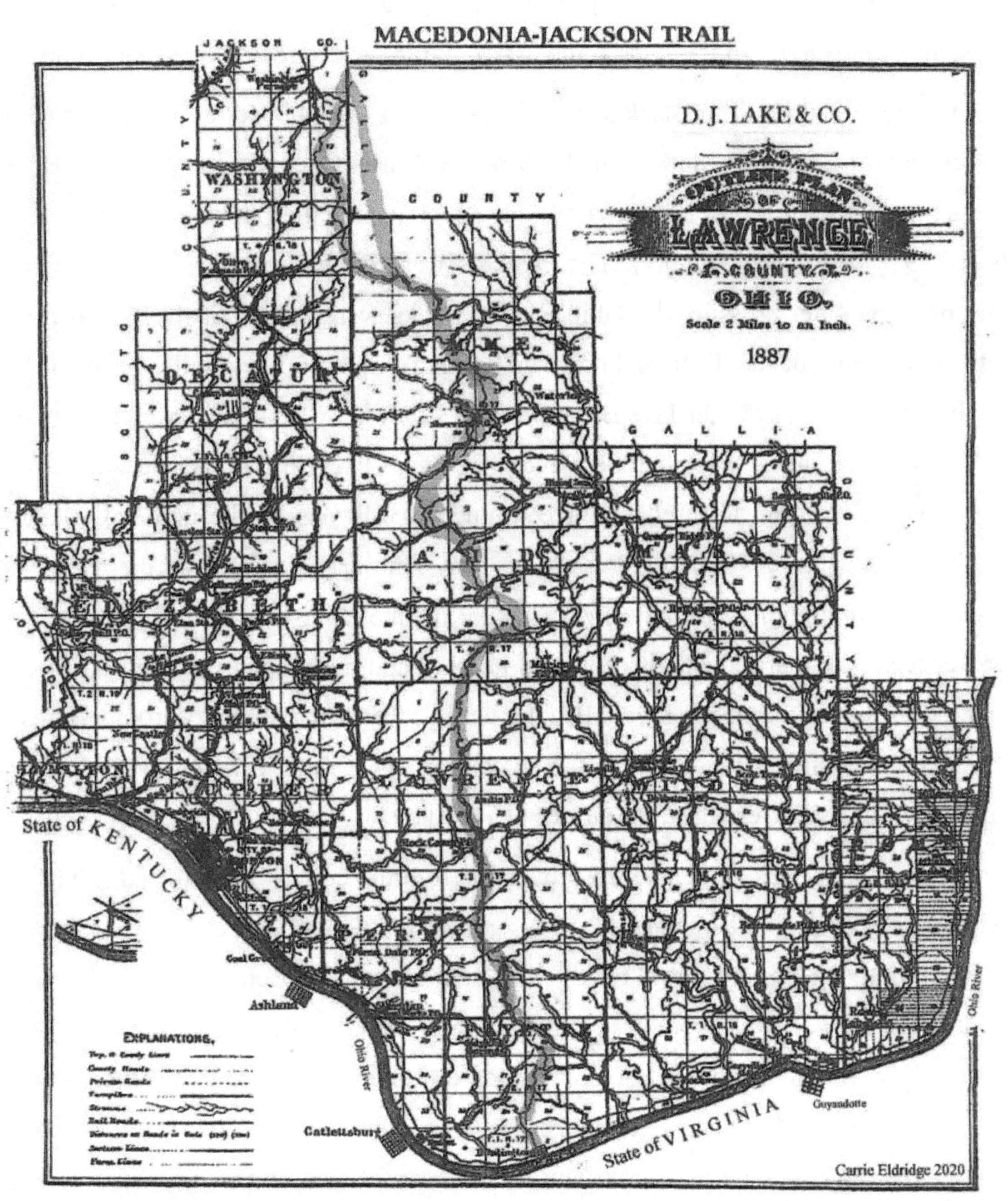
MACEDONIA-JACKSON TRAIL
D. J. LAKE & CO.
OUTLINE PLAN
OF
LAWRENCE
COUNTY
OHIO.
Scale 2 Miles to an Inch.
1887
JACKSON CO.
WASHINGTON
COUNTY
DECATUR
GALLIA
ELIZABETH
State of KENTUCKY
EXPLANATIONS.
Ohio River
Ashland
Catlettsburg
State of VIRGINIA
Guyandotte
Ohio River
Carrie Eldridge 2020

Chapter 5: Black Settlements in Lawrence County

Lawrence County had only five Black communities before the Civil War. Four of them were a few miles from the Ohio River, while number five was called Poke Patch. That settlement was about thirty-five miles north of the river at the extreme northern edge of Lawrence County.

The oldest communities with Black settlers began along the Ohio River. Southeast Ohio was created Washington County at Marietta in 1788 before Gallia County was created in 1803. It is possible the first Black settlers in Lawrence County accompanied the Quakers settlers who arrived in 1796 or 1797(Washington County). The Quakers were known to escort and protect Blacks across the frontier. After crossing the Ohio River, Blacks were automatically free people. The Black settlement near Quakers Bottom, known as Red Hill, was about two miles north of the river on a trail that became OH775. Quakers Bottom (later Proctorville) was direct across the Ohio River from the Virginia community, Guyandotte. Several hotheads lived in Guyandotte, and most of the Blacks who passed through this settlement continued North, passed through Poke Patch, and sought safer areas to live. Serious settlers were few. An early family was the Terry family, manumitted from Montgomery County, VA, in 1826. All the children moved farther west except daughter Rebecca who married Charles Johnson in 1832 and became part of the Macedonia Hill settlement. After the arrival of the Lewis Brooks family, they became the best-known residents. Lewis, Sr., was a recognized conductor for the UGRR and more than willing to protect himself, as several old newspaper articles attest. (Ironton Register 21 Mar 1863)

The second oldest Black settlement also began before the county was created. The 1811 tax list for Union Township, Gallia County (which became Union Township, Lawrence County) showed two Murphy families living on Symmes Creek near a settlement called either Unionville, Russell's Place, or later Getaway. It was about three miles north of the Ohio River. The families seemed to be brothers who represented two households: one named Henry Murphy and the other Washington Murphy. After Lawrence County was organized in 1817, there were still two families, but Henry disappeared after 1830, while Washington Murphy was part of the Lawrence County records until after 1850. Washington was a horse trader and a fighter, but he was best known for the number of days at County Court. Both Henry and Washington were victims of hate crimes. Washington also sued neighbors for trespass and fraud over his horses.

Polly Ferguson was manumitted in 1824 from Cabell County, just across the Ohio River. She stayed in the area because her son, Sampson, was not to be freed for thirteen years. Her children and grandchildren were enumerated in both the 1850 and 1860 censuses, and her granddaughter, Martha, married at 'Getaway.'

The most important Black community in the southern part of the county grew up about two miles north of Burlington, the County Seat. One of the earliest deeds recorded in Lawrence County was by a woman, a Black woman, in an era where few women owned property. In 1817, Rosanna Bryant sold one-half of her quarter section of land in Fayette Township. The land had been recorded at the Chillicothe Land Office and then at the Lawrence County Court by William Bryan (see Bryant family page 21), who also produced a receipt of payment. Rosanna's son, John, lived close by with his family, although across the Upper Township line. (Located near the current South Point exchange on US 52.) The local Black population in 1820 enumerated just twenty-three people, but about a mile north of Rosanna's property, the fledgling Macedonia Church had been meeting in homes for about ten years. No evidence exists to prove the earliest members of the church families.

The Bryant's had probably been taken across the Ohio River from either Mason County or Kanawha County, Virginia, by their owner William Bryan. Other members of the Bryan family lived along the Ohio River, where Cabell County would be created. William Bryan may have become ill on the trip to Chillicothe to record his Ohio lands, for he does not appear in records after recording the deed in Lawrence County, but once his slaves were on the Ohio shore, his people were free.

The growing community near Macedonia Church was called Macedonia Hill. It struggled along until 1829 when a large group of Blacks arrived in the county. The manumitted Wards arrived, settled, and even married into the community by 1830. When a new church building was erected in 1849, the religious community represented one hundred and twenty-four individuals. Most of the area's residents were small farmers who also did some hunting or worked odd jobs, or became rivermen.

In 1848, the future site of Ironton was a wide river bottom with a few farms. Over the next ten years, the expanding iron business would see a large influx of settlers, both Black and white. The County Court moved downriver from Burlington to Ironton in 1852, and with it, several of the businesses and local people. Manumitted Matilda Johnson was a marvelous cook, and before long, she was cooking at the leading hotels in Ironton. Her son, Gabe Johnson, sold his prosperous barber shop in Burlington, then opened a new one in Ironton. He also took his expertise of the UGRR and shared it with several of the Iron Masters to create and operate a UGRR Ironton trail to Poke Patch. By 1860, just after eight years of existence, Ironton had a Black population of more than one hundred. Its location across from Kentucky quickly became an outlet for Free and Freed Blacks traveling north along the Big Sandy River from eastern Kentucky and North Carolina, as well as escaping slaves from central Kentucky.

Poke Patch may have been the most important settlement for Blacks in the county. Located in the swamps at the head of Symmes Creek, the area encompassed the northern edge of Lawrence County, as well as Greenfield Township Gallia County. Poke Patch was never a real community. Instead, it was a collection of mixed people in their tiny homes. This isolated region became a 'station' for an escape trail (an UGRR) from the Ohio River to points north and freedom. Gallia County's Greenfield Township was created about 1818, while Decatur Township in Lawrence County was not official until 1820, and Washington Township was not until 1850. The isolated area was an excellent place to hide, ignore the law, and protect others who needed assistance. For many years, Poke Patch was far enough from the Ohio River to assure the runaways could be helped on their way north because the local 'slave catchers' did not relish the long ride or possible armed resistance. That situation changed when the 1850 Fugitive Slave Law created 'professional' slave catchers and large rewards.

Both Burlington and Quakers Bottom (Proctorville) were actively passing escaped people through their communities by 1820, if not before. Their proximity to the Ohio River and the slave states of Virginia and Kentucky assured runaways would cross the river, although the number was small compared to other sections of the Ohio River. There were few large plantations in the area, but two large rivers from western Virginia drained into the Ohio River across from Lawrence County. People who escaped managed to cross hundreds of miles of hostile territory from as far away as the Carolinas. Over forbidding mountains, they tramped down the Guyandotte or the Big Sandy rivers without aid. It was not safe to approach people even if you had freedom papers.

Rivermen probably kept lookouts on boats with willing Captains who stopped for any passenger. Some communities had white ministers and doctors involved in freedom as well as most members of the Black community. All simply believed in the rights of all men to be free.

Chapter 6: Manumission

Manumission is the legal term "to be released from slavery." A Virginian had to meet many restrictions before a slave could be freed, but there were three ways in which freedom could be granted. Two were by legal means, while the third method developed after the passage of the Northwest Ordinance.

The law required the owner to make his intention known to the county court. He had to provide surety to guarantee no freed person would be a burden to the county. The owner also had to prove the freed person could support himself or provide financial support for the rest of that person's life. The freed person had to register with the county court, carry a paper at all times proving the manumission, and had to "remove from" or leave Virginia within one year of the legal document. (Freed persons without the manumission document could be re-enslaved.)

A deed of manumission (freedom) could be issued by the county court at the slave holder's request and signed by him and two witnesses. This method was usually used to free a single person or small family (stating good service or old age.) Larger numbers of slaves were usually manumitted by the owner's will. With a will, the owner could give instructions for the dispersal of funds and designate legal assistants to assure his wishes were carried out. After death, this method freed the owner from relatives who contested the will and the courts, which could add restrictions to the manumissions. (Rarely were slaves allowed to keep lands willed them or allowed to remain in the county.)

The third method of manumission was to take your slaves and leave the state for Ohio. Many slave owners had lands in different counties of Virginia. They could be miles away before officials suspected or realized their intentions. This method usually meant the owner had few funds to meet the legal requirements, but it also gave the slaves protection as they moved across the frontier. When the party crossed the Ohio River, the owner could register the Blacks with the county court, provide the required surety, pay fees, or buy land in their name.

Manumitted slaves who arrived in Ohio had a better chance of surviving than people who ran away with nothing except their clothes. If the freed people came as a group, they had their own leaders, and often some were educated. They could become landowners and could grow crops to feed their families, even on the cheapest land around. As frontier settlers, they were on an equal footing with others who were trying to clear the lands and provide for their families. They had a place in the community even when they were not allowed to vote, be educated, or appear in court.

Manumitted Blacks had something else. They had freedom from slavery which they wanted to share. The people who settled in Lawrence County and southern Ohio decided they had to assist others who wanted to be free and set about quietly doing just that. Even today, very few people are aware of events the communities shared or of the assistance they provided. The manumitted people knew discovery meant jail, a beating, re-enslavement, or loss of life. There was a secret – it remains today.

Few people understand manumission. Yes, it was a way to free slaves you did not want to keep, but it was also a method of raising the freed slave above others in the Black community. The freed slave often acquired land or money and at least legal status, which gave him a right to work during a period when a free-born Black struggled to make a living and was subject to enslavement or being placed in the poor house. Most Blacks had to abide by all the laws concerning slavery. The worst part of manumission forced the freed individuals to leave family, friends, and home to seek a new and different life in lands they never knew existed.

Virginia manumissions appeared in many different styles and can be viewed at various internet sites or in book form as genealogy researchers locate the old and often forgotten books. Louisa County, Virginia, offered some early manumitted documents of freed Blacks who later registered in Ohio. The Reverend John Poindexter manumitted several slaves over the years, but the man believed the slave had to earn the right of manumission. In 1794 'Edy' was manumitted by Poindexter. 'Edy' purchased and manumitted her husband, Charles. In 1800 Poindexter issued a deed to free the woman 'Frankey,' only it became effective 25 Dec 1829. In 1802 other deeds would free James when he reached age 31 in 1821, and Daniel was to be free in 1820. Some of the manumissions stated: "if he reformed and was allowed to remain in the state," or "when my youngest child is educated." These manumissions refer to freed Blacks who registered in Jackson County, Ohio, in 1824. (Ohio required Blacks to register and a $500 bond for work permits.)

Manumission by Location

Manumissions much harder to locate are those "manumission by location." Owners took the slaves into free territory, thus freeing them. Frontier areas were concerned with staying alive, not record keeping. One problem with these manumissions is related to early records of any frontier area. Records are limited or non-existent. The vast Ohio Territory lay on the border of two river states (Virginia and Kentucky) beyond settled Pennsylvania; and far from eastern population centers. The area which became Lawrence County was slow to develop, nor was it an original county, but it was created from Gallia County, Ohio, in 1817. The records for Gallia County (created in 1803) are limited, as are most others in the region.

In addition, many Lawrence County residents crossed the Ohio River from Virginia, but Cabell County was not formed until 1809, and its parent county (Kanawha - created in 1789) had very few entries about slaves. The researcher finds almost twenty years of extremely limited records. Understanding the early Black population of Lawrence County requires imagination and reading between the lines. Although runaway slaves did cross the Ohio River, the number was limited before 1840. Those Blacks who appeared in the river counties were mostly manumitted and carried that proof with them. Any Black without identification could be arrested as a fugitive and returned to slavery, even if free. Most of the early Black settlers in counties that bordered the Ohio River moved away from the river as soon as possible to avoid "slave catchers."

The early black settlers in Lawrence County who remained near the Ohio River

The area that was to become Lawrence County was part of several political units before it was designated as a county in 1817. Land in the Northwest Territory was surveyed under the Federal Survey System, and the first major land sales went to the Ohio Company, which preceded to build a fort at the mouth of the Muskingum River, where they built Marietta and created Washington County. That county extended along the western bank of the Ohio River from the Muskingum River south to the Scioto River, including the area where Lawrence County would eventually be created. In 1803, Gallia County was carved from the lower portion of the Ohio Company lands. Records for anyone living in southern Gallia County were recorded as part of Union Township, Gallia County, between 1805 and 1817. The western section of the new county had been part of Scioto and Adams County.

Lawrence County was finally organized in March of 1817. Its first Federal Census was taken in 1820. That census enumerated only four Black families and four unnamed Black servants in the entire county, a total of twenty-three people. The families were 'probably brothers' Henry and Washington Murphy and their children, and two Bryant families led by Roseanna Bryant and her son John Bryant.

Early Chattel records (personal property tax records) in Gallia County show Henry and Washington Murphy in the future area of Lawrence County by 1812. Both were taxed for their property of horses and cattle. Were these Black men runaways? Had they been manumitted? The only fact for sure was Washington Murphy liked to fight, and he spent a lot of time in the courts. The 1810's land records record no Blacks, but they do show that William and Stephen Wilson (who later did business with the Bryant family) owned land in 'Union' Township, Gallia County, located in Township 1 Section 24 Range 16. (Gallia Survey) (Note: All deeds will be listed by numbers only as follows listing after 1810 - Section/Township/Range or 24-1-16 -see illustration in the appendix.)

The Second Decade of the 19th Century, 1800 - 1820

Before Lawrence County was organized in 1817, the area was the southern section of Gallia County and was designated "Union Township" when it was created in 1808. The 1800 Federal Census for the area was known as Gallipolis Township of Washington County, Territory North of the Ohio River. Race was not recorded on the 1800 census, nor could Black persons identified from later census information.

Gallia County was organized in 1803, but no Census was available for Gallia County in 1810. The county did make a replacement census by using the 1811/1812 tax lists. This substitute list names a Henry Murphy, taxed for one horse, and a Washington Murphy, taxed for 2 horses and 4 head of cattle. Both lived in Union Township (later Lawrence County), and additional information shows they were mulatto and probably brothers.

Lawrence County was created before the 1820 census was taken. It listed only four Black families and four Black servants in the entire county. The census indicated that the Murphy men lived on Symmes Creek about three miles north of the Ohio River in Union Township. The Bryant families were near Burlington on Solida Road, where it crossed between Fayette and Upper Townships.

Both the Murphy and Bryant families were joined by other families during the 1820s. First single families crossed into Ohio, but the area also attracted several large groups of legally manumitted families. Between 1828 and 1829, the first families to arrive were forty-seven family members from Pittsylvania County, Virginia, known as the 'Ward Manumission.' In late 1849 another large group entered Lawrence County. This group, manumitted by James Twyman of Madison County, Virginia, was called the 'Burlington 37,' or simply the '37.'

The Wards arrived just as the earlier residents were beginning to organize their escape routes and were soon a major part of that effort. Although the Twyman's came much later, their contribution was to cause the community to see their arrival and miss any events connected with runaway slaves or an UGRR. Each family, especially those living near the Macedonia Church, had a part to play in planning the escapes and executing the successful masquerade used to spirit people from the Ohio River into the surrounding hills and points north.

Figure 11 – Washington Murphy Event Sites

There may have been another Centerville in Rome Township, but other evidence indicates the Elliott family (maybe Washington's 1st wife) lived near Poke Patch.

Chapter 7: The Murphy Family of Gallia County and Lawrence County, OH - 1810

Containing: 1st household – 1820 - Murphy, (Henry) 26-44 & wife 45+, 1 male 0-14 and 2 females 0-14

1830   Male 35-54   1m 0-10   ---   3f 0-10 2f 10-23 1f 24-35

2nd household -Murphy, (Polly -white 45+) Washington (b1780 South Carolina – son 0-14

1830 Washington 45+ son Elliot (no wife)

The earliest Blacks recorded in the southeast corner of Ohio seem to have been the extended Murphy family, which settled about four miles north of the Ohio River on its tributary, Symmes Creek. The first records for the family appear in Gallia County's 'Personal Property -Chattel' list, which was compiled in 1811 and 1812 to substitute for the 1810 census. Just two men were listed. Henry and Washington Murphy were recorded in Union Township (the lower portion of Gallia County next to the Ohio River). An interesting fact recorded in those records shows Washington Murphy was a prosperous person for the time and place. He owned four cows and two horses, and it seems he was a livestock dealer who even boarded horses for other people. (Recorded in Law. Co. Probate Records.)

The 1820 census is a record for the same area, which became Lawrence County in 1817. That census listed only 'head of household' by name with additional family members recorded by age group. If you compare the 'chattel' information with the 1820 census for the same area, you find that there were Murphy parents about near 35 years of age, 1 male child under 10, 3 females under 10 and 2 more females under 23. A second household was led by Polly Murphy. She was over forty-five, with two mulatto males in the home, her son Elliot under fourteen, and her husband Washington, over forty-five. (Early census listed 'whites' before 'Blacks'.)

Later, information claimed Washington was born in South Carolina (OH Penitentiary Records), probably with the rest of his family. How could these brothers, one a couple with four young children have reached Ohio if they were slaves? If free, the same question? It was not a safe time for anyone to travel and much worse for Blacks. Did they travel with the Quaker group from Carolina who settled in the Union Township area? Were they manumitted by location? Were they manumitted by some unknown Carolina plantation owner? Reason would indicate they were free, for they stayed in the area despite great odds. Just read a few of the court cases involving

Washington Murphy (which began as early as 1813 and continued at least until 1855) to understand just how difficult a life he led. The question is, WHY?

The 1820 census also listed several households with Black servants, but ages only could not identify these people. About the only information available would be their attendance at church on Sunday when almost one hundred percent of the frontier population sat in a church. The only Black Church in southern Lawrence County was Macedonia on the hill.

The 1830 census showed an increase in the Black population. Some of that population may have been earlier servants who had begun their own households. The 1830 census did name Henry Murphy as head of household. Henry was married and had a son and three daughters under ten with two older daughters under twenty-three and possibly a second wife. No further census reference was made to the Henry Murphy family although Henry was involved in several court cases. In a nearby home resided Washington Murphy with one male child over ten (Elliot). His wife Polly was either dead or gone.

Besides being the earliest family in the records books, the Murphy group was involved in numerous lawsuits. This is especially true of Washington Murphy, who seems to have appeared at every court and was represented by several well-known lawyers. Most of Lawrence County was first settled by "squatters." (Those travelers who simply stopped until someone came along and either claimed the property or asked for taxes.) The tax collectors must have realized there was a lot of untaxed land in the area because, in the late 1830s, numerous land warrants were issued for Lawrence County land at the regional land office in Chillicothe.

One of Washington's early cases involved 'hate crimes' while others concerned 'trespass or assault.' He received fifty acres in Section 16 in Union Township as a settlement in one case. Nothing more was mentioned about that property, but Washington took out his own land warrant for forty-eight acres in 1838. He lost it a few years later to pay court costs. His last case was probably to recover the personal property which was sold when Washington went to prison for 'assault with intent to injure.' That case was continued for several years and then dropped by 'mutual consent.' By 1850, Washington was about seventy-five years old. He had a second wife, Rebecca, and four children to support. He was penniless when he died, but his family survived.

(More information about Washington Murphy is available at the lawrencecountyohio.com site.)

Rebecca Murphy moved her family to northern Lawrence County, where she and her children found work in the local iron furnaces. Her children quickly married, and by 1880 the large extended family moved to Vernon County, Wisconsin, where a Quaker community welcomed everyone.

Figure 12 - Great S Bend of Symmes Creek - Murphy Family lived on the north side.

Lake's 1887 Atlas of Lawrence County, Ohio

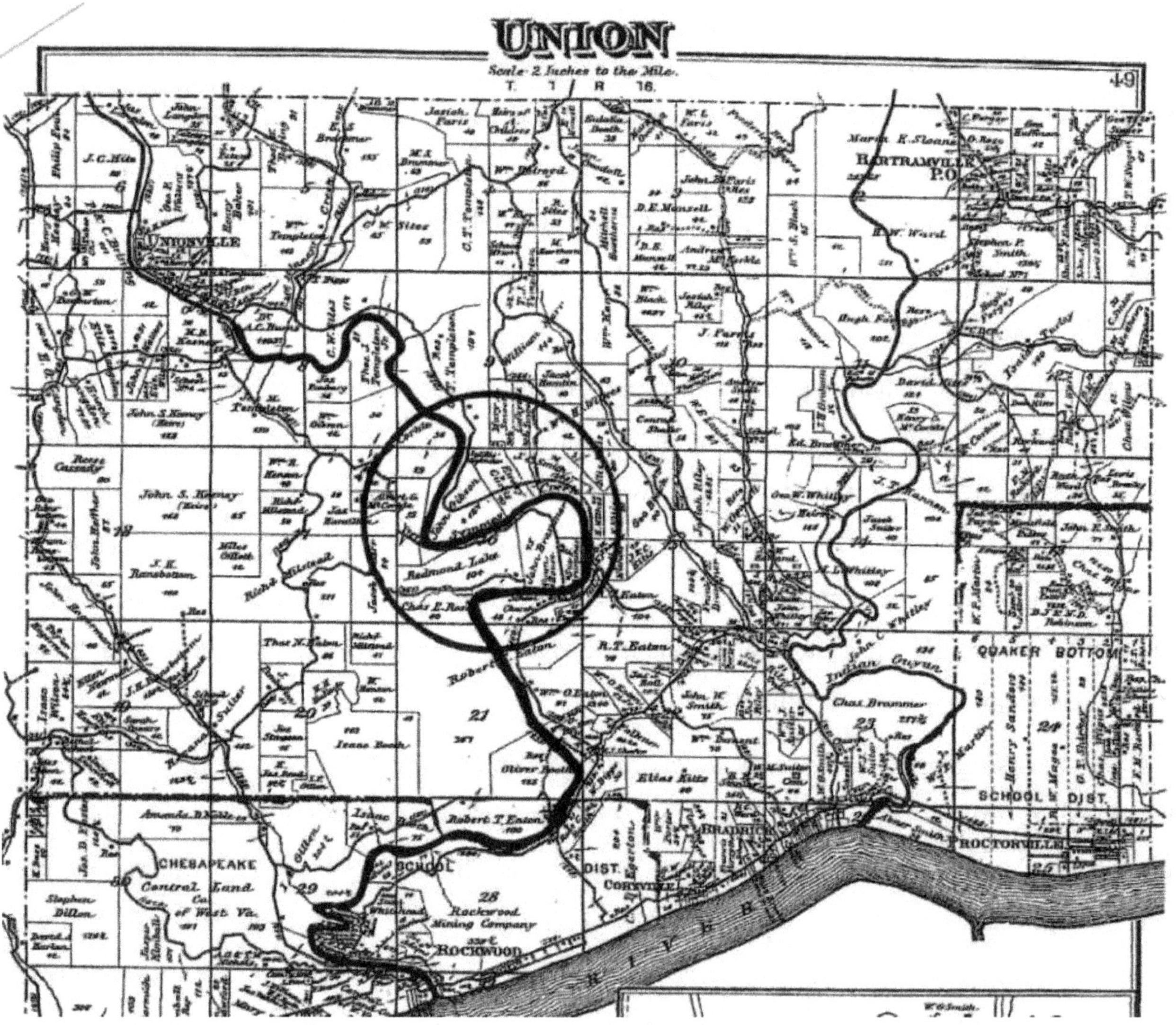

The Murphy family was the first group of Blacks located by records in the Lawrence County area. Those first records were the Duplicate Tax Records used by the State of Ohio to reconstruct the 1810 Ohio census, which had been destroyed during the War of 1812. Washington Murphy was the most obvious member of that family because he was in court frequently.

The first census for the newly created Lawrence County was taken in 1820 named two extended Murphy families under the names of Henry Murphy and Polly Murphy. Additional information would show those individuals were the Henry Murphy recorded in the 1811/12 Tax Records and the wife of Washington Murphy, a white woman named Polly.

Both Henry and Polly were involved in at least one court case. Henry sued once because he was attacked and beaten without reason. He claimed $500 damages in August of 1819, and although the jury accepted his arguments, it allowed him just $7.56 in settlement. (Lawrence County Common Pleas Ledger p 109.) Another time, also in 1819, Henry had a cow stolen, and himself abused. First, the finding favored Murphy, then later, he appealed for damages, and a jury ruled against him and denied all charges and damages. (Lawrence County Common Pleas 1834 p. 234.) Henry Murphy and his family are not listed on the 1840 census or later.

Polly Murphy was white and listed as the householder on the 1820 census because the form was designed to list the following order - white people, slaves, (then) freed Blacks. Since Ohio had no slaves, the enumerator used the second section for free Blacks. Polly was not listed on the census after 1820, but that does not mean she was dead. The Murphy women had a record of leaving and using their maiden name. Since her maiden name was not guaranteed, she was impossible to locate. Polly did appear in court, however. In another case in 1819 for the Murphy's, Polly sued Neal for the loss of a cow. The jury ruled against her and 'her false clamor,' requiring her to pay court costs. Polly vanishes between 1820 and 1830, although her son, Elliot, was living with his father, Washington, in 1830.

Figure 13 – Court Case Days for Murphy

Court Case days for the Murphy Family
Gallia County - Lawrence County

Washington Murphy –	18	100 plus
Henry Murphy –	10	13
Polly Murphy -	-	4

Washington's cases began in 1813 and continued until 1855.

There is still a small community in Lawrence County with the name "Getaway." It was first called Unionville, then Russell's Place, but acquired the name Getaway by the time of the Civil War. The community of twenty to thirty houses was near the area where the Murphy family lived, and there are several Ironton Register articles that referred to the place. Getaway was located at an old ford across Symmes Creek. The site was also the junction where two streams joined the creek. From the west flowed Rankins Creek, which headed near Macedonia Hill. From the east flowed McKinney Creek, a natural connection to the high ridge called Greasy Ridge, which led north towards Poke Patch.

For readers not familiar with the topography of southeast Ohio, a quick lesson may help them understand the area. It is part of the Appalachian Plateau and consists of steep hills and narrow valleys. The region was originally a Long Hunters paradise, and an old article from a Richmond paper stated that 10,000 bear skins were shipped from the area by 1800. All the trails followed a stream and even today, the roads are "as crooked as a dog's hind leg." Following the hunters, farmers arrived to claim lands. Some of the earliest settlers were Quakers opposed to slavery. They supported the Blacks who arrived in the area and preached against slavery. Many of the early white settlers in the county agree with their anti-slavery policies.

<u>Businesses and businessmen of Getaway from the 1850 census</u>

<u>Stores & merchants</u>	<u>Shoe shop</u>	<u>Furniture & coffin maker</u>	<u>Logger</u>
LD. Morrison	James McCorkle	Eli Thacker (minister)	J.W. Jones
George Walters			<u>Grist mill</u>
Charles Walters	<u>Shoemakers</u>	<u>Tan yard</u>	1st Samuel Langdon
Francis Russell	Joseph Beckett	Francis Russell	brought mill stones
Manoah Neal	Seldon Peters		from VA
	(mulatto)	<u>Miller</u>	2nd (?) Francis Russell
<u>Blacksmith shop</u>	<u>Gunsmith</u>	David Fudge	
Francis Russell	Seldon Peters		<u>Sawmill</u>
	(mulatto)		Ronsler Boyl
<u>Blacksmiths</u>	<u>Coopers</u>	<u>Brick mason</u>	
John Gerlach	Pleasant Ellis	William Chinn	<u>Carpenters</u>
John Wipple	John Riddle		Allen Howard
J.M Burns	(barrel makers)	<u>stone mason</u>	Anderson Laffon
Reuben Thacker	<u>Rock quarry</u>	Madison Cannon	Ira McEntre (McIntire)
John Carter	Jenkins family	(sandstone)	Stephen Daniels
Drury Arnold (mulatto)	(foundation	<u>Stone cutter</u>	Joseph Rumbold
(Black Drew)	stones)	Peter Gerlach (headstones)	

1850 Census - #1 – listed 140 households near Getaway –'its the area of service', while only 226 families lived in the entire Union Township.
(abstract) R.C. Hall article:
    "Getaway Ohio Possesses an Odd History," *Herald Advertiser,* 24 Jul 1938, Huntington, WV.

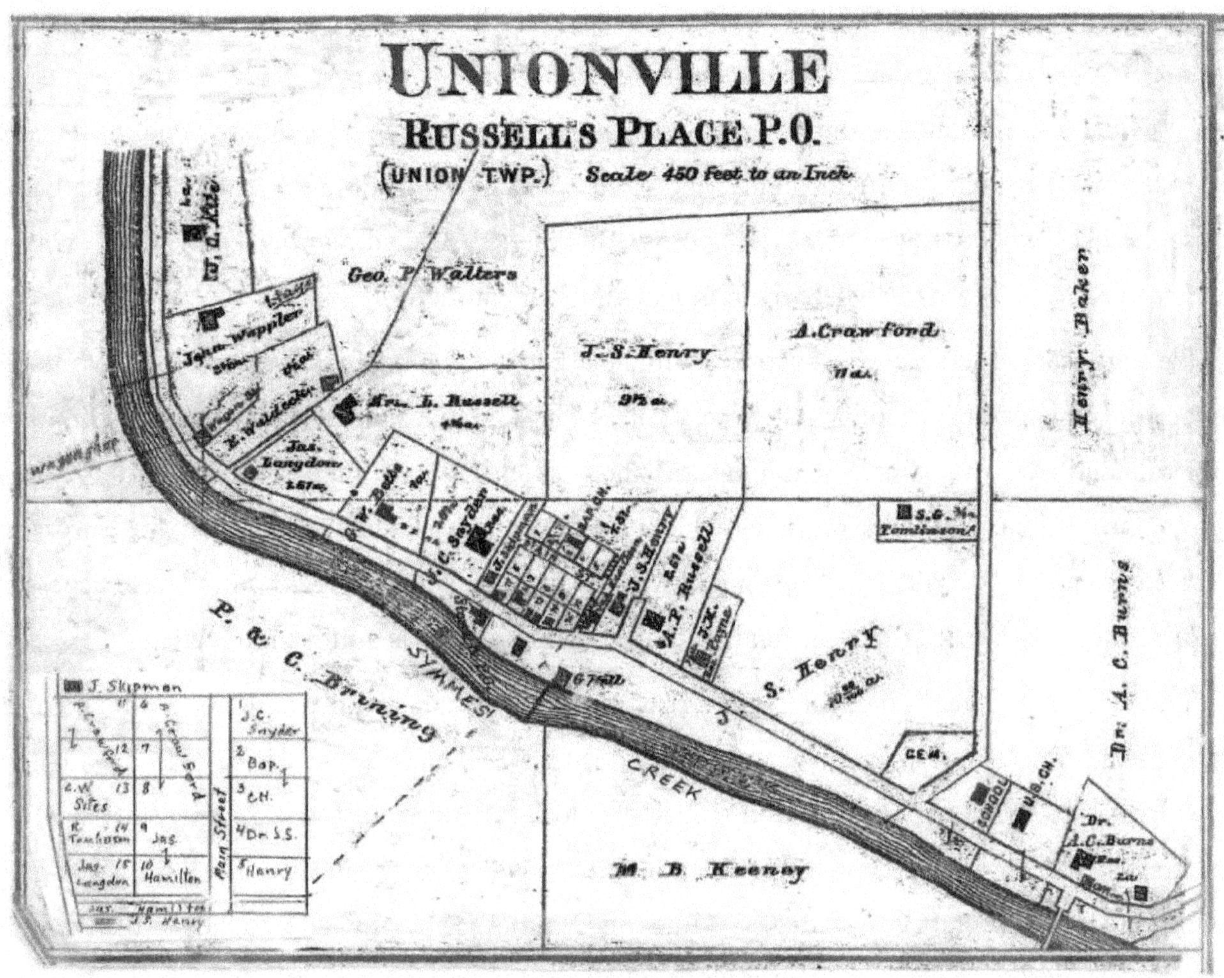

Unionville Business References – 1887 Lake Atlas - p29
Russell Place Post Office (later Getaway)

John Q Hamilton – Dealer in Dry Goods, Groceries, Notions, Boots, Shoes, Hats, Caps, Readymade Clothing, Hardware, Queensware: also first class entertainment for man & beast.
Dr. A. C. Burns – Physician and Surgeon.
Jas. Langdon – Grist Mill

A. Crawford – General blacksmith and wagon making. Repairs neatly done, Horseshoeing
Jno. C. Snyder – Dry Goods, Glassware, Wood and Willow-ware, first class Country Store. Notary and P.M.

A Community Called Getaway

Located on a tributary of the Ohio River called Symmes Creek, this tiny community was located about six miles north of the Ohio River and began while the area was part of Gallia County. Symmes Creek was supposedly named for the politician John Cleve Symmes who was an early land speculator in the lands of the Northwest Territory. Symmes and a group of friends purchased 330,000 acres between the two Miami's and settled in Dayton. Folklore claims Symmes hiked across the headwaters of Symmes Creek before 1800 as he traveled overland from the mouth of the Scioto River to Marietta, where the regional government met.

The earliest area settlers were squatters with no claim to the land, including two Black families named Murphy. The first land grants were taken in the "Congressional Lands" by the Templeton and Huff families (who still reside in the area) about 1815. The community's location ran along a high bluff on the east side of Symmes Creek, with a ferry run by Samuel Langdon at the lower end of the community. The village lay just upstream between two smaller creeks which gave access to the surrounding ridges. For the time and place, the community was a thriving location.

First known as Unionville, for Union Township, its second name was Russell's Place after Francis Russell, the largest landowner, and local postmaster. Today, the site is called Getaway. An old story says a local story keeper told a customer to 'get away,' but a more logical explanation concerns the area's location and its population. Getaway had many Quaker Brethren among its settlers as well as several Black families. Although Symmes Creek flowed into the Ohio River, the lower section of the creek was a trap for anyone looking for an escape route. There were mile-long curves between steep hills where 'slave catchers' could easily capture their foe. Once a person made it to Getaway, with its abolitionists and small Black population, several possible escape routes were available.

McKinney Creek, flowing from the east, was a natural route to Greasy Ridge which led north towards Poke Patch. (A free Black community.) (Greasy Ridge was an early hunting area where trails were covered with bear grease. The ridge was the edge of an earthquake fault that ran from the Ohio River north, without a break, for thirty-five miles before ending about ten miles from Poke Patch.) Following Rankins Creek west to its head led to the Old Jackson Road, which also offered a good trail north. Symmes Creek, when not in flood, offered a fair path after it passed Getaway. Several old news articles refer to runaways crossing the trails in the area.

WHO LIVED IN LAWRENCE COUNTY

Manumissions: Briant-1820 = (B) - Ward -1827 = # - Twyman -1849 = * (m) = minister
Fy = Fayette   Pr = Perry   Ro = Rome   Un = Union   -- CW= Civil War

Federal Census - Lawrence County, OH – alphabetized (Others listed labor- no names)

1820	1830	1840
		Bland, Sam (3)Fy
		Brassfield, Robert (3)Fy (CW.)
		Brown, Abner (3)Fy (CW.)
Upper Twp.		(B)Bryant, Geo. W. (m) (3)Fy (CW.)
(B)Briant, John (9)4&5	(B)Bryant, John (9) Fy	(B)Bryant, John (m) (6)Fy
		Fayette Twp.
(B)Briant, Rosanna (3f)		(-)Bryan, John (white) (3)Fy
	#Callaway, Josiah (3) Fy	(Wid/Josiah) #Calloway, Letty (3)Fy
		#Craddock, Jonathan (m) (6)Fy
		#Craddock, Winnie (6)Fy (Lewis d 1834)
	Ferguson, Polly (3) Un	no (ch only later)
	#Greenhill, John (4) Un	No
	Harris, Essex (3 Fy	Harris, Essex (m) (7)FY
		Harris, Timothy (6)Fy
		Howard, Henry (4)Ro
		Howard, Joseph (3)Ro
	#Johnston, Ben (7) Pr	#Johnston, Ben (8)Pr
		#Johnston, Ben Jr.(5)Pr
	#Johnston, Charles (3) Fy	No
		Miller, Jack (3)Fy
	Moss, Daniel (6) Fy	No
Murphy, Henry (5)	Murphy, Henry (8) Un	No
Murphy, Polly (3)		Murphy Archibald (6)Fy wh & blk
		Murphy, Rebecca (9)Fy (?)
	Murphy, Washington 2Un	no – (but later)
	Randall, William (3)Fy	No
	Reed, William (7)Un	Reed, William (6)Fy (CW.)
	#Roberts, Molloy (3) Fy	No
		#Roberts, Charles (3)Fy
	#Roberts, Pleasant (6) Fy	#Roberts, Pleasant (10)Fy
		Sheppard, Emilla (7) Fy
		Simpkins, Jack (8) Ro
	Terry, Sylph (8) Ro	
	#Ward, Henry (14) Fy	#Ward, Harry(same) (6)Fy
		Wiltshead, Morton (3)Un
		Witcher, Horace (2)Un

These people were the foundation of the Macedonia Church in the Burlington area. They choose to stay in an extremely dangerous area and assist others in escaping across the Ohio River.

Although the trails were probably organized in the late 1820's, the operation of an escape trail was carried out by the sons of the organizers. Several members of the Bryant family were very active, and they were joined by various Ward descendants.

Two young men from the Ward manumission, Gabe Johnson and Phil Lynch, were named in several newspaper articles as active in the underground movement. Gabe Johnston, (son of Ben Sr. and Matilda Johnston-Wards), was an acknowledged conductor of the UGRR and interviewed by Seibert, but he was not the only known person from the Macedonia community. Phil Lynch (Ward) gathered information on the river for several years at the same time Gabe kept a barber shop in both Burlington and Ironton. They, with several Macedonia ministers and assistance from the community, led or directed escapees towards Freedom.

Minister Isaac Vinton Bryant stated in his biography: "We were all involved." (He was son of William Bryant and Martha Craddock Randall.) Although William Portrait Cradic, made no statements, he lived in several communities in southern Ohio well known for UGRR activities. (He was a son of Jefferson Craddock and Juda Bryant. Both were grandchildren of Rosanna, while both Craddock's were part of the Ward Manumission.

Chapter 8: The Bryant/Briant Manumission — 1812-1818

(Bryant/Briant/Bryan interchangeable in references. – Bryant used as a convenience.)

Records reveal a Black – John Bryant and a white – John Bryan.

The Bryant families seemed to have been manumitted by William Bryan when he moved his slave Rosanna and their son John across the Ohio River before 1817. The 1820 census shows two Bryant families living along Solida Creek between Fayette and Upper Townships (near the current South Point exchange on US 52). Rosanna Bryant's household in Fayette Township consisted of three females. John Bryant's family in Upper Township (just a few feet away) listed nine persons. Like the Murphy families who lived about five miles east along Symmes Creek in Union Township, these families were different from most Blacks who crossed the Ohio River. They did not rush to leave the Ohio Valley. Facts prove they remained in Lawrence County for generations because they had a reason.

Only a possible story with a few facts:

Sometime between 1776 and 1786, William Bryan stopped by a Virginia plantation, probably on the Kanawha River, and made a deal to buy a young female slave called Roseanna. By 1790, Rosanna had a son named John, and Bryan had moved down river, first to Mason County, Virginia, and later south of the Kanawha River in the area soon to be created into Cabell County where other Bryans, likely relatives, lived. (Settling directly south of the study area in Lawrence County, OH.) His next move was across the Ohio River into the Gallia/Lawrence area.

The earliest listing for any "Bryan' in Gallia County, OH, was found among the 'wolf scalp' orders for 1811. (Jones p. 27) James Bryan may have been a brother who moved across the Ohio River before 1810. There are no other references for James Bryan except an entry in 1816 when two minor sons of James Bryan (decd.) of Mason County, Virginia, received 104 acres each from his estate. (The Gallia County area became Lawrence County in 1817.) This Bryan probably encouraged William to cross the river. William Bryan went to Chillicothe (maybe in 1816) to record and register a piece of property along the Ohio River, a part of the Ohio River Survey, where Lawrence County would be created.

The known facts: (NOTE: Land location written Section-Township-Range or S33-T2-R17= 33-2-17)

In December of 1817, William Bryant of Gallia County presented a "Certificate of Payment" (recorded at the Chillicothe Land Office) to the Lawrence County Court for a quarter section of land in Fayette Township (33-2-17). (A quarter section equaled 160 acres.)

* (Both land transfer and John's first son named William indicate William Bryan as spouse of Rosanna.)

In June of 1818, Rosanna Bryant (a Black woman according to the census) sold one-half of that lot (Sec. 33-2-17) to Stephen Ballard for $184. Rosanna, enumerated on the 1820 Federal Census, lived on the remaining half of that property in Fayette Township until her death in 1833. The census also listed her son John, his wife Susan, and their seven children in Upper Township (Both Fayette and Upper are fragmented -partial-townships which adjoin.). John's homestead was really a few feet away but across the township line. There are no census records for Gallia County before 1820, and no other records indicate when the Bryans moved across the Ohio River. The deed, the land certificate, and the 1820 Lawrence County census show Rosanna Bryant in Fayette Township (with at least one daughter {Sarah} and maybe Harriet), while John Bryant and family were in Upper Township (Rosanna's son living just across the township line).

If the records for the Macedonia Church, which claim the Church was organized by 1813, are correct, then the two Bryant families and the two Murphy families had to be among the founders of the Church. These twenty people and those three un-named servants not only started a church, but they began a tradition of community involvement, were outspoken about the antislavery movement, and lay the foundation for the underground railroad that operated along the Old Jackson Road across Lawrence County. These people connected the Ohio River communities to free settlements farther north.

In 1818, after Rosanna Bryant received a quarter section of land registered in Chillicothe, Ohio, as property north of the Ohio River, she sold half of the property to buy horses and cattle, according to the tax list. Rosanna's eighty acres of land consisted of virgin timber, was mostly hillside, and had never been cleared for farming. Her family attacked the forest and raised their families on the land. They also started a church, offered help, and provided homes and spouses to the manumitted Ward families who arrived in their community by 1829.

The Expanded Bryant Family of Fayette Township

One method of tracing this family coincided with the formation of the Macedonia Church, supposedly organized by 1813. Founding members had to include the Bryan/t families (therefore, the Bryant families had to be settled before 1813). Rosanna, her son (John), by Mr. Bryan, and possibly two other daughters played a major role in creating Macedonia Church. The Church took a great leap forward when the Ward families arrived. Pleasant Roberts and his family may have been the leaders of the Ward group who settled in Lawrence County. His wife, Hannah, died on the trip north, leaving Pleasant with five motherless children. He married Sarah Bryant in May of 1829. An 1841 deed proved Sarah was the daughter of Rosanna when she and Pleasant Roberts sold their part of Rosanna's original land in Section 33 (33-2-17). In 1834, Roberts had purchased an adjoining lot in the same section. (See Appendix Follow the Deeds.)

There were two John Bryan's in early Lawrence County, and their name spelling was not consistent. One was white, a tanner who became the county auditor was usually written 'John Bryan.' The other John was Black and mostly known as John Bryant. Although a deed was written in 1841 listed (Black) John Bryan and his wife Susan, who sold one-half of the remaining portion of the original land Rosanna had received in 1818. The buyer was William Ballard. (Stephen Ballard bought the first quarter in 1818) That deed verified (Black) John Bryan/t still owned one-quarter of 33-2-17 in 1841 and stated he had received it from his mother's will. (See Bryant Appendix)

Between 1820 and 1830, several Black families moved into Lawrence County. Daniel Mors (Moss) was on the Lawrence County census for 1830 with a family of six was living in Perry Township next to Ben Johnston (a Ward). Moss's first wife must have died before 1834 as there was a marriage for Daniel Moss and Lucy Craddock in that year (another Ward). Daniel is not mentioned again, but two daughters married in Lawrence County. In 1851, Lucy Moss married Simon Toms (a Twyman), while Eveline Moss married Levi Harris (son of Essex).

A William Randall of the unknown background was also listed on the 1830 census. He married, first, Charlotte Johnston in 1829, then in 1834 Martha Craddock (both Wards). Martha Craddock Randall was a widow by 1851 when she became the third wife of William Bryant (one of John's sons and Rosanna's grandson). The Biddy Randall, who married Abner Brown in 1836, was possibly William's sister.

Another interesting person who appeared during the 1820s was Essex Harris. He was aged '24 to 36' on the 1830 census with a wife and child. According to his son Nathan's obituary, Essex married Elizabeth Roberts of the Ward Manumission, about 1828. In 1839, Essex purchased the SW ¼ of the SW ¼ Section 35 Township 2 Range 17, where widow Matilda Johnson (a Ward) was living. In the 1890s, the Ironton Register ran an article: "Reminiscences," stating Essex Harris was remembered as the 'Blind Minister.' (Essex may have been kin to Cornelius Harris, who settled near Poke Patch about the same time. Cornelius had come from Tennessee with the Stewart family and married into that family.)

John Bryant and Essex Harris were probably the first ministers for the Macedonia Church. They were followed by John's sons William and George Washington Bryant and several ministers from the Ward manumission such as Jonathan Craddock and Charles Roberts.

There were several other manumissions to Lawrence County by 1830. Polly Ferguson was enumerated in 1830 in Union Township. That lady had lived just across the Ohio River and was manumitted in Cabell County, Virginia, by the will of Samuel Ferguson, Sr. in 1824. The will named Polly, her daughter Sealy and grandson Sampson. The women were immediately manumitted. Both women received their bed and furniture, while Sealy received a spinning wheel. Sampson was only six at the time. The will stated Sampson was not to get his freedom until 13 years from the date of the will. (1837) The 1860 Lawrence County census for Union Township listed #713 Seely Ferguson, aged 60. Household #718 listed Samson Ferguson, aged 42, his wife

Gincy, and seven children. Both homes were at Russell's Place (Getaway.) near the homes of the Murphy's and Peter's. Seely Ferguson's daughter Martha married Seldon Peters (17 Feb 1845) in Lawrence County, and the couple lived at Getaway until their deaths after 1900. They were buried nearby in the Tabor Cemetery.

The freeborn Peters family arrived in Lawrence County from Amherst County Virginia before 1845. The family of ten children was led by their mother Tursey Peters (possible a widow of Esom Peters). A mixed family of Indian and French Canadian, they settled in Union Township where son Sheldon Peters 1816-1909) was a gunsmith for more than fifty years and kept a small shop on the hillside above Getaway.

Sylvia Terry and her children were manumitted by William and Patience Terry in Montgomery County, VA in 1829. Most of the family continued West except daughter Rebecca who married Charles Johnson in 1832.

Surely, these people joined the only Black Church in the area, but the greatest addition to Macedonia Church came at the end of the decade. During 1828 and 1829, one hundred and thirty-eight Blacks were manumitted by James Ward, Sr. in Pittsylvania County, Virginia. Forty-eight of those people arrived in Lawrence County, and many settled near Macedonia Hill, where the Church was located. They also found and married many spouses from the local population.

The arrival of the families from the Ward manumission with teenagers and young adults would allow the Church and community to expand their mission of helping runaways escape. The Church was strengthened by young people who were 'daredevils.' The newcomers were quietly accepted into their frontier community by both whites and Blacks.

In 1818, Roseanna Bryant sold one-half of the quarter section of land which had been registered in Chillicothe, Ohio, as property north of the Ohio River. The eighty acres of land she kept was not ready farmland but virgin forest. The Lawrence County tax lists recorded Rosanna on both the Land Tax Records and the Property Tax Records. Rosanna used the money from her property sale to buy a $40 horse and several $8 cows for herself and her son.

These first recorded Black settlers in Lawrence County were manumitted. They owned land, paid taxes, and took their place in the community. They did not hide or move away from the river. They were free and planned to help other Blacks become free. (See Appendix #6)

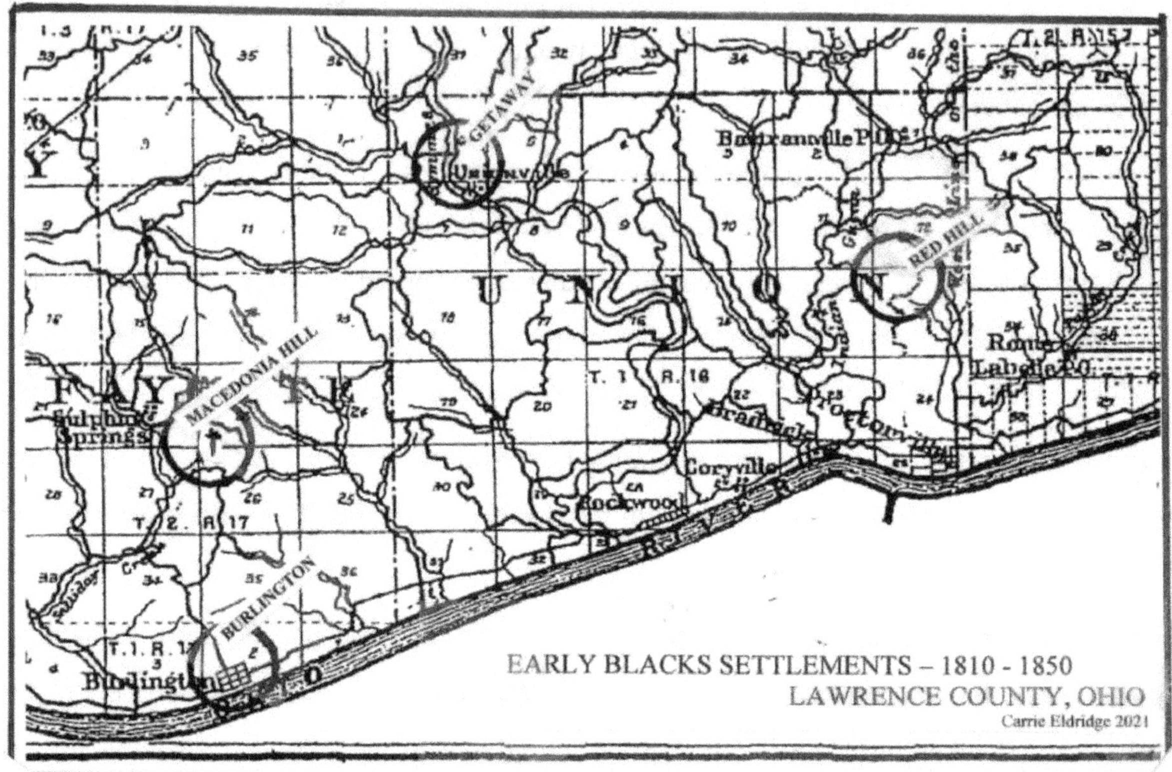

Macedonia Hill and Burlington

Unlike Unionville, which became today's Getaway, Burlington's Black settlement was not located in the community. Possibly because the land was cheaper or unclaimed or perhaps because they felt safer away from the river's edge, the families in the Burlington area built their homes about two miles North of the county seat. Almost all of them considered themselves farmers and worked small clearing around their homes. They referred to their settlement which developed near their Church on the hilltop as Macedonia Hill.

Rosanna Bryant's property, in Section 33, was about one and a half miles from the Church, which lay in the center of Section 26. Hartwell Roberts, Jonathan Cradic (Wards), and Robert Brasswell bought land in Section 26, while Essex Harris and Harry Ward (Ward) had property in Section 35 to the South, all land on the hills near the Church. Perhaps the most interesting of all the deeds was from Nehemiah Valentine to Essex Harris. Matilda Johnson, widow of 'Ward' Ben Johnson, was a squatter on the property. The Valentine deed reserved, for Matilda's lifetime, 'her cabin and yard and the cord of wood already cut.' Matilda lived in several relatives' homes and was a cook in several locations. She died at the Poor House in Scioto County.

In most cases, the Black settlers needed about ten years to raise enough money to purchase any property. Those who could buy the property allowed other members of their families and even neighbors to build cabins on the land. That is the only way to account for the large number of dwellings enumerated in the census. The settlers were farmers, although several younger Blacks held jobs as domestics or common labor, few Blacks did not live in Burlington before 1849.

That year the 'Burlington 37' arrived, manumitted by James Twyman. The land acquired by the Twyman group was just to the east and adjacent to Burlington. While not in the community, they lived much closer to the village than Macedonia Hill.

Figure 16 - Western Section 'Fry Lands'

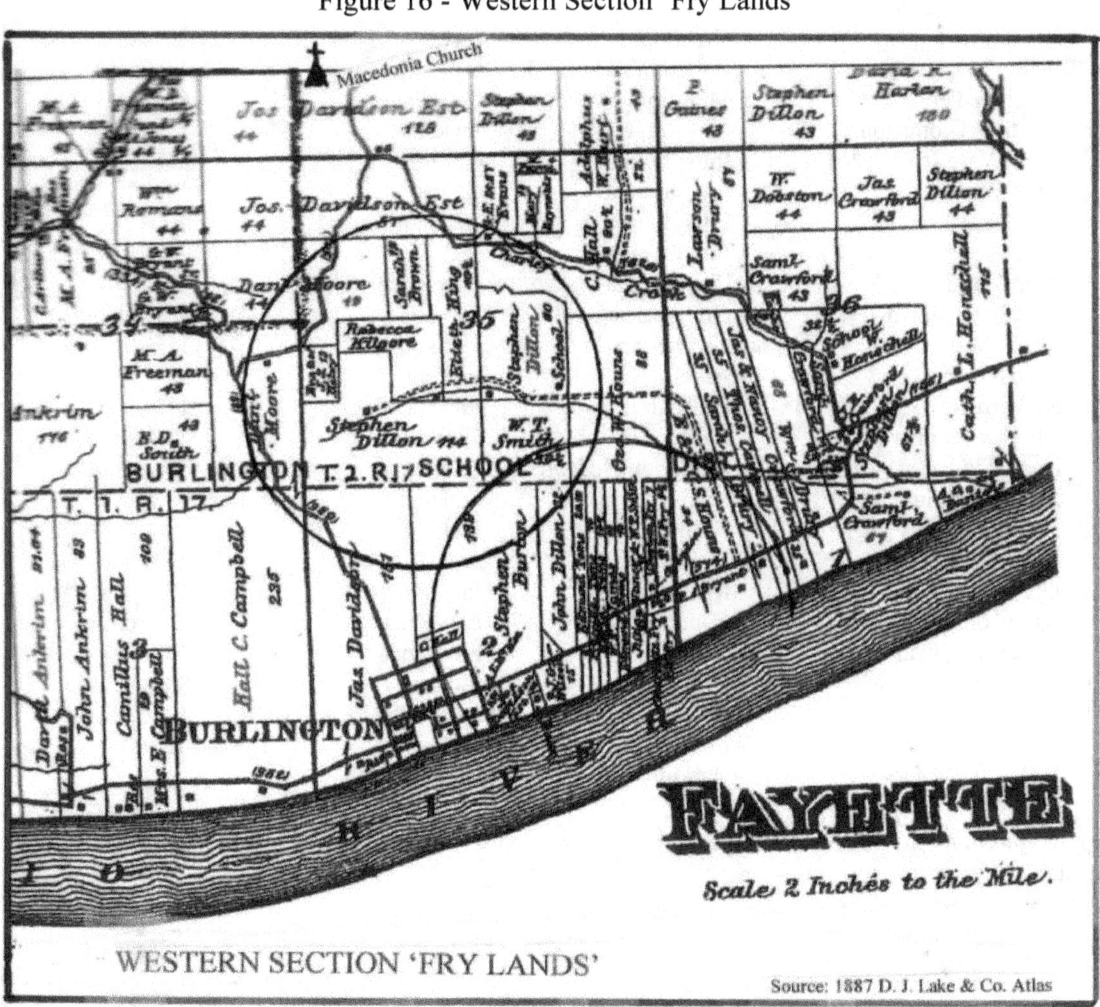

By the 1840 census, several additional manumitted families arrived in Southeast Ohio. Although not all settled in Lawrence County, several families intermarried or belonged to the church communities that worked together. Both the Ward and Twyman manumissions had a major impact in the area and concerned both Macedonia Church and the Underground Railroad.

Figure 17 – Manumission in SE Ohio

Some Manumissions to Southeast Ohio - Gallia, Jackson, Lawrence (with Ward manumission)

Year	Master	County Manumitted Virginia/ or other	County Settled	Number set/manumit ? Surname
1815	Jeremiah Ward	- Cabell	Lawrence	1 (Ferguson)
1816	Law. Aug. Washington	- Frederick/Mason	Jackson	1
1819	Thos. Whittington, Jr.	- Bedford	Jackson	1/60 (will)
1820	John Burchett	- Dinwiddie	Jackson	2
1820	Rev. John Poindexter	- Louisa	Jackson	8
1823	Alexander Catlett	- Greenup, KY	Jackson	1
1824	Samuel Ferguson	- Cabell, VA/WV	Lawrence	3
1826	William Terry	- Montgomery	Lawrence	8
1827	Hannah Thompson	- Jackson, OH	Jackson	1
1827	John Ward (total 126)	- Pittsylvania	Clinton	35
1827	John Ward	- Pittsylvania	Gallia	19
1827	John Ward	- Pittsylvania	Highland	7
1827	John Ward	- Pittsylvania	Jackson	2
1827	John Ward	- Pittsylvania	Lawrence	48
1834	Elizabeth Morrow/Wm.	- Greenbrier	Jackson	7 (husband's)
1834	James Withrow	- Greenbrier	Jackson	1
1836	John Skurry	- Amelia	Jackson	9
1839	Richard Hawks	- Dinwiddie	Jackson	1
1839	Charles Lambert, Jr.	- Bedford	Gallia	46 (1843)
1840	Lucy Claws	- Campbell/Bedford	Lawrence	1 (UGRR)
1840	Joseph Perkins, Sr.	- Louisa	Jackson	9
1844	John Hockaday	- Halifax, NC	Jackson	12
1847	James Stephenson	- Jackson, OH	Jackson	1 (Kanawha)
1847	Dr. Charles Webb	- King William	Jackson	18/52 (will)
1849	Sampson Sanders	- Cabell, VA/WV	Lawrence	1 - from MI
1849	James Twyman	- Madison	Lawrence	37 to 44
1850	Elizabeth Morrow	- Greenbrier	Jackson	8 (her own)
1852	Mary Garland	- Richmond	Lawrence	1 (12) Brooks
1855	William Ragland	- Louisa, KY	Jackson	68/98
1855	William Turner	- Harland, KY	Lawrence	5+

These manumissions are recorded in various county documents, including wills, deeds, and registration books. See Bibliography for sources of information.

Chapter 9: The Ward Manumission 1828

The Forgotten Manumission

In 1826, John Ward, Sr. of Pittsylvania County, Virginia, manumitted 136 slaves and provided for them to be sent west. (Index #3- The Ward Will and Manumission Abstract). Pittsylvania County lay on the boundary between Virginia and North Carolina, with the nearest free territory being southeast Ohio. The Ohio River was the western boundary of Virginia and several hundred miles distant. The freed individuals registered with the Pittsylvania Court, which required their name, age, physical description, and often family connections. In 1827/8, forty-eight individuals from this group settled in Lawrence County, Ohio, and were listed on the 1830 Federal Census. (See -Who lived in Lawrence County-page 13.) The other eighty-eight individuals settled in locations farther from the Ohio River in Ohio counties Gallia, Jackson, Ross, Pike, Highland, and Clinton.

The Pittsylvania County Registration Book provided ages, personal descriptions, surnames, and family grouping of all 136 persons, while Ward's 'Will' supplied information about the owner's intent. The four oldest slaves were to receive land in Virginia for their support, and all slaves over age fifteen were to receive $20 each. Special consideration was given to favorites, 'David and his sister Nancy (children of Old Molly).' Each was to receive $150, a $40 horse, and two cows. Ward also requested the County Court give permission for David and Nancy to remain in Virginia. The Pittsylvania Court did not even bother to convene, meaning that David and Nancy and the other 134 freed slaves had to leave the state of Virginia within one year of the Will's settlement.

Forty-eight freed 'Wards' settled in Lawrence County, Ohio, while others moved farther west. Siblings David and Nancy Ward lead their group of thirty-four all the way to Clinton County, Ohio, near Wilmington. They probably crossed southern Ohio on OH 73, which passed through Jackson, Piketon, and Hillsboro before it reached Clinton County. Most of that group settled in Clark Township, where the UGRR was known. Wards seemed to settle where active underground groups existed and often supplied ministers supporting the anti-slavery platform.

The Ward manumission was interesting for several reasons. The 'white' Ward family arrived in Massachusetts about 1650. It seems the family tried to populate America by itself, and several generations had fifteen children in each family. By the time John Ward, Sr. died in 1826, he had several thousand Ward relatives across the frontier, and many of them were land speculators. His uncle (Jeremiah Ward) and cousin (Thomas Ward) just happened to live in Cabell County, Virginia, across the Ohio River from Lawrence County, Ohio; while another cousin lived in Lawrence County. It is probable that John Ward, Sr. '1826' knew what his former slaves could expect in their new homes in the western wilderness.

Pittsylvania County was on the Carolina Road (US 15 & US 29) that led to central North Carolina. Travelers could return north by those roads to their junction with the James River and Kanawha Turnpike (US 60). This route led to the Ohio River at the mouth of the Guyandotte River in Cabell County. The extensive Ward family holdings across the frontier would have allowed the freed slaves to move from holding to holding, gathering supplies, and receiving protection without alarming the local officials who wanted no more Blacks. The 'Black' Ward families who settled in Lawrence County included ten Craddocks/Cradics, eleven Johnsons, ten Roberts, and nine Wards. After reaching Ohio, many of the settlers chose spouses from families already in Lawrence County.

Another outcome of the Ward manumission was the rapid increase of Lawrence County's Black population. In 1820, there were just twenty-seven Blacks in Lawrence County, consisting of four families with only sixteen children. The forty-six manumitted Ward slaves represented five additional families and twenty-eight children. These families pooled their $20 allotments, and each family purchased at least one horse to till the land and one cow to help feed their relatives. (Lawrence County Personal Property books.)

Between 1827 and 1852, almost thirty marriages connected the original settlers and the Wards. Not only did the Macedonia Church receive forty-six new members, but those members added at least five children for each family group, or 150 children in a twenty-year period. As increasing numbers of slaves tried to escape north, the Macedonia community was strong and had enough young people to begin guiding runaways north. (See Index #4.)

Having an underground escape route required helpers in other areas. The map on page 28 shows other counties where freed Wards settled. All these counties developed strong assistance groups who directed escapees onward to the next station of an underground railroad. (UGRR) Almost all the areas were also associated with the Anti-Slavery Baptist Churches and had ministers and elders connected to Macedonia or Union churches. (Appendix 7-Macedonia and Ministers.)

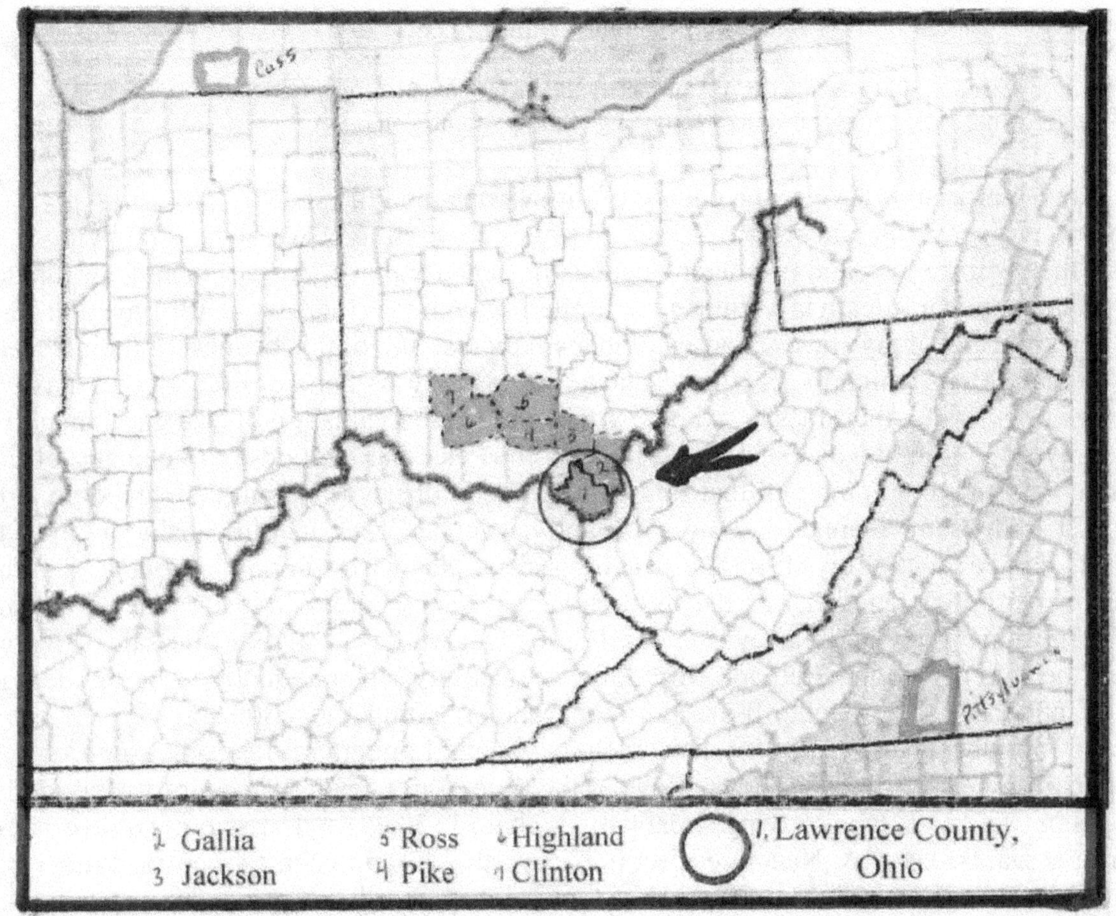

Figure 18 – Counties with Manumitted Wards

JOHN WARD, SR. – WILL AND MANUMISSION

The Forgotten Manumission

Pittsylvania Co. VA probated 20 Nov 1826 - WB1-pgs 109-112
(abstract - pertaining to the manumission only)

I, John Ward, Sr. (1826) of the county of Pittsylvania and the state of Virginia-----

Item 9: It is my will and desire that all my slaves now living or which may be living at the time of my death be free, and I do hereby bequeath to each and every one of them their freedom immediately upon my death in as full and unlimited a manner as the laws of Virginia will admit of. But should any of my slaves choose not to avail themselves of this bequest of their freedom with the conditions which the law may annex, then it is my will and desire that they have the privilege of choosing their master, who may take then at the valuation of two good men to be chosen by my executors, and should the females thus electing to choose to keep any of their children with them: it is my will that said children be at liberty to obtain their freedom at the age of 21 in the same manner. It is my wish and particular desire that in consideration of the general good conduct of my slaves Davy and his sister Nancy (testimony left blank) that they should be permitted, together with the children of said Nancy to remain in the state of Virginia, hereby meaning Davy and Nancy, the children of Old Molley. I give to the said Davy and Nancy the sum of one hundred and fifty dollars. I also give them, equally to be divided, my tract of land that I first bought off of Henry Pickral, containing about 300 acres.

I give to four old slaves, Will, Sam, Ned & Ben, the land I bought of the Cook estate.

I give to all my slaves over 15 years of age at the time of my death the sum of twenty dollars (excepting Davy and Nancy having already given them $150 each). I give to my above-named favorite servants, Davy & Nancy, each a horse worth $40 and each two cows. Pittsylvania Court Records 1823-1827 state David Ward and Nancy Ward and her children George and Joseph petitioned the court in 1826 to remain in Virginia.

The motion continued into 1827. The court refused to even meet, let alone give permission. The 1830 Ohio census shows these four people in Clinton County, OH, with thirty more of the manumitted Wards. (Between Chillicothe and Dayton)

Figure 19 – Will – John Ward, Sr.

The Pittsylvania Court did not even meet to consider Ward's request to allow some of the slaves to remain in the county. That meant all the 135 people had to be out of Virginia by 1 Jan 1828 (one year after the will was probated). The slaves numbered 70 to 170 were registered at the 1827 January Court. Slaves numbered 173 to 194 were registered at the February Court, while numbers 195 to 202 were certified at the March Court. Milly Tucker (Number 203) was registered on 20 April and Number 204, not until 18 June, and he was recorded born free. Was he accidentally added to the Ward list?

<u>Abstract of the rest of John Ward's (1826) will.</u>

1. To John Smith, Ralph Smith, Sallie Leftwich, and Paulina Clayton, $300 each. $1200
2. To the children of Elizabeth Smith Leftwich (decd.) $300 to divide equally   300
3. To the children of Mildred Smith Jones (decd.) $300 to divide equally   300
4. To Matilda, Sally & Dosha Callaway $300 each   900
5. To Seth Barber, a tract of land called Mayhew's old tract, plus tract bought of Shadrach
6. Mustain and adjoining tract purchased off of Thomas Hutson   ....
7. To Carter Barber, tract on Beech Tree Creek where James Lester lives.   ....
8. To John Dillard, out of my estate, $1200   1200
9. To nephew Robert A. Ward – the full amount he owes me and no more.
10. To Matilda Adams, Lucinda Rutledge, Julian Barber, Henrietta Barber, John Barber, William
    Barber, Robert Barber, and Jeremiah Edwin Barber (ch of Patsy Barber)
11. All my interest in Toll Bridge across Staunton River.
12. Manumission and bequeath to slaves (see above)
13. To nephew John Ward, Jr., tract on Staunton River in Campbell County-   1200 to 1600 acres
14. Also, tract on James River above Lynchburg in Amherst County -   750 to 800 acres
15. Also, tract on Pigg River & Frying Pan Creek, Pittsylvania County
                        I purchased off of Walter Coles   600 to 700 acres
16. To nephew Lynch Dillard, all tracts on Staunton River at the Pocket   being 1424 acres
        a. Also, all tracts on Straightstone Creek in Pittsylvania County –   1500 to 2000 acres
        b. Also, a tract in lower Pittsylvania adjoining George West-   300 to 500 acres
        c. Also, the Frank Smith tract and adjoining lands on Sycamore Creek –   500 to 1000 acres
17. After payment of all debts, etc. .... All residue of any type of property to go to
18. Nephews John Ward, Jr. and Lynch Dillard named executors. 30 Jul 1826
                        John Ward, Sr. $50,000 bond - Security
                        Will probated: 20 Nov 1826, Pittsylvania Co. VA

The Ward executors had to sell any property bequeathed to the slaves to have money to move them. The trip required wagons, clothing, and food from "lower" Pittsylvania County, VA, to the Ohio River (the point where Ohio, West Virginia, and Kentucky now meet). It was at least 400 miles over some of the most rugged terrain in the eastern United States. An average day's travel was ten to twenty-five miles, and the route probably followed the Carolina Road and the James River Turnpike. Ward owned property along both these routes, which would have provided provision, refuge, and safety on the long trip. The freed Wards located in five Ohio counties: Lawrence 48, Clinton 34, Gallia 14, Pike 12, and Highland 7.

The extended "white" Ward family had many land speculators and owned land west of the mountains. Did the former slaves stop on other Ward property or receive help from other members of the Ward family? Western Virginia was a frontier in 1827, with a limited population, limited resources, and most definitely limited records.

Ward Manumissions (registered) -1827 - Pittsylvania Co. VA = PCVA # –

LAWRENCE COUNTY   Residents only – (See Appendix #3 for additional information.)

Will - John Ward, Sr.'1826' - Pittsylvania Co. VA -1826-7 manumitted 134 individuals

Registration # PCVA	Name		1827 age	known OH location source
-80	Roberts, Pleasant		38	Lawrence Co. OH 1830 census Fayette Twp.
-81	"	Hannah -wife	33	" d 1827/8 – Pleasant m Sarah Bryant 18 May 1828
73	"	Betsey -ch	17	"
74	"	Elvy (f) -ch	16	"
75	"	Pauline -ch	14	"
76	"	Laura -ch	13	"
77	"	Penelope -ch	10	"
78	"	Charles -ch	8	"
79	"	John -ch	3 (in June)	" (John Hartwell)
84	Johnson, Benjamin		58	Lawrence Co. OH 1830 census (35 - 55)
85	"	Benjamin, Jr. s/Ben	25	" only 7ch - 4m-3f
-195	"	Matilda Wife (Ben - Sr.)	31	" (by census w/older Ben) obit 1871
-196	"	Nancy -ch	6 wks	"
-197	"	Charlotte -ch ?	16	"
-198	"	Dorcas -ch?	14	"
-199	"	Moses -ch?	10	"
-200	"	Sucky (f) -ch?	5	"
-201	"	Gib (m) -ch?	2	" (Gabe)
86	"	Jerry - s/Ben	18	?
87	Ward, Harry		30-40	(Henry) Lawrence Co. OH - 1830 census
88	"	Lydia - wife	45	" (15 on census) - Fayette Twp.
89	"	Sary(Sarah) - ch	12	"
90	"	Bob - ch	9	"
91	"	Anderson -ch	7	"
92	"	Judith -ch	3	"
93	Craddock, Lewis		75	d (on trip?)
94	"	Winney - wife	45	(head) Lawrence Co. OH - 1840 -1850
95	"	Jefferson -ch	?	m Judah Bryant 20 Nov 1831 (Cradwick)
96	"	Lucy -ch	16	m Daniel Moss (27 Feb 1834) Law. Co.
97	"	Martha -ch	10	" (also 1850)
98	(Craddock), John -ch		12	Jonathan '40-'50 m Permelia Bentley(7 Dec 1837)Law.
99	"	Cory Ann -ch	8	m Geo. W. Bryant (29 Mar 1827) Law. Co.
100	"	Permilia -ch	5	" (also 1850)
101	"	Mouring -ch	3	m Robt. Brassfield (28 Aug 1839) Law. Co.
102	Craddock,Mary -ch		3m	Lawrence Co. OH 1830 (1850)
103	Greenhill, John		75	Lawrence Co. OH 1830 census
104	"	Sylvia -wife	60	" (4) Union Twp.
130	Callaway, Jack (Josiah)		48	Lawrence Co. OH 1830 census
131	"	Letty -wife	45	" (3) Fayette Twp.
132	"	Polly -d/Jack	9	"
137	Ward, Joseph -s/Nancy		12	" also 1850 Law. Co. OH
138	Ward, Molly		60	Lawrence Co. OH 1830 census
139	Ward, Amanda		4	?
140	Lynch, Phil		15	Lawrence Co. OH 1850 census To Clinton back to Law. Co.
141	Lynch, Chaney (f)		12	Clinton Co. OH
168	Johnson, Charles		28	Lawrence Co. OH 1830 census-probably s/Ben & Matilda
190	Powell, William		70	Lawrence Co. OH 1840 census
202	Roberts, Molly		70	Lawrence Co. OH - 1830 census (3f)

Total 48

Families arrived in the "wilderness" of Lawrence County. They had to build their own cabins, while some families shared living quarters with current residents. (see Appendix 3 for all Ward's manumitted.)

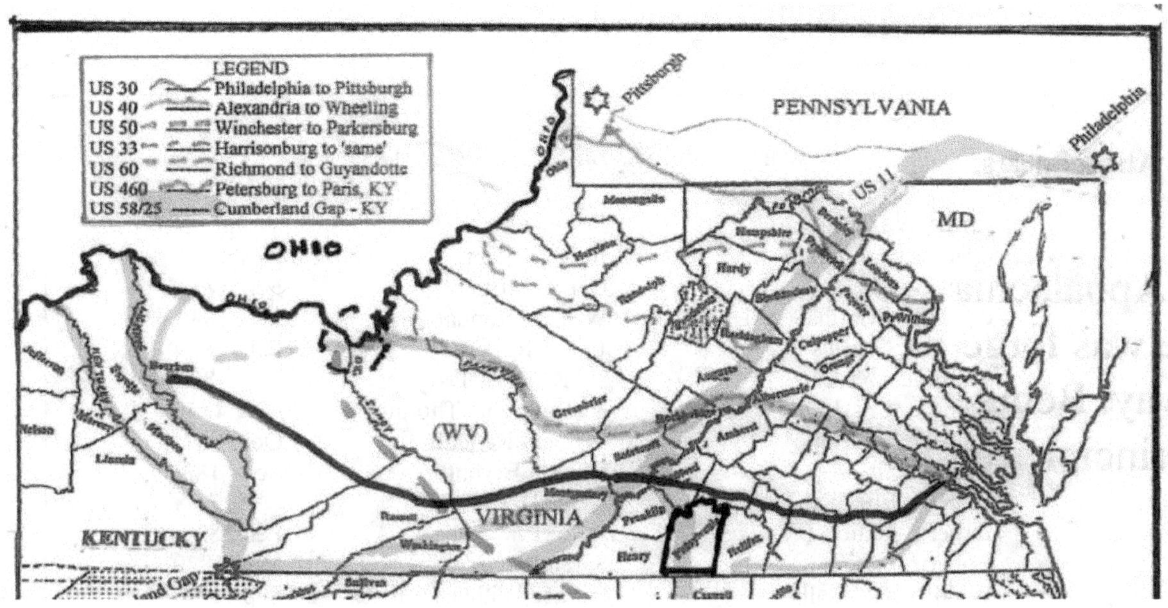

Figure 20 - Ward's Trip North

The logical trail would have been north on US 29 to the junction with Virginia State (US 60), which connected Richmond to the Ohio River. (US 60 met the Ohio River at Guyandotte, opposite Lawrence County at Proctorville.)

Marriages Were Necessary

When the freed Wards arrived in Lawrence County, there were no houses for them. Each family had to cut the trees, notch the logs, raise the walls, and roof the cabin if they wanted a place out of the weather. As in other frontier areas, the new arrivals moved in with existing families until a cabin was built. The marriage records show the results of close quarters.

There was also the requirement to replace a father or mother who died on the trip north. Living conditions were primitive in any frontier area. Childbirth claimed many young women who left children behind; accidents were frequent and doctors unavailable,

The 1830 census listed all these individuals except Lewis Craddock, age 75, and Amanda Ward, age 4, both of whom probably died on the trip north. Another death was Hannah Roberts, who left six children. Her husband, Pleasant, married Sarah Bryant on 18 May 1828.

Ward Manumission Marriages by 1835

Freed Ward	Spouse	Marriage date
Cradwick, Jefferson	Judah Bryant	20 Nov 1831
Craddock, Lucy	Daniel Moss	27 Feb 1834
Craddick, Martha (2nd)	William Randall	5 Oct 1834
Johnson, Charles	1st Ely Roberts	26 Feb 1829
Johnson, Charles	2nd Rebecca Terry	11 Nov 1832
Johnson, Charles	3rd Katherine Thornton	24 May 1840
Johnson, Charlotte	William Randall	4 Oct 1829
Lynch, Phil	Rosetta Bryant	26 Sep 1833
Roberts, Elizabeth	Essex Harris	1827/28
Roberts, Pamela (Pauline)	John Gilkerson	12 Feb 1829
Roberts, Pleasant	Sarah Bryant	18 May 1829
Widow Letty Callaway	Horace Withers/Witcher	27 Sep 1840
Aged 58	aged 86 (1860 census birth 1754)	

(See Index #4 for Lawrence County Black marriages through 1856.)

Please note: These early marriages were with the Bryant family or members of the Macedonia Church.

These marriages continued as family members came of age. During this period to about 1850, other Blacks were moving into area. Some were manumitted; others were runaways seeking freedom. The latter group passed through Lawrence County or settled in the area called Poke Patch at the northern edge of the county. The Providence Association of the Antislavery Baptist Church and its members aided those runaways with supplies, information, directions, and even personal conductors headed to the next "station."

Figure 22 – Madison County, Virginia

Madison County is on the eastern side of the Blue Ridge.

Picturesque, rural, and isolated.

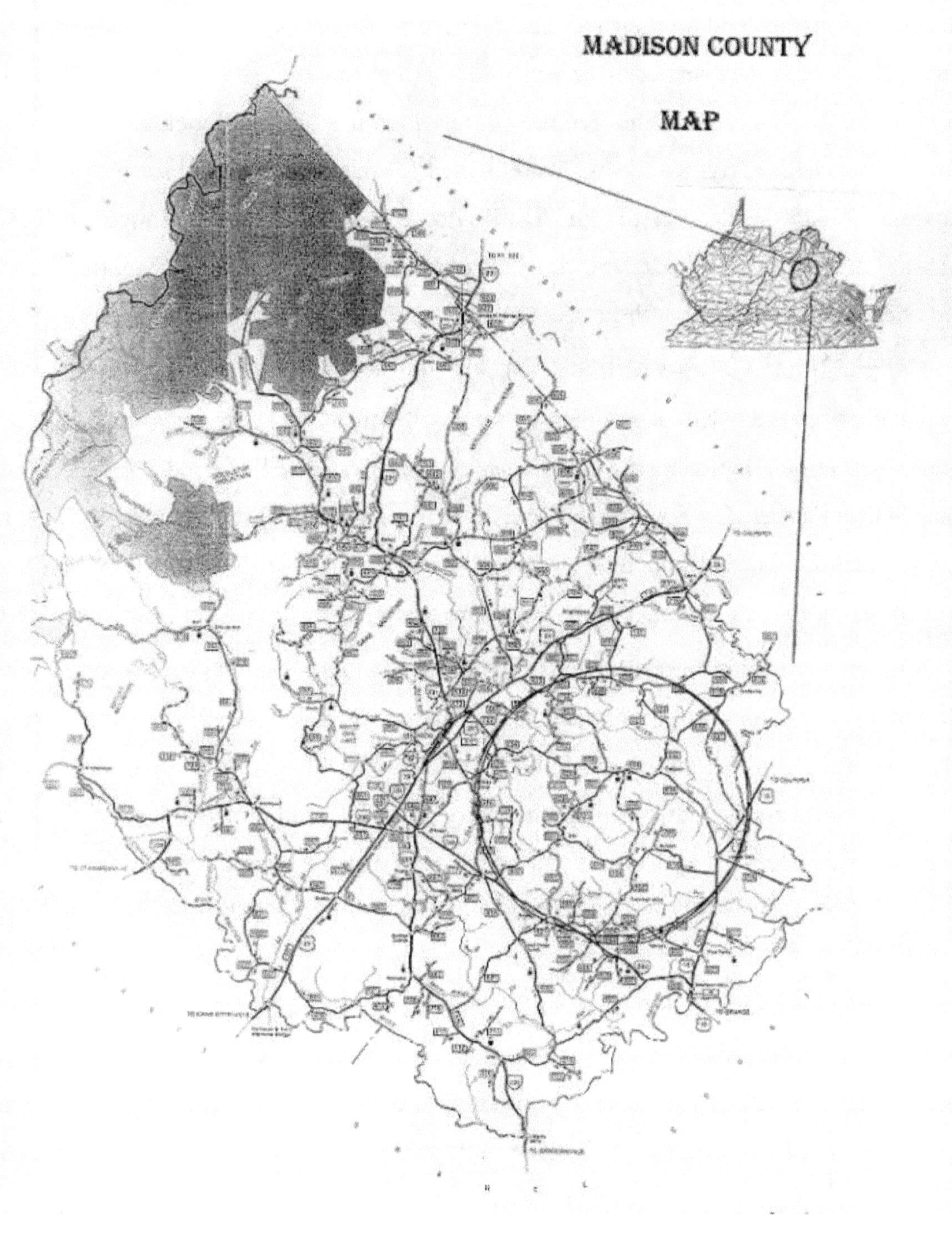

Chapter 10: Twyman - The "Burlington 37" 1849

James Twyman Manumission

The 1849 will of James Twyman of Madison County, VA, named 37 slaves to be manumitted "with others unnamed and all their increase." These freed slaves were accompanied to Lawrence County, OH, where they settled near Burlington, (the county seat) in Fayette Township. Few researchers realize under-aged children were rarely identified in legal documents. This is the case in the Twyman will. Forty-six persons were named for manumission and forty or forty-one came to Lawrence County instead of just the 'Burlington 37.' Property division records filed with the Common Pleas Court in 1870, federal census records, and Lawrence County marriages and deaths provide most of the names, but these records also leave some unanswered questions.

In addition to the '37' named in the will, the following children were emancipated in 1849. (All people were listed with ages given in the 1850 census and surnames of the 1860 census.) Edmund aged 6 and Daniel aged 3 (son of John and Maria Toms), Eliza aged 2 (daughter of Jane Toms Jackson), Alexander aged 1 (son of Beck [Rebecca] Toms Killgore), William aged 2, Beck, grandchild, James, grandchild, Sarah, grandchild, (born in 1850 after arrival), and William "Traveler" Smith aged 9/12 (A son of Nancy Toms Smith born on the trip, but not recorded in 1850 census or recorded incorrectly.)

The Lawrence County property division case states that all the slaves were the "children of Noah and Winnie Toms/Twyman," and it also names as heirs "Peggy – name unknown" and "Walker Toms," "both remaining in Madison County, VA." Listed in the will are "Eleanor" and "James," who both disappear from all further records; and Washington (James) listed as "missing," but later claimed deceased by his brothers. (To further complicate matters, a "Nancy Twyman aged 70" was living with the Frye family in 1850, and the 'Burlington 37' Cemetery is the resting place of William Edmund Toms with dates 1804 - 1878.)

Recorded as 'parents of all,' Noah and Winnie Toms/Twyman (70 and 75 respectively) were not supposed to come west. According to the original will, extra funds were provided for their invalid support. The couple must have found it impossible to be left behind when all their family was leaving. Supposedly they had the following children, grandchildren, and great-grandchildren, all of whom received shares of the original Lawrence County purchase.

The children of Noah and Winnie were: Violet Toms/Twyman -50 (wife of Simon),

Charles Thomas- 50,

unknown mother of James' brothers (no share),

Yellow John Twyman- 45,

Walker living in VA,

Maria Toms- 42 (wife of Short John),

Thomas Walker Fry-40,

William Dykes- 37,

Peggy living in Madison County, VA,

James (from will-no share)

Lewis Twyman-31.

Families of Noah/Winnie's children:

Violet Twyman, husband Simeon (Toms) and sons Ambrose and Abraham,

the four James brothers-Washington, Robert, Lawrence, and Albert,

Thomas Walker and Charlotte Frye with daughter Barbara Gaunt and her children

Horace Twyman and Susan Wilson,

Maria and Short John Toms with their fifteen children and grandchildren:

Nancy Smith, son Ambrose, daughter Julia and her son William Traveler Smith,

Jane Jackson and daughter Eliza,

Beck Killgore and son Alexander,

Henry, Elizabeth, Mary Ann, Ellen, Lucy Ann, Priscilla, Eleanor, Edmund,

and Daniel Toms

grandchildren Beck Toms (no share), James Toms (no share)

and Sarah Brown (probably the daughter of Elizabeth who was 16).

JAMES TWYMAN'S WILL – MADISON COUNTY, VA
Abstract pertaining to his slaves
Will written 1 Aug 1848 – death recorded 8 Feb 1849

1st: I hereby emancipate and set free all my slaves (except the invalid slaves Noah, Winney and Joe for whose support provision will be made hereinafter) to wit: Jenny, Amanda, daughter of said Jenny, and Frances Ann, daughter of said Amanda, Simon and Violet his wife and their sons Abraham and Ambrose, Walker and Charlotte his wife, Barbara, Horace and Susan, Short John and Maria, his wife, Nancy, Julia, Jane, Beck, Henry, Elizabeth, Mary Ann, Ellen, Lucy Ann, Persiller, Eleanor, Charles, James, William, Lewis, Bob, Washington, Lawrence, Albert and Yellow John and all others not herein named, if any, together with all their future increase wherever born before or after my death. …… Noah, Winney, and Joe to be free if they so desire.

2nd: 200 acres to be held in trust for use and benefit of Jenny, Amanda, and Frances

3rd: I give Isaac S. Twyman, James W. Twyman, and Lewis B. Williams $18,000 to be invested for the support of Jenny, Amanda, and Frances Ann – the remainder of funds at their death to be divided among their descendants.

4th: Jenny, Amanda, and Frances Ann to have all my silver plate, clock, watch, household furniture, 2 good horses, 4 milch cows, all types of fowls, and a supply of provisions to support them for one year after my death.

5th: Amanda and Frances Ann to receive their own $800 each

7th: I place $3,000 to be held for the support of Joe, Noah, and Winney. If any desire freedom, then at least $500 be applied to locate them in one of the free states if they wish to leave with my other slaves, then $1500 should be added to the sum provided for removal.

8th: I bequeath $1000 each to Isaac S. Twyman, James W. Twyman, and Lewis B. Williams for them to faithfully execute my wishes for my slaves.

9th: I bequeath to my executors $10,000 for the removal of my slaves emancipated (except Jenny, Amanda and Frances Ann, for whom provisions have already been made) to one of the free states and to purchase home or homes for them together and provide provisions and clothing and all necessary tools to support them for one year.

Executors named: brother Anthony Twyman and nephew William H. Twyman
James Twyman - signed 1 Aug 1848 – death - 8 Feb 1849

Brother Anthony Twyman was head of the extended Twyman family, and he agreed to accept the Will. Other members of the family objected to the manumission and tried to break the Will. Their objections concerned bequeaths to Jenny, Amanda, and Frances Ann and the main reason those women took the cash willed them and left Virginia. (See Appendix 7.)

Chapter 11: Twyman Families Moving West

The Lawrence County lands purchased for the manumitted slaves were referred to as the FRY LANDS and so identified by the surveyor's office. Supposedly, the properties were purchased in the name of "Walker Fry et al.," but his name is not the first listed on any transaction. Family tradition says Walker was the plantation foreman. (The possibility exists that he was Twyman's ½ brother.) Others claim someone came before the group and selected the land for purchase. Nine individual properties composed the Lawrence County purchase, and it would have taken time and trouble to locate lands closely situated to one another if not adjacent. Since the deeds do not name Fry first, it is a logical conclusion that the representative who came ahead of the group was Walker Fry. If he was indeed the plantation manager, he would have been able to select useful land and have been able to negotiate and bargain for its purchase.

It is known that at least one of Twyman's nephews accompanied the manumitted slaves to Ohio, but the Twyman estate dispersals list expenditures for only one trip. It seems improbable that land was not selected prior to the arrival of the manumitted slaves and several thoughts support this theory. 1) Why was Lawrence County, Ohio, selected? 2) Why were the slaves moved without a determined destination? 3) How was so much semi-adjoining land found accidentally?

Figure 24 - Twyman Settlement Area

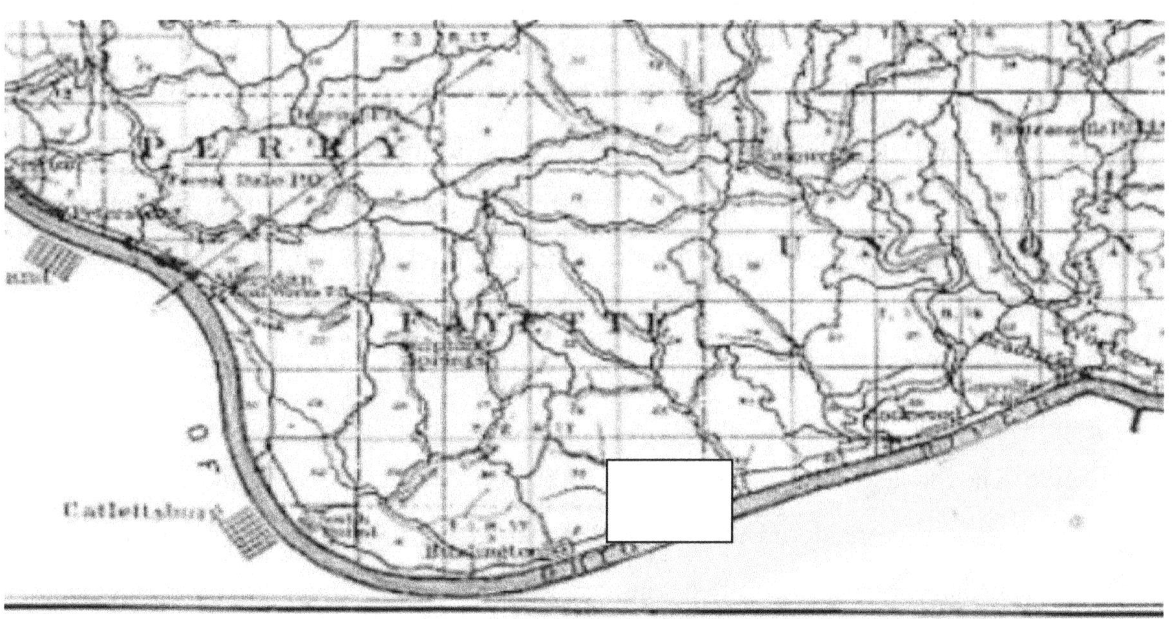

Section of Lawrence County, Ohio, where the Twyman families settled.
East end of the Burlington community along the Ohio River.
Properties in Fayette Townships 1 and 2

Between the time James Twyman executed his will, his death, the court probate, and the move west, many events happened to the newly emancipated slaves. As requested in the will, several slaves completed 'for hire' contracts, and their wages were paid to the estate. Everyone had to appear before the county court to be registered and to have manumission papers signed and filed. While there was a delay in printing copies of the will for each person, the adults gathered supplies and packed them in the wagons prepared for the trip. Another delay came procuring tents and camping supplies, but finally, farewells were said to friends and family, and the trek began.

The distance from Madison County at the eastern foot of the Blue Ridge to the Ohio River was about 400 miles. On good days they traveled about twenty miles, first south along the Foothills Trail, and then west on the James River and Kanawha Turnpike. It took more than two weeks of tedious travel as they crossed the Blue Ridge and then the more difficult Appalachian Mountains before they emerged into the open fields of Teays Valley in western Virginia and reached the mighty Ohio River. There were several river landings on the Virginia shore, and the settlers may have crossed the river on a steamboat. The children were impressed by the boat because no one had ever ridden a steamboat before or even seen one.

The manumitted slaves did not travel alone. Twyman had requested his nephews make the trip to Ohio for both protection and guidance. However, the land sale was arranged, and Isaac Frampton produced two separate deeds, which included nine parcels of land deeded to all the freed slaves as a group. Hopefully, each tract of land had a house, but stories handed down told of one large house and several small ones to hold all the people. The 1850 census showed five family groups, while the 1870 Property Division indicated their locations. A map of the area today shows the property lay west of the Sybene curve of US 52 and continued along the road for a mile to the edge of Burlington. Within that area lay the schoolhouse lot, Charlotte Lane, and the '37' Cemetery which remain today.

James Twyman stated that the land should be for the entire group. Most plantation owners of the period thought of their slaves as a single family who would need all its members working together to survive. The master believed he was doing the people a favor by giving title to the land to all of them. Few masters considered there were individual families or that each person might want to own a piece of land. The former slaves, in turn, did not realize how much land they needed to produce food for themselves or having products to sell.

The Lawrence County land sold to the Twyman's was only partially cleared and located on the swampy river bottom or up the side of the numerous hills. It was not prime real estate, but each person wanted his share. By 1870, the group decided to go to court and divide the land. It was a complicated problem, but the ensuing cases gave the names of all the Twyman people and even included those deceased or remaining in Madison County.

After all the court cases, each lot equaled about 15.61 acres. Barely enough to raise a large garden, those lots were also too small to divide and pass on to the children. Some members of the '37' sold their land as soon as they could.

Lawrence Co. OH Deed Book 12 - pages 137-8   31 Oct 1849
Isaac Frampton and wife Jane of Wayne Co. VA   (spelling original)
To Simeon, Violet, and others   (underling added by author)

Know all men by these presents that Isaac Frampton and Jane Frampton, wife of said Isaac Frampton of the county of Wayne and state of Virginia in consideration for the sum of six thousand dollars to us in hand paid by Simeon, Violet, Abraham, Ambrose, Walker, Charlotte, Barbara, Horace, Susan, Short John, Maria, Jane, Beck, Henry, Elizabeth, Mary Ann, Ellen, Lucy Ann, Persilla, Eleanor, Edmund, Daniel, Cilla (daughter of said Jane), Alexander (son of said Beck), Nancy, Julia, William (son of said Nancy) Charles, William, Lewis, Washington, Lawrence, Albert, Yellow John, Bob, Noah, and Winna during their natural lives and then to their heirs, forever, for the following premises situate in the County of Lawrence and the state of Ohio and in the township of Fayette and described as follows:

The East part of fractional section No. 2 in Range No. 17 and Township No. 1. Beginning at stake on the Ohio two hundred and forty-three poles easterly by the said river from the South West corner of the said fractional section at the South East corner of Barton's heirs land thence running North 69 degrees East one hundred and thirty-three and two-thirds poles to a stake the South West corner of land formerly owned by Yager now owned by George Kouns, thence due north along said Kouns' line to the back line of the said fractional section to a stake, thence West on the said back line to such a point as will be running due south therefrom to intersect the stake at the place of beginning, thence from a said point south to said first mentioned stake, the place of beginning. Excepting and reserving out of the about granted premises the following parcels of land heretofore sold and surveyed by William Lynd to wit: 5 ½ acres to Elijah Frampton.

Also, 6 acres 2 rods and 1 pole to William C. Johnson, the <u>above two described tracts</u> are taken from the South West corner of said tract = containing one hundred and fifty-four acres more or less. (154a less 5 ½ a and 6a 2rod 1 pole = 143 ½ a – more or less)

Also, the South East quarter of the North West Quarter of Section 35 Township 2 of Range 17 saving and excepting one acre out of the North West corner sold to Arty Carter and one acre sold to Abner Johnson off the West side of said tract. (40a – 2a = 38a)

Also, one acre of the same side was sold to Anna Robinson, containing forty-one acres more or less. Also subject to a life lease heretofore grant to Samuel Blankenship and wife for about 15 acres on said lot.

Also, part of the South West quarter of the North East quarter of Section 35 Township 2 of Range 17 being all that part of the said quarter section that lies south of the top of the ridge: commencing at the corner of the said Isaac Frampton and (   ) Randall the center corner of Section 35, thence north with the West line of the said quarter to the top of the ridge about 35 rods to a stake about one rod West of a Black Locust 12 inches in diameter, thence Easterly along the top of said ridge flowing the marked or blazed trees with the meander of the top of said ridge till it strikes the East line of the said quarter about 10 rods North of the South East corner thereof to a Hickory tree 8 inches in diameter, thence south to the said South East corner of the said quarter, thence West along South line of the said quarter to the place of beginning containing by estimation twenty acres more or less.

Also, the West half of the South West quarter of S35 T2 R17 containing 87 acres and 14/100.

Also, the South East half of the South West quarter of S35 T2 R17 containing 88 acres and 72/100.

Also, the South West quarter of S35 T2 R17 containing 43 acres and 22/100.

Also, the East half of the North West quarter of the South West quarter of S35 T2 R17 containing 23 acres and 86/100.

To have and to hold said premises with the appurtenances unto the said Simeon, Violet, Abraham, Ambrose, Walker, Charlotte, Barbara, Horace, Susan, Short John, Mariah, Jane, Beck, Henry, Elizabeth, Mary Ann, Ellen, Lucy Ann, Persilla, Eleanor, Edmund, Daniel, Cilla (daughter of said Jane), Alexander (son of said Beck), Nancy, Julia, William (son of said Nancy), Charles, William, Lewis, Washington, Lawrence, Albert, Yellow John, Bob, Noah and Winna during their natural lives and then to their heirs forever. And said Isaac Frampton for himself and his heirs does hereby covenant with the said Simeon, Violet, Abraham, Ambrose, Walker, Charlotte, Barbara, Horace,

Susan, Short John, Mariah, Jane, Beck, Henry, Elizabeth, Mary Ann, Ellen, Lucy Ann, Persilla, Eleanor, Edmund, Daniel, Cilla (daughter of said Jane), Alexander (son of said Beck), Nancy, Julia, William (son of said Nancy) Charles, William, Lewis, Washington, Lawrence, Albert, Yellow John, Bob, Noah and Winna their heirs and assigns that he is lawfully seized of the premises aforesaid that the premises are free and clear from all encumbrances whatever and that he will forever Warrant and defend the same with appurtenance unto the said Simeon, Violet, Abraham, Ambrose, Walker, Charlotte, Barbara, Horace, Susan, Short John, Mariah, Jane, Beck, Henry, Elizabeth, Mary Ann, Ellen, Lucy Ann, Persilla, Eleanor, Edmund, Daniel, Cilla (daughter of said Jane), Alexander (son of said Beck), Nancy, Julia, William (son of said Nancy) Charles, William, Lewis, Washington, Lawrence, Albert, Yellow John, Bob, Noah and Winna their heirs and assigns against the lawful claims of all person whatsoever. In testimony whereof, the said Isaac Frampton and Jane Frampton have hereunto set their hand and seals this 31st day of October in the Year of Our Lord one thousand eight hundred and forty-nine.

Executed in the presence of Elias Nigh & J.M. Bryan   Isaac Frampton (seal)
The State of Ohio Lawrence County   Jane Frampton (seal)

154a less 5 ½ and 6+ acre = 143 ½ a - 41a less 1a & 1a & 1a = 38a - 20a plus = 20a
87 14/100a plus = 87 14/100a - 88 72/100a = 88 72/100a - 43 22/100a = 43 12/100a
23 86/100a = 23 86/100a   total 444 20/100 more or less for $6,000 or $13.50 per acre

Figure 25 – Government Survey

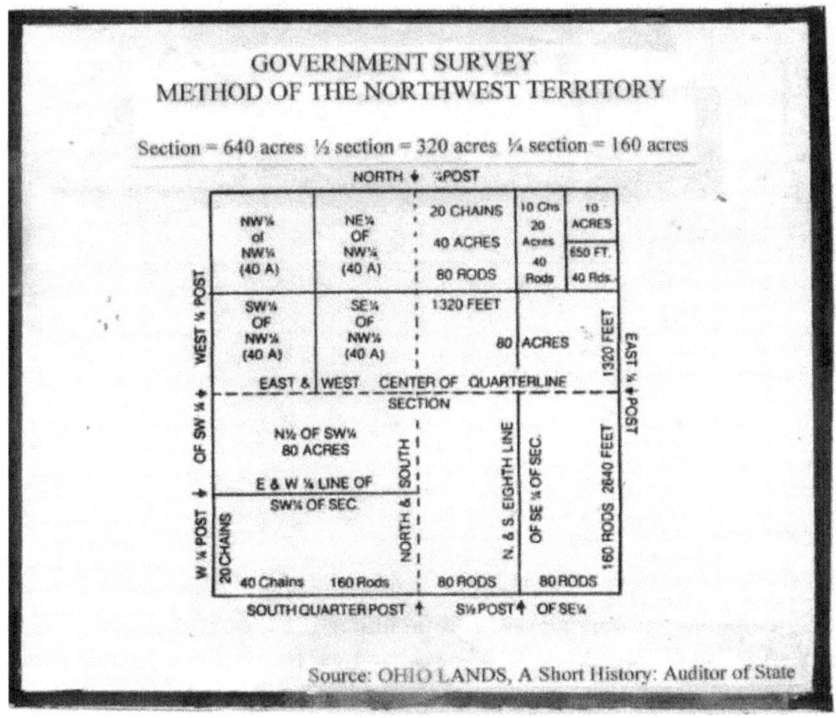

WILL of JAMES TWYMAN (death 8 Feb 1849) – "all slaves manumitted plus all increase."

1) Joe (invalid)   stayed   funds provided for care - died in about 1 year
2) Jenny- house slave   -stayed   mother of Amanda
3) Amanda-house slave   -stayed   daughter of Jenny and mistress of James Twyman
4) Frances Ann   -stayed   daughter of Jenny and Twyman

		1	2	3	4	5	6	left heir	death
5) Noah (invalid) came	70	x	x	x	x	x	d(decd.)	x	1858 cem
6) Winney (invalid) came	75	x	x	x	x	x	d	x	1854 cem
7) Simon Twyman	55	x	x	x	x	x	d	x	1864 cem
8) w/Violet "	50	x	x	x	x	x	d	x	1850 cem
9) s/Ambrose "	15	x	x	x	x	x	d	x	1860 cem
10) s/Abraham(Abram)"	13	x	x	x	x	x	d	x	1860 cem
11) Walker w/Charlotte	40	x	x	x	x	x	x		1898 will
12) Charlotte h/Walker	47	x	x	x	x	x	x		1892
13) Barbara Gaunt	(26)	x	x	x	x	?	x		see appx.
14) Horace Twyman	13	x	x	x	x	x	x		1911 dc
15) Susan Wilson	4	x	x	x	x	x	x		1941 obit
16) Short John Toms	49	x	x	x	x	x	d	x	64-in '60
17) Maria "	42	x	x	x	x	x	x		59-in '70
18) Nancy Toms Smith	27	x	x	x	x	x	x		1896
19) Julia Smith(James)	10	x	x	x	x	x	x		
20) Jane Toms Jackson	24	x	x	x	x	x	x		
21) Beck Toms Killgore	22	x	x	x	x	x	x		1896
22) Henry Toms	19	x	x	x	x	x	x		1911 dc
23) Elizabeth Toms King	16	x	x	x	x	x	x		
24) Mary Ann Toms	14	x	x	x	x	x	d	x	1857 cem
25) Ellen Toms Shelton	12	x	x	x	x	x	x		42-'80
26) Lucy Ann Toms	9	x	x	x	x	x	d	x	1858 cem
27) Persiller Toms	8	x	x	x	x	x	x		1890 dc
28) Eleanor Toms	-	x	x						1850
29) Charles Thomas	37	x	x	x	x	x	x		75–'80
30) James (vanishes)		-	x						?
31) William Dykes	37	x	x	x	x	x	d	x	1853 cem
32) Lewis Twyman	31	x	x	x	x	x	d	x	1856 cem
33) Bob James	30	x	x	x	x	x	d	x	1850
34) Washington "– missing		x					d	x	1849
35) Lawrence James	24	x	x	x	x	x	x		1886 dc
36) Albert James	22	x	x	x	x	x	x		
37) Yellow John Twy-	45	x	x	x	x	x	d	x	p1870 cem
inf 38) Edmund s/J&M	6		x	x	x	x	x		1918 dc
39) Daniel B. s/J&M	3		x	x	x	x	x		1917 dc
40) Eliza d/Jane	2		x	x	x	x	x		1927 dc
41) William s/unk	2				x				
42) Alexander s/Beck	1		x	x	x	x	x		
43) Wm. Traveler s/Nancy	9/10		x	x		x	x		1931 obit
44) Beck	gr ch				x				
45) James	gr ch				x				
46) Sarah (Brown)	gr ch				x				

On census or other documents – not in will – children under 12: Edmund 6, Daniel (David) 3, Eliza 2, William 2, Alexander 1, William Traveler 9/12, Beck, James, Sarah. Questionable-(? Nancy 70, census, Rebecca 26 -maybe Barbara? – James will. as adult, Eleanor - ch d 1850?)

Chapter 12: Thomas Walker Fry and Aunt Susan

By all accounts, Thomas Walker Fry was the leader of the '37'. Aunt Susan was his granddaughter and the keeper of the family history. Family memories and news articles all claim Fry was the most important person. Usually called Walker Fry, he seemed to have been a half-brother to James Twyman and was probably the overseer of the Twyman Plantation before coming to Ohio. He was also a broom maker, a creditable carpenter, and a capable hedge doctor, but he was best known as a minister in Madison County.

Macedonia Church had been in existence for forty years when Fry and the other freed Twyman arrived in Burlington. Walker Fry and most of the group quickly joined the only Black Church in the area. He was associated with Macedonia for the next fifty years, regularly preaching in numerous locations and attending Association gatherings until his death in 1898. After the Civil War in 1866, he was credited with the organization of Mount Pisgah Church at Red Hill just north of Proctorville in eastern Lawrence County.

Thomas Walker Fry was also one of the ministers associated with the underground railroad trails. Just one of several members of the Macedonia congregation, Fry was able to move around the region as both a minister and a 'hedge doctor' who could treat people a white doctor would not. Intelligent and experienced in handling people, Fry probably gave directions, passed out supplies, and misdirected search parties.

His granddaughter, Susan Twyman Wilson Gordon, was just three years old when she arrived in Lawrence County. First living with her grandparents, then moving to northern Ohio with her mother before returning to the Ohio Valley; Susan had many experiences to remember and repeat. Events were etched in her young memory and expanded over the years as many visitors appeared at the Fry home. Her great-grandparents were Noah and Winnie Toms, who had spent seventy-five years in slavery. Their joy in freedom encouraged Susan to remember all their stories and to pass them along to younger members of the extended family.

Susan was born in 1847 to Barbara (recorded on the census as Rebecca), a daughter of Walker Fry and his wife, Charlotte. Barbara was one of the first Twyman's to leave Lawrence County, and she sold her share of the land before she left. Marrying a Moses Gaunt, she took Susan to Huron County, Ohio, before 1870. Barbara may have died in 1876 when Susan returned to Lawrence County to live with her grandparents again. Susan first used the name Wilson, but soon married

Isaiah Richard Gordon and had two daughters, Iona and Barbara. Susan spent the rest of her life in Lawrence County, dying in 1941 at age 96.

The only Twyman person to keep the name was Susan's brother Horace Twyman.

Ten years older than Susan, he lived with his Fry grandparents until he was twenty-one. In 1870 he was living in St. Louis, MO, five years later, he had a daughter in Cairo, IL, but by 1880 he was again in the Fry home living with his wife Susan and children Edith (Gussie) and Alexander.

After his grandchildren returned to Lawrence County, Walker Fry sold each, Susan and Horace, one acre of his portion of the Divided Lands. Susan spent the rest of her life in Ohio while Horace moved his family south across the Ohio River to the Guyandotte section of Huntington, where members of the family took jobs in the C & O railyards.

Susan passed her love of history to several of her grandchildren, who kept the stories alive. Owen Pleasants, a son of Iona Gordon Pleasants, and Susan Reynolds Spencer, a daughter of Barbara Gordon Reynolds, like their grandmother, lived into their nineties and always had a story on their lips.

Figure 26 – Charlotte & Walker Fry with granddaughter with Susan about 1892

#2046 – Document #3 page 215 – Recorded in Record of Wills #5 p45
Filed 7 Feb 1899 by W.T. Smith & Mary. K. Smith
Admitted to Probate 22 Apr 1899

In the name of the Benevolent Father of us All, I, T.W. Fry of Burlington, Lawrence County, Ohio, do hereby make and publish this; my last will and testament.

1st I give and devise to the heirs of Horace Twyman, To wit: Augusta Twyman, Alexander Twyman, Maud Twyman, Lottie Twyman, Jasper Twyman, Moses Twyman, and Cora Twyman, All the lands Owned by me embraced in lot #1, containing 9 acres more or less, Said lands now on the county records as Fry Lands and others; the heirs to share alike. I also give all my personal effects to the above named heirs of Horace Twyman, and that no appraisement or sale be made of same.

2nd I give and devise to the heirs of Susan Gordon, To wit: Iona Gordon and Barbara Gordon, all the lands in lot #2 now owned by me, lying north of the pike and joined on the west by the lands of W.T. Smith. I further desire that the road on the west side of these lands leading from the pike to the river not be changed to inconvenience my relatives and neighbors.

I appoint W.T. Smith Executor of this my last will and Testament in Testimony hereof, I have hereunto set my hand and seal, this 6th day of July 1898.

his
Thomas W. X Fry
mark

Signed and acknowledged by said T.W. Fry as his last will and testament in our presence and signed by us in his presence.
Wit: M.K. Smith -W.T. Smith (William Traveler Smith)

****

Horace Twyman family;
Augusta Twyman, 'Gussie' m William A. Lane of Guyandotte
Maud m Nelson B. Layne of Guyandotte
Charlotte (Lottie) m James Carlos Justice of Burlington
Cora m Hugh Lane of Guyandotte
'WT' - William Traveler Smith and wife one of the '37', a teacher and secretary at Macedonia.

****

In 1823, twenty-six years before his death, James Twyman executed the following deed to his father in Madison County: (Reference to Thomas Walker Fry's name and Peggy in Virginia.)

Figure 28 - Deed of Gift

Know all by these presents that I, James Twyman of Madison County and the State of Virginia, for and in consideration of the natural love and affection which I bear William Twyman of same county and state as well as for further consideration of one dollar in hand paid by the said, William Twyman …

by these presents do give and grant unto the said William Twyman…. a negro woman slave by the name of Peggy and three children by name Jacob, Joe & a small one not named, formerly the property of Elizabeth Fry, wife of Joshua Fry…… 13 Nov 1823

Deed of gift recorded 27 Nov 1823   signed James Twyman   (seal)

Elizabeth Fry was the sister of James and William Twyman, Jr.
Deed referring to 'Peggy, still in Madison County' listed in 1870 Property Division.

The Twyman manumission happened over 170 years ago, but because there were extensive legal documents and family members who kept the history alive, information about the Burlington '37' was easy to locate. Walker Fry, born in 1810, lived in 1899. Aunt Susan, born in 1847, lived to be 96, dying in 1941. Her grandchildren, Owen Pleasants and Susan Reynolds, lived almost as long, dying about 2010. The important fact was who they knew and the stories they kept alive. Aunt Susan lived with or near her grandparents for fifty years, and the same held true for her grandchildren.

The original '37' had limited education, but they saw their children and grandchildren become teachers. They began life in slavery, but from the will of James Twyman, they became free landowners and proceeded to improve their life. The land connected them to the community and encouraged most to stay along the Ohio River even after the Property Division.

Many of the records and pictures in this volume were shared by Owen Pleasants and his wife Emajean in 2003. Both individuals were descended from the '37'; Owen from Aunt Susan and Emajean from William Traveler Smith.

Figure 29 – Owen & Emajean Pleasants, 2003

Chapter 13: Macedonia Church

The Importance of a Freed Community

The heart of the Black community in Fayette Township in Lawrence County, Ohio, was the Macedonia Church, located on a high ridge known as Macedonia Hill. That church began in the homes of its members between 1811 and 1813 and was probably the first Black church in Ohio. Since Roseanna Bryan/t owned property nearby, it could be assumed that the first meetings began at her home, and her son John most likely led the meetings. Unable to join the local white churches, the congregation choose from their own members to provide their elders and ministers. By 1819 enough Blacks had settled in Lawrence County to create three churches that joined together to form an association.

The original *Providence Anti-slavery Baptist Association* was formed by the Macedonia Church, located two miles north of the Ohio River at Macedonia Hill, the Big Rock Church, probably about ten miles north of the river near Rock Camp, and the Union Church, near the community of Poke Patch at the northern edge of the county and thirty miles from the river. A few years later, the association was recorded as the *Providence Anti-slavery Missionary Baptist Association.*

Any church was an integral part of pioneer America in the Nineteenth Century, and most slave masters considered it their duty to bring religion to their slaves. Religious instruction was an accepted routine of the time period when Sunday was a day of rest for master and slave alike. Religious services were often handled by the master, but sometimes a slave would be allowed to lead the services and even receive some education to read the Bible. These Black ministers married the couples, baptized the children, and preached the funerals in an era when few white ministers would not or, legally, could not provide those services. These plantation ministers, already important, became community leaders after crossing the Ohio River.

The Macedonia Church struggled in its first decade with few members and no money. The arrival of the freed Wards in 1828 was probably the answer to many prayers. Not only did adults join the church, but there was a multitude of children to add strength and direction. The Ward's, like most manumitted Blacks, arrived with little money and few supplies. The established families shared their homes until new cabins could be built and a small church was erected.

Records from the early period of the Macedonia Church are almost non-existent, but the Providence Association held annual meetings, some of which were held at Macedonia. Comparing those association meeting minutes with census records and county court records makes it possible to recreate some of the evidence of the church's development. History claims the first Providence Association was created in 1819 and consisted of Macedonia Church (the Mother Church), Big Rock Church, and Union Church, all in Lawrence County.

The earliest Providence records which exist are for the second Providence association, which was organized in Jackson County in 1835. Macedonia Church is not even mentioned, but two other Lawrence County churches were members of that second association. Union Church, the Black church at Poke Patch, was named, but the other was a white church located on the top of Greasy Ridge, known as Mount Pleasant. That church had been founded in 1807 and joined the association because of its anti-slavery platform, and the church probably supported an escape route that followed Greasy Ridge.

The first families of Macedonia had to be the first Black settlers in the county, whether they were listed in the records of settlers or as squatters out in the woods. Both the Bryant and the Murphy families arrived shortly after 1810. With other unidentified settlers, they organized a Baptist Church in their homes and then created their own association when the white churches would not acknowledge them.

Rosanna Bryant died in 1833, and her son, John, was not mentioned after 1841, but leading members of the Macedonia Church in the 1850s were the sons and grandsons of that family. William Bryant (John's oldest son) was named in the 1856 Association records, and the census noted he was a Baptist minister in 1880. His brother, George W. Bryant was listed as a minister on the 1850 census while both brothers were active in the Association records.

Later William's son, Isaac Vinton Bryant, became part of the records from the 1870s to the early 1930's. A noted minister and educator who served in Huntington, West Virginia, he joined several of his cousins, children of John's daughters, as active members of the Macedonia Church. Juda Bryant married Jefferson Craddock. Their son, William Portrait Cradic, preached across southern Ohio then moved to Columbus where he died in 1912. Susannah Bryant married Charles Roberts, a Ward, who became a Macedonia minister and baptized many members in southern Ohio. He was listed in twenty-second minutes of the *Providence Anti-Slavery Association* in 1856, as well as the 1884 membership records for Macedonia Church.

Another source of information was the Macedonia Freewill Cemetery, where primary burials between the original cedar trees are several members of the Bryant family. Many original members no longer have head stones. (Historical Marker and Burials of the Macedonia Freewill Baptist.)

A community of freed Blacks had an advantage over Blacks born free. The emancipated Blacks were legal. They had freedom papers, a little money, and often their work bonds were paid by the former owner or waved. On the early Ohio frontier along the Ohio River, they were also usually accepted as simply other settlers. In the case of the Macedonia settlers, they were also smart enough to stay out of the public view and selected their church site on the ridge above the Ohio valley, where they would have plenty of notice if a raid was planned. Slave catchers were a fact of life, many laws prohibited Blacks from their complete freedom.

All of Ohio's settlers wanted to be farmers and either purchased small tracts of land or simply 'squatted' some place and tried to raise enough food to feed their families. A squatter had no rights to the land which could be sold, forcing him to move. Often the 'squatter' built a cabin and plowed a few acres, then sold his 'improved claim' to the next 'squatter' who came along. The practice was a time-honored frontier custom that lasted until the tax collector appeared.

Located on the northern shore of the Ohio River and in a free state was a further benefit to the Macedonia Blacks. They were able to gather information about events along both sides of the river from riverboat men, settlers and movers, and their young people working as domestics.

That information was shared with a few trustworthy persons, and action was taken as needed to locate, provision, and direct escaped slaves to reasonably safe trails past Burlington and into the wilderness that existed in southern Ohio.

Figure 30 – Re-dedication 1889 – *Ironton Register*

Figure 31 – Macedonia Facts

MACEDONIA FACTS

1807-1813 – the founding of Macedonia meeting in members' homes.
-            Only 23 known settlers by 1820
1810-1817 – location manumission of Rosanna and John Bryant
1813-1830 – probable minister – John Bryant
1819   – formation of *Providence Anti-slavery Baptist Association*
1827-1828   - manumitted Ward's arrival
1830's   – John Bryant joined by Essex Harris, Pleasant Roberts & Jefferson Cradic
1831   – Association's name became Providence Missionary Baptist Association
1840's   – John's sons William and George, with C.W. Roberts, J.J. Cradic
1849   – The Twyman "37" arrive led by Thomas Walker Fry, minister
1856-1857 – Providence Association minutes list Macedonia ministers & elders:
            W. Bryant, J. Cradic, T.W. Fry, C.W. Roberts, and W.P. Cradic (s/Jeff)
1868   – 33rd Providence Association held at Macedonia (*Ironton Register* 30 Aug)
                "One to two thousand people, both black and white, attended."
1879   – 44th association meeting held at Macedonia
1880-1882 – a bell post, used to call the riverboat, placed on the Ohio riverbank
1884   – church minutes survive
1889   – Macedonia rededicated Church building (*Ironton Register* 21 Nov)

As the years passed and the Ward manumission members joined the church, several became ministers. Jonathan Craddock was only twelve when the families arrived in Lawrence County, but J.J. Cradic was listed as a Macedonia Minister in 1856 and 1857. He later had a church in Scioto County and, in 1879, represented Ironton at the association meeting. Charles (C. W.) Roberts was also a representative in 1856 and 1857. An educated guess would suggest the fathers or brothers of these men led the church during the 1830s and 1840s with the Bryant brothers. (Jefferson Craddock married Juda Bryant in 1831, Pleasant Roberts married Sarah Bryant in 1829, and Essex Harris married Elizabeth Bryant in 1828.)

Figure 32 – Known and Inferred Macedonia Ministers

1810-1820 – John Bryant – son of Roseanna Bryant
1820-1840 – Essex Harris (son-in-law), Jefferson Craddock
    (son-in-law & Ward), Pleasant Roberts (son-in-law-Ward)
1840-1860 – Wm. Stewart (Union), Wm. Bryant, Geo. W.
    Bryant, – (both s/John), I.V. Bryant (s/Wm.) J. Cradic, C.W.
    Roberts, W. P. Cradic (s/Jefferson), J.J. Cradic [all Wards],
    T.W. Fry, Henry King (m Twyman), T.W. Smith (Traveler)
    (all Twyman)
Also in southern Lawrence County: L.W. Johnson – Ironton
J.D. Noel and G. McDaniel - Quakers Bottom
Wm. Stewart – Union Church minister - taught at Macedonia
in 1848, attended Lawrence County meetings in 1856-57
but already living in Cass County, Michigan.

Depository for the Providence Association materials of the American Baptist - held by the Samuel Colgate Historical Library, Colgate Rochester Divinity School, Rochester, NY. (Recently moved to North Carolina.)

By 1849 when the Twyman group arrived, the Macedonia Church was well established and was just completing its first "real" church building. The addition of new people brought several assets. The leader of the Twyman manumission was Thomas Walker Fry, an established minister who quickly joined Macedonia. The new settlers also came with money and property.

Much of the property purchased for the Twyman group lay in a corridor from the Ohio River to Macedonia Church on the forested ridge. That land created a safe passage for any slave crossing the river. The expanded congregation made improvements to the church building at Macedonia Hill, but more important was recognition received throughout the nearby Ohio valley. Macedonia became a "Mother Church" in all three states of Ohio, Virginia, and Kentucky as its members moved out to form new congregations in the surrounding area.

The 1830s and 1840s saw the church grow, and as Association records prove, it began to produce numerous ministers and elders. It also secretly expanded its anti-slavery stand by creating and maintaining an escape route for runaways. The Macedonia Church and its members lived along the route of the Old Jackson Road, which connected the Ohio River to the county seat of Jackson County, about thirty-five miles to the north. A great road (really an Indian path which the County Court ordered surveyed and established between 1 Jun and the last of July in 1817 – Lawrence Co. 1817 Common Pleas Book #1)), it crossed Lawrence County along most of the ridges and steep hills, but it led from slavery to freedom. If the runaway slave, aided by church members, could reach the Ohio ridge where Macedonia stood, it was possible to make his way to freedom.

Just thirty miles north of Burlington, beside the Old Jackson Road, sprawled an area called Poke Patch. Poke Patch was a loose little community settled by free people, freed slaves, runaways, mulattoes, whites, and native Americans which lay in the woods about halfway between Olive Iron Furnace in Lawrence County and Gallia Iron Furnace in Gallia County. It was also a recognized 'station' of the Underground Railroad (UGRR). (Siebert)

About thirty-five miles from the Ohio River, runaways could reach the area from Burlington, Ironton, Quakers Bottom, and even Pt. Pleasant. There, a large group of 'conductors' would protect the runaway and send him onto the next 'station.' Its distance from the river meant few slave catchers were willing to make the long trip, nor did they care to confront a large group of angry people who lived there. Direct contact between Macedonia Church at Burlington and the Union Church at Poke Patch existed between the ministers and missionaries who traveled among the hills looking for lost souls. Several of the Poke Patch Stewarts taught and preached at Macedonia, while Macedonia ministers attended Association meetings throughout the area.

The Old Jackson Road was used by the itinerate ministers, teamsters and their assistants, and farmers going to market, but it could also be used as a guide to the north. The road seemed to follow the North Star. Between 1820 and 1850, the road was heavily used for many purposes, from its terminal on the Ohio River at Burlington. It certainly was not a modern road but a dirt trail that wound through dense forest and climbed many hills. That lonely, crooked path led directly north, making it a guide for the escaping slave trying to find Poke Patch.

In 1852, Lawrence County seat moved its county seat from Burlington to the new community of Ironton. A new 'Jackson Road' followed the Iron Railroad and the Iron Furnaces north along a route that became Ohio 93. The 'Old' Jackson Road was soon forgotten by all except conductors for the Underground Railroad and the escapees who ran along the trail.

Figure 33 – Road Along the Iron Furnace Trail

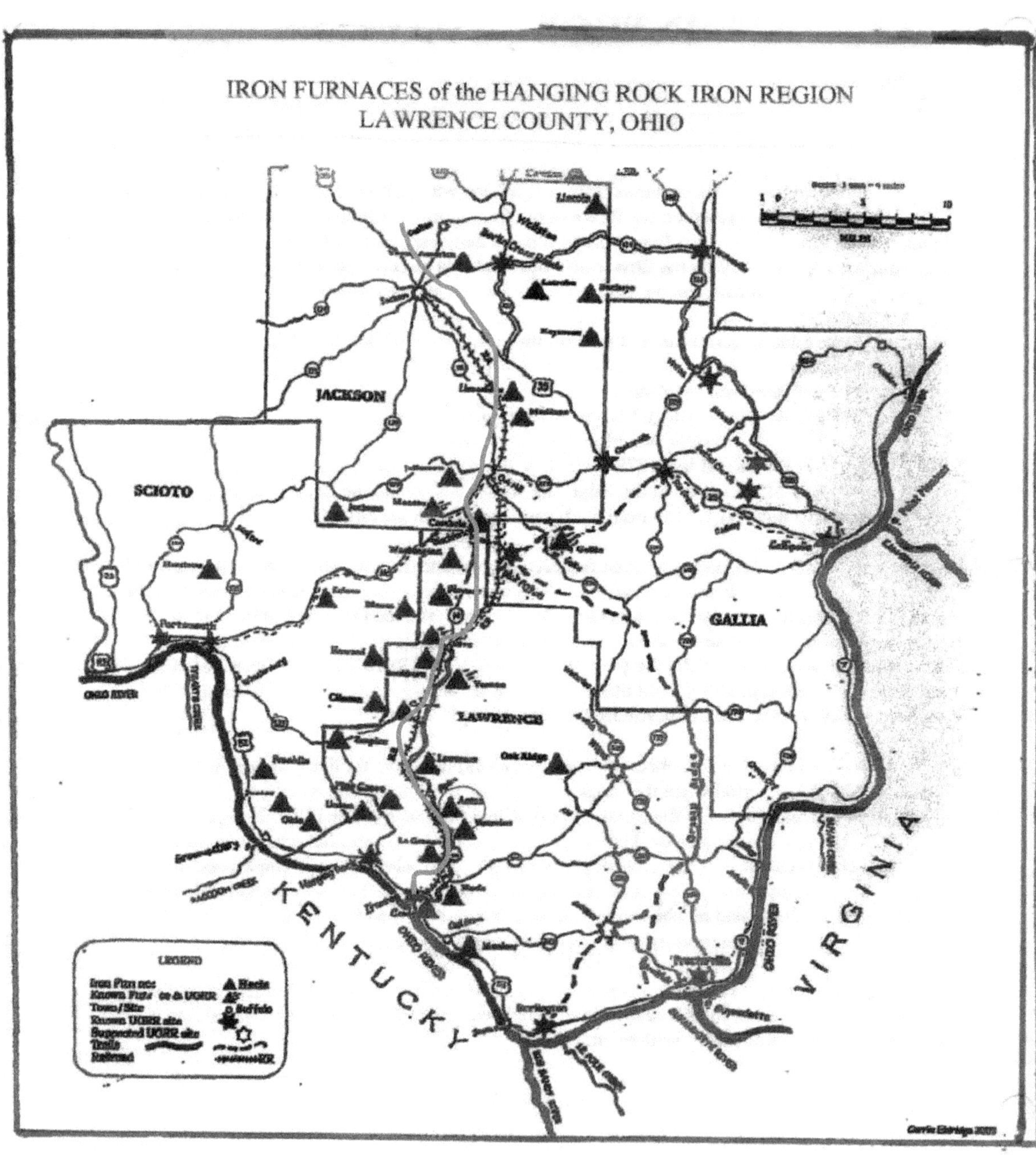

SCIOTO GAZETTE
1810
Chillicothe, Ohio

$50 REWARD
Ran away from subscriber, a negro
man named Ben, 17 years of age,
5 feet, 6 to 8 inches high, branded
on each cheek thus: "T.W"
(T and W are joined together)
For horse stealing.
Any person taking him up and
bringing him home to Thomas Ward
in Cabell County, Virginia, near
the Big Sandy shall be entitled to the
above award with all necessary travel
ing expenses, or confine him in any
jail so that I can get him again.
Thomas Ward

Recorded 20 /Dec 1967
Bryon T. Morris – OUT OF PAST –
Wayne County News

This 1810 reward was posted by
Thomas Ward, Sheriff of Cabell Co. VA
He was a nephew to the John Ward of
Pittsylvania County, VA who sent his
Manumitted slaves to Lawrence Co. Ohio.

The Fugitive Slave Law of ----------
Stated a slave was property and the owner
had a right to recover him from any location.
The 'hated' Fugitive Slave Law of 1850
made the same statement, but demanded
everyone had to help recover that slave on
penalty of fine or imprisonment. Many, who
would have looked the other way, began to
assist runaways and hinder 'slave catchers'.

Much has been written about the life of a slave, even those who had been freed faced a difficult, uncertain life. The *Scioto Gazette* reward advertisement was very common. Worse, the owner had only to name a person a runaway slave, no questions asked. This meant anyone could be accused, jailed, and put into slavery. The members of the Providence Association did not want that to happen to their people.

Information about "a route and method of escape" (an underground railroad) in Lawrence County was collected in the 1890s, many years after the fact. The researcher, Professor Wilbur Siebert, relied on written questionaries distributed by students as a class project. Most of the information in Lawrence County was gathered from Ironton and the Iron Industry area. Although the Iron Industry began in the late 1820s, the town of Ironton was not begun until 1848, and Siebert may not have known of Burlington's early importance. Unless the residents from Burlington had moved to Ironton, no mention was made of the Old Jackson Road or the people who operated any trails from the central part of the county. One factor involved in gathering information was fear of retribution even after fifty years, and some students were threatened.

The Macedonia Church was the only Black church along the Ohio River in Lawrence County. Most of the Blacks living in Rome, Union, Upper, Perry, and Lawrence, as well as Fayette Township, would have attended the church. The limited Black population in the rest of the county was represented by just five families centered around the Iron Furnaces in Decatur Township in 1850. They probably attended the Union Church.

Siebert's book, *The Underground Railroad in Ohio*, did include interviews with persons who had been involved in Lawrence County, but because the interview area ignored the old county seat, Burlington, many possible workers were not recognized or contacted. Among the published interviews was one by Rev. Jacob Cummings, who claimed he was born in 1835 and lived along Symmes Creek. He named some of the associates along the 'railroad' as G.W. Bryant, William Bryant, and W. P. Cradic (all named as ministers of the Macedonia Church). Cummings also wrote about Gabe Johnson, "who kept the underground depot for years." Gabe was part of the Ward Manumission who worked on the river and kept a barber shop, first in Burlington and later in Ironton. (See Appendix #3 Wards) In September of 1894, Gabe himself was interviewed and stated: *"I worked the UGRR in Cincinnati until 1854-55 and knew everything that was going on there. I was the first man that established anything like a systematic road here in Ironton with a man named James Ditcher." (Siebert)*

Gabe also told about: *"Phil Lynch of Burlington (another Ward) and two white ministers, a Presbyterian named Beaman and a Methodist named Stephen Wilson (partner to the Bryans) were into it." (Siebert)* Phil was known as a great whistler and may have passed messages with his singing and whistling as he worked in the community. (IR 15 Aug 1895)

When the Siebert interviews were recorded, a researcher should notice many of the names mentioned were already dead, and there was no way to verify the stories. Since the interviews were taken by students with questionnaires, just how did they collect the information? Did they stand on the corner and pass out papers? Was there an article in the papers asking people to come forward? Stories were told about the students being harassed and threatened as hate and fear lingered in the area. The question remains: How many others still living in the 1890s could have added to the information if someone had asked for an interview?

There were three major sections of the UGRR in Lawrence County. In addition to UGRR activities in Burlington between 1820 and 1860, and the Iron Furnace trail north from Ironton during the 1850s; the eastern section of the county had a trail originating at Quakers Bottom (Proctorville). That trail used Indian Guyan Creek, Greasy Ridge, and Symmes Creek to aid people north. (Poke Patch lay in the headwaters of the Black Fork of Symmes Creek.) Settled by several Quaker families from North Carolina before 1800, the area was known as Quakers Bottom for many years before the current name of Proctorville was adopted. The families and their church were against slavery in any form and were more than willing to assist escaped slaves on their way north.

Quakers Bottom lay directly across the Ohio River from Cabell County, Virginia's main river port of Guyandotte, at the mouth of the Guyandotte River. Although that river ran through exceptionally rugged terrain, it headed just to the west of the Great Valley of Virginia and offered another route to the Ohio River and the Northwest Territory. The eastern escape trail may have been as old as the 1798 settlement, but it was also the closest to settled Cabell County and its contingent of 'slave catchers'; and the slave-holding population who lived in eastern Cabell County. It was safer for a runaway to go downriver a few miles and to cross the Ohio River just above Burlington at either the 4 Pole (creek) or 12 Pole shoals. (Virginia creeks with long sand bars.)

Several Quaker homes in the area were reputed to have tunnels and secret rooms, but most likely, the hiding was done under rock houses and cliffs away from the settlements where small farms supported large families.

One Black family of note lived in the Red Hill community, on the hill north of Quakers Bottom. Lewis Brooks, Sr., and his family raised produce for the market. His family had been manumitted in 1852 by Mary Garland of the Richmond area, but the father, Lewis, belonged to another plantation, and although manumitted, the master's family fought the will. Freed by the Court, Lewis, his wife, and ten children were sent to Lawrence County in 1852 and settled north of Proctorville on OH 775. In one remembered incident, trouble came his way late one night when Lewis Brooks was ready. Toughs tried to break into his cabin, but Brooks severely whipped several of the invaders, thus discouraging future raids on his livestock and gardens. (According to Siebert's interviews, his home was a UGRR station.)

There were several Quaker families in early Lawrence County who opposed slavery. Many of the residents of Unionville (also called Russell's Place and Getaway, about six miles out of Symmes Creek) were descendants of the first settlers. Some became Baptists when the Quaker ministers continued west. That may have happened to the white Pleasant Valley Church, far out Greasy Ridge which began in 1807. For several years that church was a member of the (Black) Providence (Anti-Slavery) Missionary Baptist Association. It was situated in an excellent place to forward runaways along Greasy Ridge to Poke Patch. (Greasy Ridge was a single ridge from the Ohio River almost to Poke Patch.)

Quaker Brethren, Methodist, or Baptist, a fair number of Lawrence County settlers and their ministers supported the abolitionist movement. Most were never involved in the UGRR, but they despised the Fugitive Slave Law and quietly looked the other way, left food or clothes by the path or misdirected hunting slave catchers. Although a few local people from Virginia helped catch local runaways, most of the real 'slave catchers' were professional hunters working for the reward which was created by the Fugitive Slave Law of 1850.

An autobiography by the Reverend William Portrait Cradic written in the 1890s.

****

I was born in Lawrence County, Perry Township, seven miles above Ironton, on 8 May 1835. My parents were Jefferson and Judea (Bryant) Cradic. My father died when I was 2 ½ years old. I was converted and united with the Macedonia Baptist Church back in Burlington. I was baptized by Reverend Thomas N. Stewart and was ordained in 1866 to the pastor, Triedstone Baptist Church, Ironton. I pastored there for 16 years; the membership grew from 12 to 217. I was a member of Providence when some of the members started the Mt. Olive Association in West Virginia. I was with the underground railroad, and it was only known to those engaged in it from Gallia, Lawrence, and Jackson Counties. Our business was to hide and render assistance to those seeking freedom from slavery. I have in my possession a copy of the papers made by a John Ward and signed by the clerk of Pittsylvania County Court House, Virginia, on 7 Apr 1827, to free my father. Signed: *William P. Cradic.*

****

Source: 150th Anniversary Souvenir Book of the Providence
<u>Regular Missionary Baptist Association 1984</u>
William P. Cradic was the son of Ward slave Jefferson Craddock #95,
and the grandson of Lewis and Winnie Craddock # 93 and #94.
Jefferson <u>Cradwick</u> married Juda Bryant on 29 Nov 1831, a daughter of John Bryant.
W.P. Cradic died in Columbus, OH in 1912.

****

Figure 35 -

W. P. (William Portrait) Cradic
Couresty of Chris Saunders

Figure 36 - Old Union Church at Poke Patch – circa 1900 -1925

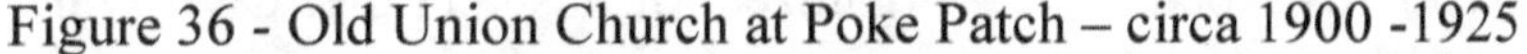

Ford McKeel, Nicy Scott, Tom Mathews, Fitz Keels (source Lou Keels)

1807-13 - Macedonia - oldest Black Baptist in Ohio (Mother Church)
      Big Rock before 1819 (Possibly on Rock Camp Rd. church named Triedstone.)
         Rock Camp began in 1815 – an old hunter's camp
      Union – 1819 at Poke Patch on Lawrence/Gallia/Jackson line. (near current Black Fork)
1821 -   Providence Anti-Slavery Baptist Association was founded by these 3 churches in 1821.
1821 – John Bryant and Pleasant Roberts, ministers

1807 - Mt. Pleasant Baptist Church –(white) North end of Greasy Ridge founded 1807
1819 – James B. Stewart preached first sermon at Union Church.
1820 - James B. Stewart – (census) Gallipolis - (brother of the clan)
1820-30 - Bryant, John may have been a minister. (inferred) with brother-in-law Pleasant Roberts
      John presents Rosanna's will in 1833, sells property in 1841 - vanishes
1830-50 - Blind minister - Harris, Essex – IR article –Remember LORE
1835 - Mt. Pleasant (organized 1807) joined with Union (organized 1819) 4 others Jackson Co.)
1835 – 2nd Association - Providence Missionary Baptist Association formed in Jackson Co.
1845 - Macedonia – Wm. Bryant and Geo. W. Bryant come of age
1848   Stewart, Rev. William at Macedonia Church (Missionary) (brother to James B.)
1848   Stewart, John S. taught Singing School at Macedonia Hill (m Eliza Ann Harris)
         (maybe a daughter of Essex Harris - Burlington) (she was b/Bedford Co. VA
1849   Fry, Thomas Walker - after 1849 (Twyman) Burlington, minister at Macedonia
         Later Red Hill- Proctorville – organized Mt. Pisgah (after Civil War)
1850   Cradic, Jonathan (Ward) preaching
1856 & 1857 Macedonia ministers: W. Bryant, J. Cradic, T.W. Fry, C. W. Roberts, W.P. Cradic
      Union ministers: R. Beverly, J. Coker, and H. Ligans, 1857: Jno. J. Stewart
      Wm. Chavous, and R. Beverly (Providence Association Minutes)
      1855-56 William Stewart was preaching in Law. Co. OH and living in Cass Co. MI.
      1855 - W.P. Cradic, s/Jefferson Cradic, grandson of Rosannah Bryant preaching
      1856 – Roberts, Charles W. (Ward) preaching
      1879 -Isaac Vinson Bryant s/Wm. & 3rd wife, Martha Craddock Randall, preaching
1879   44th Annual Session Providence AS Missionary Baptist Association held at
      Macedonia: Moderator- P.H. Williams (Gallipolis), Clerk- W.T. Smith (Burlington),
         Treasurer- W.P. Cradic (Ironton)

Wm. Bryant	- Burlington, Lawrence Co. OH	F.C. James	---------WV
T.W. Fry	- Burlington, Lawrence Co. OH	J.K. Brown	---------WV
I.V. Bryant	- Burlington, Lawrence Co. OH	A.L. Zimmerman – Piketon, Pike Co. O
J.J. Cradic	- Ironton, OH	J.L. Ward	- Wheeling, WV
W.P. Cradic	- Ironton, OH	J.M. Cousens	- Gallipolis, OH
N. Barnett	- Ironton, OH	P.H. Edwards	- Gallipolis, OH
L.W. Johnson	- Ironton, OH	W.F. Ellison	- Pine Grove, Gallia Co.
H. Cox	- Hillsborough, Highland Co. OH	B. Jones	- Richmondale, OH
B. Sales	- Roxebelle, Ross Co. OH	J.D. Noel	- Quaker Bottom, OH
M. Ahlter	- Rutland, Meigs Co. OH	G. McDaniel	- (Quaker Bottom, OH)
J.W. Walker	- Omega, Pike Co. OH	N.W. Viney	- Lancaster, OH
H. Carter	- Omega, Pike Co. OH	K.L. Carter	- Camba, Jackson Co. O
J. Furguson	- Middleport, OH	W.C. Dickerson	- Circleville, OH
P.H. Williams	- Middleport, OH	W. A. Meredith	- Zanesville, OH

1880-1882 – Barnet, Nelson
> A bell post stood on the Ohio shore. Ringing the bell called a boatman to
> Ferry churchgoers across the river from West Virginia and Kentucky

1882 – 47th meeting Providence Association held Bethel, Morgan Twp. Gallia Co.
> 1884-1896 Macedonia preserved Church Minutes

1890 – (54th) meeting Providence Association held Macedonia – Lawrence Co. OH
> (Notes from Providence Association minutes and 1884 Macedonia Minutes.)

Beginnings of Macedonia Church

1807-13 - Macedonia - oldest Black Baptist in Ohio (Mother Church)

> Acts 16 10-17: Leave at once for Macedonia a land to the north

- black slave – go be saved in Macedonia.

Due North of Macedonia, at the apex of Buffalo Creek and Rankins Creek, stands a church called Sunrise. It stands on a point called High Top. From that site, the North Star is just visible on the horizon; a brighter star, a degree to the left, shows a ridge leading north. About 4 miles along that North line off Twp 117 and along Rock Camp Road stands a church once called Triedstone Baptist (maybe Big Rock). Rock Camp community began about 1815, probably settled earlier by long hunters (some were Black) who camped under the cliff overhangs called rock houses.

> Isaiah 26 16: I am the cornerstone of a sure foundation.

> Do not scoff so that your bonds will not be tightened.

From Triedstone (Big Rock?) Church, the Old Jackson trail followed Dog Fork Creek for several miles again 'due north.' It passed close to the Oak Ridge Iron Furnace site (built in 1856). Beyond the furnace lay about 15 miles of dense forest enclosing the hidden community of Poke Patch, which sprawled along Dirty Face Creek, a branch of Symmes Creek. It was home to runaway slaves, free Blacks, Indians, whites, and mulattoes of each race. People passed through the area or settled for a few years.

> Union Church – at Poke Patch named for its 'united' congregation.

> It united the various races into one church. - To unite, to become whole.

Providence Anti-Slavery Missionary Baptist Association was founded by these 3 churches in 1821. In 1831, a new association formed farther north, dropping the 'Anti-slavery' and adding Missionary to their name. (150th Anniversary Program, Providence Association Minuets.)

Macedonia Connections using the 1879 Association list

~ original Law. Co.   *Ward   #Twyman   @free/Poke Patch

~Wm. Bryant   - Burlington, Lawrence Co. OH   1820 Grandmother, Rosanna, original settler
~ Geo. W. Bryant -Burlington, Lawrence Co. OH   William's brother
#T.W. Fry   - Burlington, Lawrence Co. OH   1849 (Twyman) – '37
I.V. Bryant   - Burlington, Lawrence Co. OH - Isaac Vinton - s/Wm. Bryant & Martha Cradic Randall
#W.T. Smith   - Burlington, Lawrence Co. OH   1849 (Twyman) - '37 - "Traveler"
*J.J. Cradic   - Ironton, OH   1827 (Ward) *Jonathan Craddock
W.P. Cradic   - Ironton, OH   s/ Juda Bryant & *Jefferson Cradic m 1831
Chas. W. Roberts - Ironton & Burlington   Ward – married Susannah Bryant dau/John
          N. Barnett   - Ironton, OH
          L.W. Johnson   - Ironton, OH
          G. McDaniels   - Quaker Bottom, OH (Proctorville)
          J. D. Noel   - Quaker Bottom
          H. Cox   - Hillsborough, Highland Co. OH
          B. Sales   - Roxebelle, Ross Co. OH   others
          M. Ahlter   - Rutland, Meigs Co. OH   B. Jones   - Richmondale, OH
          J.W. Walker   - Omega, Pike Co. OH   K.L. Carter   - Camba, Jackson Co.
          H. Carter   - Omega, Pike Co. OH   N.W. Viney   - Lancaster, OH
          A. L. Zimmerman- Piketon, Pike Co. OH   W.C. Dickerson- Circleville, OH
          J. Furguson   - Middleport, OH   W.A. Meredith - Zanesville, OH
          P.H. Williams   - Middleport, OH
          P.H. Williams   (Gallipolis)
          P.H. Edwards   - Gallipolis, OH   F.C. James   ---------WV
          W.F. Ellison   - Pine Grove, Gallia Co. OH   J.K. Brown   ---------WV
          @J.M. Cousens - Gallipolis, OH   J.L. Ward   - Wheeling, WV

When the Baptist association of Western Virginia refused to admit the Black churches of
Southern Ohio, three Black churches, led by the Macedonia Church, north of Burlington, formed
their own Providence Antislavery Baptist Association. From this beginning, numerous churches
were founded, and an organization was formed to guarantee that other Black persons could live a
life of freedom if they could escape slavery.

Chapter 14: The Providence Association

Burlington was the county seat of Lawrence County – from 1817-1851
Gallipolis became the county seat of Gallia County in 1804.

	Church	Minister	Location
1821	Macedonia	(John Bryant)	Burlington, Lawrence. Co. OH
		(Pleasant Roberts)	Burlington, Lawrence, Co. OH
	Big Rock?	(possibly Rock Camp, Lawrence Co.)	
	Union	James B. Stewart	Poke Patch, Lawrence Co. OH
		Richard Stewart	"
		William Stewart	"
1835		Eld. Robertson Townsend – no church	
	Chester	Dea. Thomas Everton	--
		Lewis Chase	--
	Mt. Zion	John Cron	Jackson Co. OH
		Peter Kingery	"
		Sartin McCommis	"
	Mount Pleasant	Jesse Corn	Mason Twp. Lawrence Co. OH
	(white)	William Corn	"
		Jephta Massy	"
		Silas Shewmate	"
		Jacob Ward	"
	Paint Creek	Eld. Gabriel Hargo	Gallipolis, Gallia Co. OH
	Providence	Frances Champlain	Milton Twp. Jackson Co. OH
		Thomas Parker	"
		James Saddler	"
	Union	Eld. James B. Stewart	Poke Patch, Lawrence Co. OH
		Richard Stewart	"
		William Stewart	"

Sources: Wilma Fox's 150th Anniversary Program, Association Minuets – see Bibliography.

Figure 37 - Mount Pleasant Baptist Church

1835 member Providence Association – white membership located 2nd crossing of Greasy Ridge & OH 775.
Organized in 1807 – Bell tower is part of the original church.

PROVIDENCE ASSOCIATION MINISTERS (con't)
Elder (Eld.) – (Licentiate (Lic.)

With programs for both 1856 & 1857 – changes or additions to 1857 are in italics.
Information held by Records of the Providence Anti-Slavery Missionary Association held by Samuel Colgate
Historical Library, Colgate Rochester Divinity School, Rochester, NY. See Bibliography.

1856	(Providence)	not represented	
	Bethel	J. Cousens *xx*	Morgan Twp. Gallia Co. OH
		J. Ellison xx	"
		G. D. James	"
		Howell James	"
		Eld. Wm. C. James	"
	1857	*F. James*	
	1857	*S. Jones*	
	Calvin Center	Eld. William Stewart	Cass Co. Michigan (Stewart from Poke Patch)
	Franklin	Kendall Lee	Jackson Co. OH
	Lebanon	B. Jackson	Warren Co. OH (NE Cincinnati)
	Macedonia	W. Bryant	Burlington, Lawrence Co. OH
		J. Cradic *(Craddoc)*	"
		W. P. Cradic *(Craddoc)*	"
		T.W. Fry	"
		C.W. Roberts	"
	New Hope	A. Bunch	Springfield Twp. Gallia Co. OH
		A. Dabner *xx*	"
		H. McDaniel *xx*	"
	1857	*R. Carter*	
	1857	*G. McDonald*	
	1857	*H. McDonald (?)*	
	1857	*Wm. Viney*	
	Paint Creek	J.T. Berry *xx*	Gallipolis, Gallia Co. OH
		J.W. Couzens *(Jas. W.)*	"
		L. Holmes, Jr. *xx*	"
		Joseph Jones	"
		H.M. Williams	
	1857	*H. Williams, Jr.*	"
	1857	*O. Viney*	
	1857	*A. Ward, Jr.*	
	2nd Baptist	D. Jones	Columbus, OH
		A. Lewis *xx*	"
		L. Scott *xx*	"
		T.N. Stewart *xx*	"
	1857	*A. Alestock*	
	1857	*J. Goens*	
	1857	*J. Johnson*	
	Salem *1857*	*Jos. Cousens*	---
		S. Ford, Jr.	
		S. Ford, Sr.	
		Thos. Ford	
		P. Gillmore	

Providence Association Ministers (con't)
Elder (Eld.) – (Licentiate (Lic.)
With programs for both 1856 & 1857 – changes or additions in 1857 are in italics.

Sharon	W. Dolby *xx*	Jackson, OH
	S.P. Newman	"
	R. Raglin	"
	J.L. Smith	"
	James L. Smith	"
Shiloh	W. Dickerson	Portsmouth, OH
	Wm. Cook	"
Union	R. Beverly	Poke Patch, Lawrence Co. OH
	J. Coker *xx*	
	N. Liggans *xx*	
	Wm. Chavous	
	J. Stewart	
Wilmington	Benjamin Jackson	Clinton Co. OH
Zion	F. Bryant	Jackson Co. OH
	H. Carter	"
	B. Jones *xx*	"
	J. Jones	"
	R. Jones	"
1857	*T. Wingo*	

Elected: Asst. Secretaries: F. Bryant, J.L. Smith - Clerk: Eld. T.N. Stewart

Mentioned: M. Carter, Lemuel Scott, Isaac Howell, Susan Scott (Macedonia) Lic. B. Sailes

Eld. T.N. Stewart, Eld. William Stewart (Moderator), Francis James Asst. clerk, Jonathan

Craddoc (pastor at Shiloh in Portsmouth), Eld. Wallace Shelton (delegate Union A.S. Asso.)

Eld. G. Hargo, Harrison Cox (a blind preacher)

Several new families arrived in Lawrence County between 1850 and 1860 and joined Macedonia. One family illustrates the problems that Blacks faced crossing the frontier.

Eli Atwell was born in North Carolina between 1804 and 1807, according to census records. By 1840 he had crossed the Blue Ridge into Washington County, VA. Ten years later, he married a Nancy Cooper in Smith County, VA, where he was enumerated as a mulatto Blacksmith. By 1860, he had made his way down the Big Sandy River and crossed the Ohio River to Lawrence County with his wife and nine children. Atwell was listed as a minister at Macedonia, but by 1880 he had moved to Jackson County, OH, and was living with a son.

Another son, Samuel, was a minister in Macedonia.

Figure 38 - Union Church Homecoming

21 Aug 1938 – Black Fork, Lawrence County, OH

(Poke Patch)

Chapter 15: The Stewart Family and 'Clan'

Greenfield Township, Gallia County - Decatur Township, Lawrence County
'Clan' – a group of families related by marriage

Equally important to the development of religion and the UGRR in southeast Ohio was the creation of the small community of Poke Patch. Located at the northern edge of Lawrence County, it spread across the county line into Gallia County. Its settlers were freeborn Blacks, freed slaves, runaways, Indians, frustrated whites, and mulattoes of each group. Early dominated by the extended Stewart family, this community had established its own church by 1819 and joined with Macedonia and Big Rock to create the first Association of Black Churches in Lawrence County. The Poke Patch congregation named their church "Union," for it was a union of all races of people.

The Stewart Family and the Union Baptist Church began locally at about the same time. A brief history of the extended Stewart family and the beginning of the Union Church will show how they intertwined. Poke Patch was located about thirty-five miles north of the Ohio River. The Stewart family formed the main "station" of the fledgling UGRR trail, probably as early as 1820. To better understand the development of both church and trail, the reader needs a brief history of the Stewart family. When the family moved to Michigan about 1855, their exodus endangered the local UGRR movement and probably ended it.

[Several internet sites list a Stewart family history that has been abstracted for this book's purpose. This family appeared in King William County, Virginia, before 1750. Edward Ned Stewart (1721-1801) married Frances Dungy (1707-1840?) about 1755, then moved to Powhatan County, VA. (Frances died at 133?).] (Frances spelling used for women – Francis for men.)

Ned & Frances's 'oldest' son, John Peterson Stewart (1757-1817), married twice: first a Dinah (1779) (mother of the first six children), then to Frances Dungey (1776-1840) in 1800-1. Father Ned died in 1801 in Powhatan County, VA, about the time the slave uprisings threatened the state. By 1810 John P. and Frances were moving their family to White County, TN, accompanied by several other Powhatan families. John P. Stewart died in 1817, quickly followed by two sons, Thomas in 1818 and Elisha in 1821. His wife, Frances Dungey Stewart, remained in White County with her sons Elisha and William for several years, but the oldest remaining son, James B., and wife (another) Frances Dungey Stewart had moved to Gallipolis in Gallia County, OH, between 1813 and 1818 instead of joining the family in Tennessee. Their son John J. was born at Gallipolis in 1818.

Note: Information is abstracted from Ancestry. Please check for accuracy.
Stewart, John Peterson – m 1st Diana (1779 d 1798) m 2nd Francis Dungey (1801 -certificate-Powhatan Co.)
The family lived in Powhatan, VA until 1810-White, TN, 1825-Gallia, OH-1858, and Cass, MI currently.)

Children b. Powhatan Co. VA to White Co. TN	*son- Stewart, James B. & Frances Dungey @ 1811*
To Gallia Co. OH – to Cass Co. MI	1812-1895 Thomas b VA m Susanna d Cass Co. MI
1780-1818 Thomas m Margaret Crowder – both d TN	1813-1885 James W. b VA m Cassels d Jackson, OH
1783-1852 James B. m Frances Dungey – d Gallia	1818-1892 John J. b OH Elizabeth A. Harris d Gallia.
1786-1823 John m Polly Carter – he d Wyandot, OH	1821-1894 Isaac Perry m Marinda Dungey d Cass
1786-1821 Elisha m Lucy Creacy 1803 he d White, TN	1830-1904 Jacob D. m Emily Evans d Columbus
1792-1860 Elizabeth   m Peter Coker   d Cass ------------Coker, Peter & Elizabeth Stewart (lived w/Toliver)*
1798-1858 William (Rev.) m Mary Dungey – d Cass	lived in White, TN, Gallia, OH d Cass, MI
1800-1885 Richard W. m Barbara Crecy d Cass	son John m Mary Rickman TN, OH, MI
1801-1860 Susannah m (Wm ?) Dungey d Gallia	son Elisha m Susanna Harris TN, OH, MI
1802-1854 Littleberry m Mary Woods d Gallia	son Thomas m Agnes Newman TN, OH
1804-1846 Rebecca m James S. Bowen d Gallia	son James m Delila Harris TN, OH, MI
1810-1870 Mariah m James Crandolph d Gallia	son Michael m Sarah Hughs TN, OH
	son Toliver TN, OH d Douglas Co. KS*
	son Wm. C. m Delilah Eliza Harris TN, OH, IN

__1800-1885 Steward, Richard W. & Barbara Creacy__
    1850 in Gallia to Logan Co. by 1856, then to Cass Co. 1858 with three wagons, children, and livestock.
    (Sons Littleberry and William were in Cass County, MI, by 1854 looking for land.)
    With Sarah Stewart Hill & 3 children, Frances Stewart & husband William Chavous & 5 children
    Ann Stewart, (nephews) George W. Stewart, Joseph A. Stewart, and Henry Hawks
    1850 Census: ch-Littleberry 22, John 20, James 18, Lucy 15, George 13, Barbara 11, Joseph 9

__1801-1850/60 Susannah Stewart Dungey, in 1850, lived with her son William (who went to Cass)__
    Wm. Dungey Sr., supposed son of Frances Dungey prior to marriage to John P. Stewart (possibly brother)
    Dungey, Richard - b 6 Apr 1794 (Cumberland, VA) d 5 Jul 1871 m Nancy Penn 1800-1883 – both d. Cass
        ch 1) Sarah Ann 1819-1910 m Uriah Rickman – both b White Co., lived Gallia Co., d Cass Co.
        2) Marinda 1820 b White Co. d 1877 m Isaac Perry Stewart (s/James B.) both d Cass Co.
        3) Irene 1822-1904 b White Co. TN, 4) Nancy E. 1824-1897 m Richard W. Stewart (to Cass)
        5) John T. 1825-1897 b White Co. TN d Civil War
        6) William 1825-1888 __b White Co. TN__
        7) Anderson 1828 -1901 b Gallia Co. OH   8) Martha Ann 1829-1903 b Gallia Co. OH
        9) John R. 1834- 1867 b Gallia d Cass,   10) Geo. W. 1835-1909 b Gallia Co. OH
        11) Matilda 1836-1860 b Gallia Co. OH   12) Margaret 1838-1870 b Gallia d Cass
        13) James Edward 1842-1877 b Gallia d Cass   14) Thomas 1845-1900

The 1820 census of Gallipolis, OH, listed James B. "Stuart" with eleven in the household, which probably included his seven children and sister-in-law Lucy and her children (widow of Elisha). By 1830 James B. Stewart and assorted family members had moved to Greenfield Township and the Poke Patch community. The Stewart family's household included James B. at its head, probable sister-in-law Lucy, and his siblings: Richard, Littleberry, and Maria. By 1840, his mother. Frances Dungey Stewart and Rachel Stewart (another sister-in-law?) had their own households. (Frances did not die in TN but in Gallia County, OH, between 1840 and 1850.)

James B. Stewart and his wife Frances Dungey Stewart had five sons: Thomas H. in Powhatan County, VA (1812-1895), James W. in Powhatan County, Virginia (1813-1885), John J. Gallipolis, OH (1818-1892), and two sons born in Greenfield Township, Gallia County, Ohio: Isaac Perry (1821-

1894) and Jacob D. (1830-1904). All married in Gallia County and were members of the Union Baptist Church, and several of the family were ministers.

Father James B. Stewart preached the first sermon in Greenfield Township (probably in 1819 at the church's inception.) He was an Elder of the Providence Association of Churches from (at least) 1835 until his death in 1852. Several of his relatives also became ministers. In 1856, his son, T. N. Stewart, was Clerk of the Association. James B.'s brother Richard moved his family to Logan County, OH, then Cass County, Michigan as a preacher. During 1856/57, brother William was preaching in Gallia County, Ohio, while he claimed Cass County, Michigan, as his home. A fourth brother, John, died in 1823 while a minister to the Indians of northwest Ohio, and John Peterson Stewart was also reported to a minister.

Two more facts about this 'frontier clan' should be mentioned. The website – www.freeafricanamericans.com tells the history of Free people of color in Tidewater, Virginia. They were families of white, Black, Indian, and mulatto mixed persons. They had few rights but were usually better educated than slaves. Although free, they were required to obey all the laws which restricted slaves. Among these Free families are listed many surnames later in Poke Patch, Ohio. These Free families made their way across the frontier and lived for a while in one area or another before some continued to Canada. Checking historical events in early Virginia and Tennessee show periods of violence by and against slaves. Several events occurred just prior to the Stewart 'clan' leaving an area. {1800-1805 slave revolts in Virginia, 1815-1820 deprivation by the Morrell Gang in Tennessee, and 1850 passage of National Fugitive Slave Law in Ohio}

Finally, the Stewarts of Poke Patch and many of their neighbors and church members were active supporters of the underground railroad in southeast Ohio. Poke Patch was a recognized station with many connections farther north and west. Wilbur Siebert's books listed members of Stewart's extended family as conductors. Several trails ran to the Poke Patch "station" from the Ohio River, and the Missionary Baptist Church Association connected its churches to numerous trails leading north.

Between 1819 and 1852, the Old Jackson Road ran north from Burlington on the Ohio River through Poke Patch to the county seat of Jackson County. As the Iron Industry developed and the Lawrence County seat moved down river to Ironton, a new road (OH 93) connected the Iron Furnaces. It joined a railroad running north to Jackson and Wellston, Ohio. Even the Quaker Trail from Proctorville passed along the Greasy Trail headed for Poke Patch.

Siebert's book, *The Underground Railroad in Ohio,* has an interview that states: "I remember the last runaway family, they were captured and returned to slavery around 1860." The reader must assume the hated Fugitive Slave Law had finally made it too difficult for the Stewart family to operate. Between 1855 and 1858, at least thirty families, all kin to the Stewart family, moved to Cass County, Michigan. Although a few 'conductors' remained, that escaping slave family found little help at the nearly empty 'Poke Patch Station.'

The Poke Patch community lay between Olive Furnace in Lawrence County and Gallia Furnace in Gallia County along branches of Dirty Face Creek, Negro Creek, and Black Fork all tributaries of Symmes Creek. (Named for the black swamp water – not the people.) The low-lying land where settlers built their homes was mostly owned by Iron Master John Campbell and Company, which sold the men small lots.

Figure 39 - 1850 Non-Population Census Gallia Co.

1850 NON – POPULATION CENSUS –AGRICULTURE GREENFIELD TOWNSHIP, GALLIA COUNTY, OH	
Chaves, Jane 20a - $ 900	Rickman, Sarah 60a - $3,000
Coker, James 80a - $3,000	Stewart, Isaac 200a- $7,500
Coker, John 80a - $2,500	Stewart, James 44a - $1,000
Dungee, Andrew 40a - $1,500	Stewart, Littleberry120a-5,000
Dungee, Richard 60a - $2,000	Stewart, Lucinda 200a-$6,000
Dungee, William 120a - $3,500	all the land had mineral rights

For many years, men worked making iron by day, while by night, they ferried runaway and fugitives from the Ohio River crossings to safe trails leading north. Although several of the Iron Masters were avid abolitionists, Poke Patch ironworkers did most of the Underground Railroad work. The Fugitive Slave Law and its threat of large fines and imprisonment deterred the rich men from greater involvement while forcing the working 'conductors' to seek a safer area farther north.

Was this the reason the extended Stewart family moved to Michigan? By the late 1850s, rewards for catching slaves had increased, and the whole Stewart family was recognized in the area as abolitionists or more. Although the Underground Railroad members were a 'semi'-kept secret, perhaps safety concerns about the growing number of 'slave catchers' alarmed the family. Siebert's interview with James Ditcher indicates the only runaways he ever lost were the last ones about 1860. That loss happened two years after the extended Stewart family moved to Cass County, Michigan, and the Underground Railroad lost the major station at Poke Patch and most of its conductors.

STEWART FAMILY MEMBERS ASSOCIATED WITH THE UGRR

Old Man Cratoff	(James Cradolph married Mariah Stewart)	died Gallia Co. OH
William Chavous	(married Frances Stewart)	died Cass Co. MI
John Coker	(married Mary Rickman)	died Cass Co. MI
Peter Coker	(married Elizabeth Stewart)	moved Cass died KS
Tolliver Coker	(son/Peter and Elizabeth Coker)	to KS
William Coker	(married Delilah Eliza Harris)	died Cass Co. MI
Elizabeth Dungee	(widow)	
Richard Dungee	(m Nancy Penn	to Cass
William Dungy	(married Martha Stewart)	died Cass Co. MI
Mathew Pleasants	(married Rachel Stewart (Susanna?)	died Cass Co. MI
Stewart, Isaac	(married Marinda Dungy)	died Cass Co. MI
Stewart, Jacob		
Stewart, James B. –	(Rev.) married Frances Dungy	died Gallia Co. OH
Stewart, J. M.	(married cousin Mary J. Stewart	died Cass Co. MI
Stewart, John	(married Eliza A. Harris (Taught at Macedonia) went to Cass
Stewart, Littleberry	(married Mary Wood)	to Cass by 1860
Stewart, Lucy	(wid-Elisha)	
Stewart, Maria	(m James Cradoph)	died Gallia Co. OH
Stewart, Richard	(Rev.) m Barbara Creasy-Powhatan Co. VA died Cass Co. MI
Stewart. Thomas	(married Nancy Richman)	died Cass Co. MI
Stewart, William	(Rev.) both Union & Macedonia	died Cass Co. MI
	(married Mary Dungy)	

Sources: Sands, James. *Gallipolis Tribune.* 3 Feb 1985, 23 Feb 1997
Siebert, Wilbur. *The Underground Railroad in Ohio*

Figure 40– Stewart Family & UGRR

The Stewarts were survivors. The move to Cass County may not have been the first time the family had moved in the face of danger. At the time Grandfather Edward Ned Stewart died in Powhatan County in 1801, several slave revolts were rocking the Virginia communities. Crossing the Virginia frontier in 1810 was a hazardous undertaking even when the family chose a site in Tennessee previously settled by other Blacks from Powhatan County. The frontier was never a safe place, but about the time John Peterson Stewart died in 1817, stories from White County, Tennessee, reported an outlaw named Morrell who lived in the area near the Stewarts. He and his gang harassed the local trails for unprotected travelers. Part of his criminal "business" was capturing Blacks and selling them, then stealing them back and selling them again. When the victims had been sold too many times, their bodies disappeared into the depths of a local cave. Three members of the Stewart family died in Tennessee just before the remaining family moved to Gallia County, Ohio. Perhaps moving was a good idea.

The possible Trails from Powhatan, VA, which led the Stewarts and relatives west.

1810 - US 1 south through Petersburg (which had a large group of Stewart families)
      US 58 West towards Cumberland Gap to US 11 - US 70 (old Nashville Rd) (530 miles)
      Sparta, White County, TN - Crowder family from Powhatan Co. VA were local officials)
      son #1 Thomas Stewart m Margaret Crowder in TN.
1816/7 - James B. Stewart went west on the James River Turnpike (US 60), crossed the Ohio River and
      settled at Gallipolis, Gallia County, OH, by 1818 and moved to Greenfield Township after 1820.
1820+ - After a father and two brothers died in TN, the extended family moved to Gallia County, OH.
      From Sparta north (near) US 27 to Lexington to US 60 (many slaves) to Tri-state -
      Or to Knoxville North US 25 to US 60 at Mt. Sterling to tri-state (few slaves) 340 miles
1855, the whole family moved to Cass County, MI. Richard (from Highland Co.) used three
      wagons for his extended family, moving to Cass Co.
Poke Patch to Cass Co. US 32 west to Piketon – OH 124 to Highland/Logan - OH 73 to Xenia US 68
to junction 33 to Fort Wayne to Elkhart to Cass (300 miles) Total distance 530 + 340 + 300 = 1130 miles

Figure 41 – Following the Stewart Clan

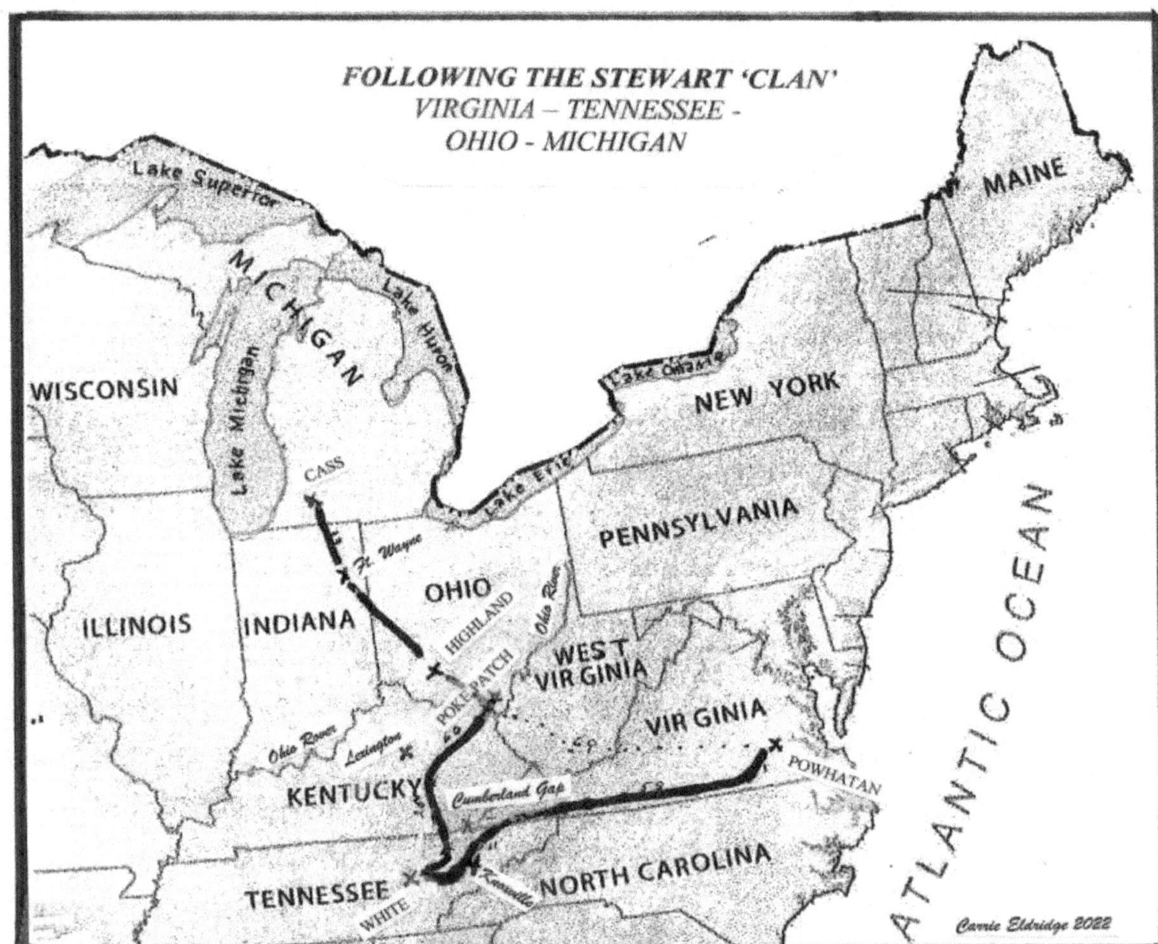

POSSIBLE ROUTE OF TRAVEL
Powhatan Co., VA – west of Richmond via US 1 south To US 58 west to US 11 SW Knoxville to US 70 - 530m
White Co. TN near Sparta East to Knoxville US 25 north to US 60 & Ohio River – 340m
Ohio- Poke Patch (Gallia/Lawrence) Ohio west US 32 through Piketon to OH 73 to Highland Co.
    Then Xenia via US 68 to US 33 west to Fort Wayne, IN and north - 300m
Cass Co. MI -US 33 to Elkhart, IN and north across state line to Cass Co. MI

Chapter 16: The Poke Patch Station of the Underground Railroad

A Waystation for Burlington, Proctorville, and Ironton

Finally, the pieces were in place for a successful operation of both the religious communities and a system to protect a meaningful escape route from the Ohio River. The people were the manumitted Blacks who watched the Ohio River banks and the multiracial families living in the forest on the upper reaches of Symmes Creek who ferried the escapees farther north. From at least the mid-1830s to the outbreak of the Civil War, runaways followed the Old Jackson Road, Greasy Ridge, or OH 93 through the primeval forests of southeast Ohio, where they found to aid and assistance from the regional association's churches and ministers.

Wilbur Siebert gathered the information for his book: *The Underground Railroad in Ohio* almost fifty years after events took place. Even then, few people were willing to provide information about the stations and conductors. For a freedom trail to exist, it had to have "locators," people who lived and worked along the Ohio River. It had to have "supporters," people willing to risk their lives to provide food, shelter, information about trails, and even personal assistance following trails north. Few of these people were identified by Siebert.

The early communities along the Ohio River, such as Burlington and Quakers Bottom, had to be in contact with other like-minded people in northern communities. Although much of the white community supported "freedom for all," few would risk their lives along trails they rarely traveled to help people who meant nothing to them. The only group of people who could be found along the trails were missionaries looking for lost souls. The fact that the local Black community banded together to create an Association of Anti-slavery Missionary Baptists gave their ministers an excuse to travel. Meeting ministers on the trails was a regular and accepted occurrence for farmers and hunters. Traveling from church to church, these men could collect information and provide warnings as they passed along.

The Black communities along the Ohio River was located near the mouth of several streams, including Symmes Creek, Little Guyan, and Buffalo Creek. Each creek was almost directly across the Ohio River from other streams on the Virginia side. All the streams created sandbars in the river, which offered low water crossing points or slowed the boats. The Black "locators" kept watch at crossings and would notify the "supporters" when refugees crossed the river so runaways could be quickly hidden or passed onto the trails headed north. Poke Patch was not just a passthrough location. It was far enough from the Ohio River to allow the runaways to rest among the scattered homes hidden in the swamps before continuing their trip north, or even settle.

Reports given to Siebert show both Quakers Bottom (Proctorville) and Ironton had safe houses, hidden rooms, dedicated workers, and numerous people looking for runaways. Abolitionists existed among the Iron Masters and their wives, many of whom were born in New England. Methodist and Presbyterian ministers, their congregations, and numerous Quaker families were opposed to slavery and shared their expertise with runaways. If whites were caught, a fine, possibly the inside of a jail, awaited, but their life would not be in jeopardy.

The situation was different near Burlington. The freed black congregation of Macedonia Church faced the possibility of being sold into slavery if they were captured and identified for aiding a slave to escape. However, little information is available about the Burlington area, where a select group of young Black men served as ministers, worked on the river, and participated in other occupations that met the public. These men and their families also worked the Underground Railroad.

Figure 42 – Escape Trails and Iron

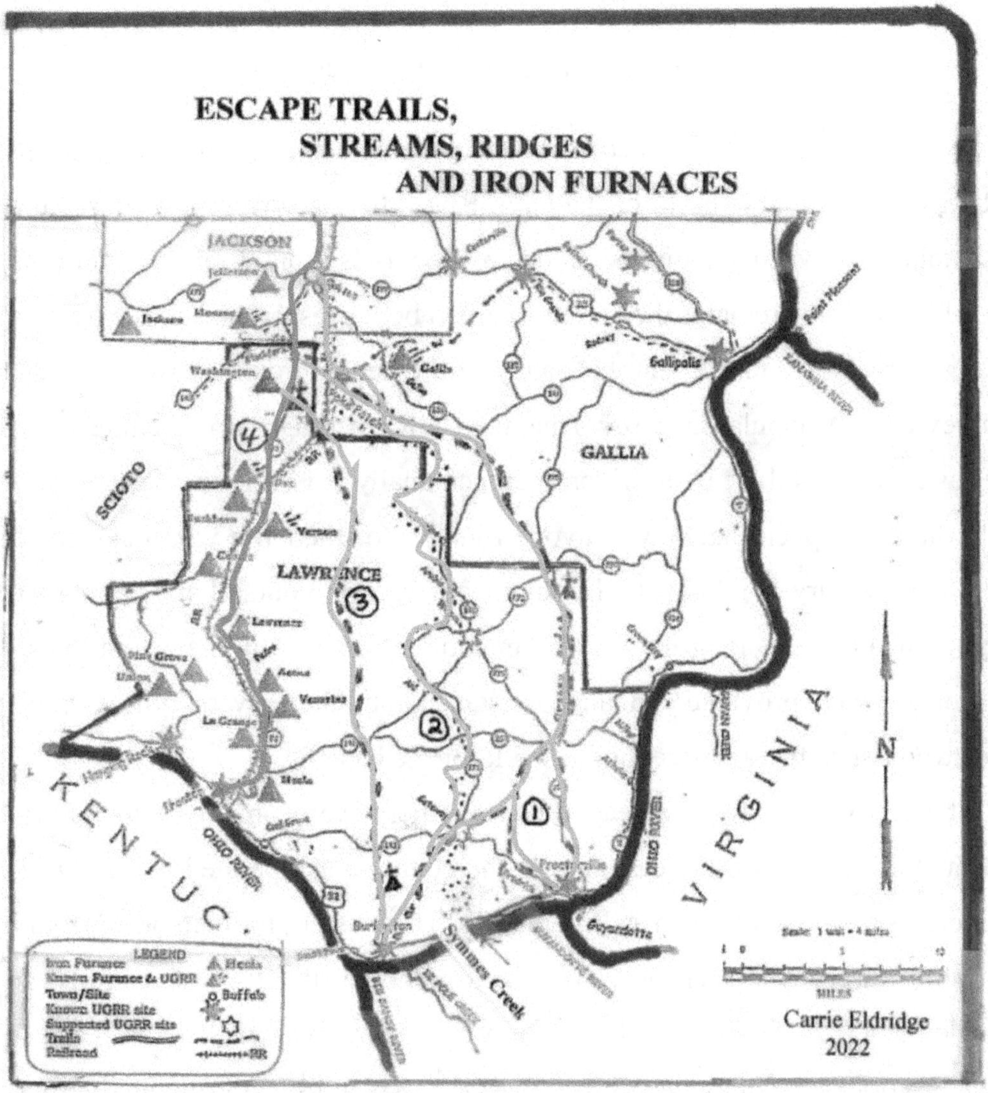

(1) Quaker Trail (2) Symmes Creek Trail (3) Macedonia Trail (4) Iron Furnace Trail

John Campbell, and his associates, owned eight of the furnaces, and by 1860 he was hiring Black workers for many different jobs. The workers could furnish someone with a floppy hat, a shovel, or an ax, and few people would question another worker. There were also numerous "charcoal kilns" in the nearby forest where assistance could be passed along.

The passage of the 1850 Fugitive Slave Law disrupted the UGRR trails. To be caught meant fines and jail for white men. For the Black workers, being caught might well mean being trapped, incarcerated, or sold, for they had no rights in Court. About 1855, the main group of the regional UGRR was the Stewart family near the northern edge of Lawrence County. They gathered family, in-laws, and neighbors and left the area, resettling in Cass County, Michigan.

Chapter 17: A Freedom Trail

The Underground Railroad in Lawrence County, Ohio

To this day, only a small amount of correct information exists about the Underground Railroad. The UGRR was only available north of the Ohio River. It was surrounded by secrecy, fear, and hate. Anyone talking or writing about the hidden escape trails found limited resources. Today, the main source of information remains the Wilburt Seibert books researched and written around 1900. True, he was much closer to the event, but many of the people involved were still alive, and the hate was still evident. A popular idea exists that the UGRR was a group of 'white' people who met the escapees as they crossed the Ohio River, then personally led everyone north to freedom.

It simply did not happen that way. Anyone running for their life who managed to cross the Ohio River was very wary of all people. Living meant trusting yourself and having a healthy fear of anyone you encountered along the way by making sure you saw them first. Yes, there were white abolitionists who provided aid and assistance, but there were others from the Black communities who risked life and freedom to work for the UGRR.

Seibert's books would have the reader believe there were only two major trails through Lawrence County. The trail on the east side of the county was operated by the Quaker families around Quakers Bottom, later known as Proctorville. The western trail led north from Ironton and followed the iron furnaces to Jackson County and points north. Both these trails did exist, but neither was the main trail across Lawrence County for several reasons.

The Quaker community was just across the Ohio River from the main riverport in Cabell County, VA. This area probably aided escapees before 1830, and Charles Wilgus of Proctorville bought land and settled his son on the trail north where OH 775 and OH 141 intersect, but any local escapees were quickly identified, and slave catchers easily crossed the Ohio River by the ford or took a steamboat to the Ohio shore. The pursuit was quick and often successful.

Yes, the Ironton area had several Iron Masters who were known abolitionists, and yes, they personally involved themselves in escapes. The problem lies in the fact that Ironton was not begun until about 1850, the Iron Railroad only went ten miles; and only a few furnaces, operating during the height of the UGRR period (1835-1855), would protect escapees. There was a noted lack of Black residents enumerated by the census around the furnace sites before 1850, although increasing new furnaces and jobs encouraged many Blacks to migrate by 1860.

Figure 43 – Iron Furnace Dates

Lawrence County Iron Furnaces Dates

Union	1826	Centre	1836
*Pine Grove	1828	LaGrange	1836
Little Etna	1832	Vesuvius	1836
*Mt. Vernon	1833	*Olive	1846
*Lawrence	1834	*Washington	1853
*Hecla	1834	Jackson Co.	1836
*Buckhorn	1835	*Gallia Co.	1844

*William Campbell Furnace - Abolitionist

Before the Stewart "Clan" moved out of Ohio, the area where they lived was known as Poke Patch or the Stewart Town. It was mainly settled by Free Blacks from eastern Virginia and the coastal Carolinas. James B. Stewart separated from his family when most of his siblings moved to Tennessee, He arrived in Gallia County, Ohio, before 1818, when his son John was born. James B. Stewart was a preacher as well as a Free Black. He gave the first recorded sermon in Greenfield Township in 1819. He probably also helped create the first Providence Anti-Slavery Baptist Association with Macedonia, Union, and Big Rock churches two years later.

The Iron Furnace industry of western Lawrence County offered an opportunity to work outside the farm, that did not exist beyond the iron ore area. Because transportation was slow, roads non-existent, and wagon loads small, the industry built several small furnaces near the sources of the raw materials. Poke Patch sprawled into three counties and had more than a dozen furnaces within a ten-mile radius of easy travel. Jobs like iron digging, coal tunneling, timber cutting, and charcoal making accepted any worker - without color or creed.

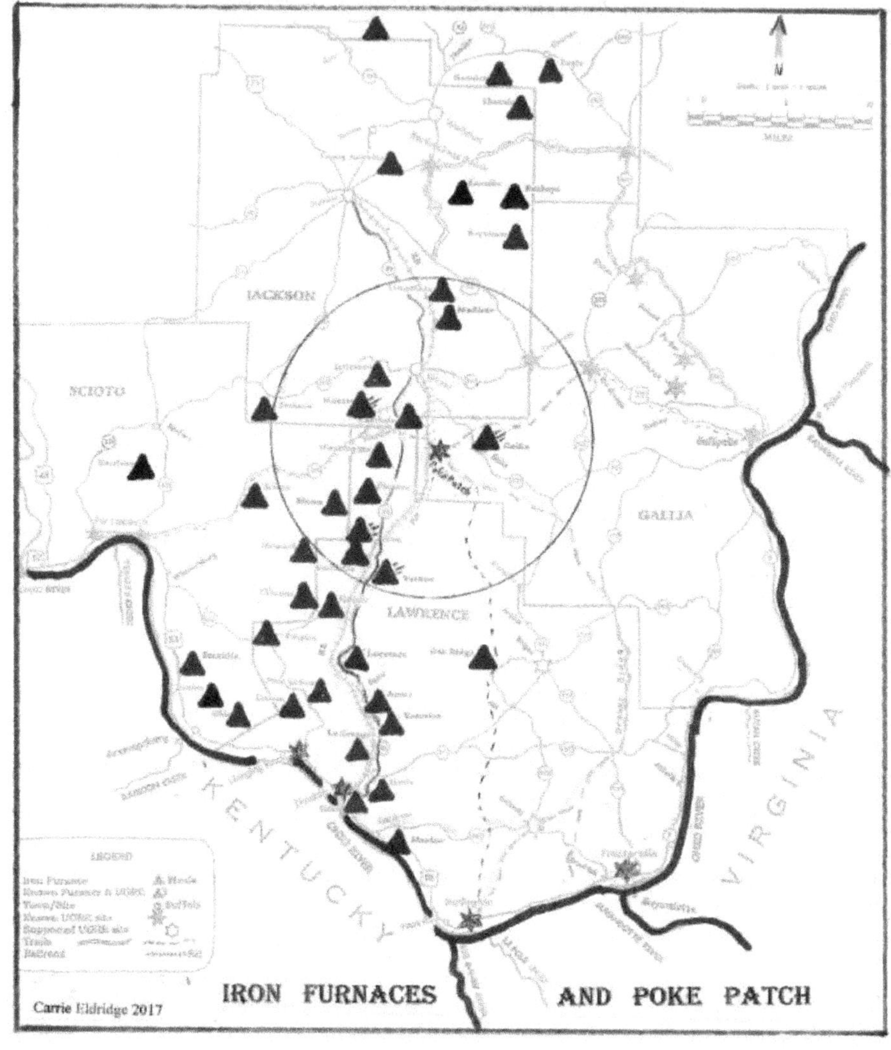

The UGRR Connection

Certain events had to be present to create and operate an escape route that would successfully move runaways from the Ohio River banks to safe areas beyond the marauding 'slave catchers.' There had to be a location for the event, people to risk their lives, connections to safer areas, and the opportunity to succeed. Although the criteria were met at several locations along the Ohio River, most of the people involved did not guarantee success in their lives.

The Black settlers of Macedonia Hill knew it was their responsibility to aid other people. They had been given the gift of freedom, and they realized that gift must be passed on and protected. Although the Murphy families were probably involved in some way, the main task fell to the members of the Macedonia Church to fulfill their legacy.

The Bryant family became the first leaders of the community and the church during the 1820s when there were only 576 people living in Fayette Township. With only fifteen people per square mile, it was a simple matter to move from the riverbank covered with the brush to creep past one or two people cutting wood or milking a cow along the trail leading to Macedonia Hill. No records show how many escapees shared the small cabins and scant meals before being shown the road north. Facts show Fayette Township's Black population continued to grow, as did faraway Poke Patch. An untold number of Blacks had to arrive and pass through the river area before anyone to reach Poke Patch. The location near the county seat and at a river port provided an opportunity that was exploited.

As the 1820s ended, the large group of slaves, manumitted by John Ward, arrived in Lawrence County. These new arrivals had no money, but their assets were a strong back and freedom. Many families shared a cabin with those already in the area, and others quickly built shelters, claiming the land as squatters. They became part of the Macedonia Church and understood the necessity of protecting their freedom. The additional people, especially young males, encouraged the church members to change their community involvement. Macedonia Church had encouraged an association of churches to better serve their congregations. Some people realized the association's name, which included "Anti-slavery," would alert unwanted attention to the church's activities. By 1831, the name had changed to the Providence Missionary Baptist Association. The church elders appeared to train ministers to expand into new churches while completely ignoring the subject of slavery. The white population accepted the change.

The church association created a communication system between the numerous churches, which encouraged its ministers to travel the area as missionaries. These men could carry messages, alert conductors, and notify stations of new escapees in the area while they tended their flock or held revival meetings and conferences. The connections between churches, especially between Macedonia and Union created along the Old Jackson Road, assured the escapees an improved chance of eluding capture until they could reach Poke Patch. Once there, the enterprising Stewart family provided sanctuary with food and shelter for a brief time before sending people north to the next station.

The involvement of the ministers and churches almost guaranteed success for the Black communities who had promised to protect their freedom. The information about the hidden road was ideally known only by a few. Reality says everyone in the congregation assisted the effort, BUT - it was a secret to be kept safe – 'forever.'

Like Macedonia Church near the Ohio River, the Union Church was the main support body of the Poke Patch area. Over the years, Union Church had several locations in Lawrence and Gallia counties, but all were near the Old Jackson Road connecting the Ohio River at Burlington to the interior and Jackson, the county seat of Jackson County. That road survey was issued by the Lawrence County Court in 1817. (Road survey ordered in 1817-1821 Clerk of Court of Lawrence County filmed by Family Search FS 8198780.) The Old Road was a highway only in your mind, for it was a horse-wide dirt path through the forest between the two county seats. It allowed the interior farmers an outlet to the Ohio River and better markets. It also gave traders, peddlers, and traveling ministers a marked trail along the streams, ridges, and forest glades that covered all of Lawrence County.

Early Lawrence County had a small population, and long periods passed before travelers met and passed even when it was the main road. After the Lawrence County Seat was moved to Ironton in 1852, the Old Jackson Road was all but abandoned in favor of the new highway, OH 93 which serviced the railroad and Iron Furnaces between Ironton and Jackson.

Between 1800 and 1850, people arriving in eastern Lawrence County came across the Ohio River from old Virginia where most settlers had relatives on both sides of the river. They also migrated down the Ohio River from New England with its abolitionist views. That migration pattern changed after 1850 as Kentucky's population grew, and the Cumberland Gap Road was still the western trail for many frontiersmen. At the same time, the county seat change in Lawrence County focused on the western side of the county around Ironton and the Iron Furnaces. In the 1850s, runaways from the numerous Kentucky plantations crossed the Ohio River near Ironton, where that group of the UGRR shuttled people towards Poke Patch.

That political change meant the area along the river at Burlington offered other runaways a better chance to reach the Old Jackson Road and to cross the county unseen, for the Ironton area drew many Burlington businesses and residents down the river. That migration left lots and farms vacant along the Old Road.

Across the Ohio River, there was also an attitude change in Cabell County, VA, concerning slavery. In the late 1840s, one large landowner sold all his slaves while another manumitted his to Michigan. Many of the remaining slaves had lost family and friends and were unhappy with their situation. The remaining slave owners in the area felt endangered and feared losing their property.

At the same time, the passage of the Fugitive Slave Law of 1850 emboldened young 'hot blood' to become "slave catchers" to make easy money. The Quaker Trail out of Proctorville probably saw fewer runaways because it was so close to Guyandotte, VA, where slaveholders had increased surveillance around their property.

The changes in trail locations, area attitudes, and certainly the passage of the Fugitive Slave Law were more than enough reasons for the Stewart family to leave Ohio. They left behind a very limited number of conductors and no station for the UGRR. The very fact that the entire family left may be the reason quite a few references name the Stewarts. Once they were gone, no one could harm them. As the whole nation moved toward war, Lawrence County had lost its ability to successfully assist people along the UGRR. (See Appendix 10 for information about Cass County, MI)

Afterword

There were three major escape trails for Black runaways through Lawrence County, Ohio, with the fourth one following Symmes Creek when it was not in flood. Each trail had a different sponsor and traveled through widely separated sections of the heavily forested county. Limited information about a Quaker Trail, north from the Proctorville area of east Lawrence County, and a western trail from Ironton, following the Iron Furnaces north, have been documented before.

This study is about the third trail. The Macedonia Trail from the Ohio River at Burlington, north along the Old Jackson Road, past Macedonia Church, then thirty-five miles north to the northern boundary of Lawrence County to an area called Poke Patch. This trail was organized by manumitted Blacks who were members of the Macedonia Church. They joined together with two other organized Black churches in the county to create an association of Black churches with a missionary zeal against slavery.

Part of their mission was to gather information, another was to provide aid and assistance, and next to arrange a system of transportation and cooperation between like-minded people (an underground railroad) and assist those people to freedom. Supported by their ministers, aided by quick-thinking young men and women, the local Black churches organized and operated an unknown and even unsuspected UGRR from the heart of the county seat to various points north. That extended trail of freedom moved across Ohio, Indiana, Illinois, and Michigan to eventually end in Canada.

The small local Black communities, found near Burlington, kept to themselves, made friends, and obeyed the laws. Although many white residents were abolitionists, only a few were willing to help people running from the law. The Black community endangered itself and took risks not demanded of free people. Some moved away from the river, taking to the freedom trail themselves, but most of the manumitted people of Lawrence County stood their ground. They quietly accepted the raiding 'slave catchers' who invaded their homes to look for unknown runaways. They took jobs that often caused them misery so that they could gather information. They shared their food and homes even if there was little to share. Having been given the gift of freedom through manumission, they were determined to help others seek their own freedom.

The Macedonia Trail began at the Ohio River, where the local people discovered they had to be quiet, unnoticed, and complacent if they were to successfully operate a freedom trail. Most of the Macedonia membership did not seem to do anything, but Bryants, Roberts, Johnsons, Cradics and others succeeded in putting the runaway on the Old Jackson Road and even provided diversions to help him on his way. How!

Diversions hid movement. People listened to Ole Washington as he ranted in Court, heard singing at the church, watched a good fist fight, or shared moonshine on a cloudy night. Your cook had questions that kept you from looking down the road, or the barber had a good story to tell. Did a load of firewood arrive when you least expected it? The hired man worked late one evening and came to your door to tell you he was finished. Did you miss the shadows that crept past the barn? A few minutes of delay could mean the difference between escape and capture.

Figure 45 - Identified workers of Lawrence County's Underground Railroad

<table>
<tr><td colspan="2">The following Burlington information was given in the Ironton Register in 1890 by John G. Wilson s/Stephen Wilson – both lived near Macedonia Hill and supported Blacks.
Burlington</td></tr>
<tr><td>B-Bryant, G. W.　(Macedonia minister)</td><td>W – Rev. Jacob Cumming</td></tr>
<tr><td>B-Bryant, William　minister</td><td>W – Dr. Camillius Hall</td></tr>
<tr><td>B-Cradic, W. P.　　minister</td><td>W – Presbyterian Rev. Gamaliel Beamen</td></tr>
<tr><td>B-Lynch, Philip - whistler</td><td>W – Methodist Stephen Wilson</td></tr>
<tr><td colspan="2">B-Johnson, Gabe-barber – both in Burlington and Ironton</td></tr>
</table>

<table>
<tr><td>Ironton – numerous Iron Master abolitionists</td><td>Conductors</td></tr>
<tr><td>W-　Campbell, John</td><td>B-Ditcher, James 'The Red Fox'</td></tr>
<tr><td>W-　Kelly – wife & servants</td><td>B-Gabe Johnson – barber & porter</td></tr>
<tr><td>W-　Peters, John</td><td>- Matilda Johnson – cook Clark Hotel</td></tr>
</table>

Quakers Bottom/Proctorville – East Lawrence County adjacent to Cabell County, VA. Settled late 1790's.

B – Lewis Brooks　W- *H.E. Adams　* C.M.Pease　*Isaac Miller　(Jesse Baldwin)　(Charles Wilgus)
　　　　　　　　*J. Kimball　* A.S. Proctor *Judge Wes Reckard　(William Russell)
　　　　　　　* All signed an abolition amendment 28 Feb 1856 – *Ironton Register*

<table>
<tr><td>Poke Patch – major station
B-Holly, Benjamin</td><td>Leading conductors</td></tr>
<tr><td>B-Stewart Brothers and sisters (# = ch of John P. Stewart)</td><td>Old Man Crandolph</td></tr>
<tr><td>　　Jacob & John (s/William)</td><td>　-James m to Mariah Stewart</td></tr>
<tr><td>　　James B. ch #2 – minister, 1st sermon at Union</td><td>Mathews, Pleasant – Susan Stewart</td></tr>
<tr><td>　　Isaac & Thomas (s/James B.)</td><td>all the Stewart sons</td></tr>
<tr><td>　　William (Union Baptist minister) (ch #6)</td><td>(Led family to Cass County.)</td></tr>
<tr><td>B-Coker, Peter m -Elizabeth Stewart (ch # 5) and their sons</td><td>later lived with Tolliver Coker</td></tr>
<tr><td>B-Chavis, Wm. m Frances Stewart (da/Richard ch #7)</td><td></td></tr>
<tr><td>B-Crandolph, James m to Mariah Stewart (ch #10)</td><td>(Cratoff-Cradock) Olive Furnace</td></tr>
<tr><td>W-Iron Master Stafford at Gallia Furnace　……………</td><td>'Black' manager - James Stewart)</td></tr>
<tr><td>W-Gallia Methodist Church</td><td>B- Clawa, Jacob at Buckhorn Furnace</td></tr>
<tr><td>W-Seeley at Buckhorn Furnace</td><td></td></tr>
<tr><td colspan="2" align="center">Sources: Seibert, newspaper articles</td></tr>
</table>

Each of the Free or Freed groups in this study had a part in the development of their freedom trail. Freed by location, the Bryant's were instrumental with beginnings of Macedonia Church. At the same time, the Murphy family seemed to accept the role of diversion. The large group manumitted by John Ward strengthened the church, provided new ministers, and had young men and women who created families and provide workers. These early families had limited land and resources, but they had a determination to help others obtain the freedom they had acquired. In the years between 1810 and 1850, they established themselves in the community and began assisting runaways away from the river to areas of safety farther north.

The establishment of the Association of Black Churches gave the ministers a reason to travel across the area, providing information and hope. Without the UGRR Station at Poke Patch, runaways would have been captured because distances to other safe areas were extreme. The extended Stewart family had generations of experience in evading capture while bending 'Black Laws,' which tried to crush them.

When the oppression finally became the Civil War, numerous young men raised in Lawrence County joined the Union forces in both Lawrence County, OH, and Cass County, MI. Some gave their lives; others gave their support. The Emancipation Proclamation and the Sixteenth Amendment did away with slavery, but the people who operated a freedom trail already knew what freedom meant. They became the teachers, ministers, the leaders of their communities, and the future.

Appendixes

Appendix #1 Lawrence County Families - Murphy by 1812

Henry Murphy and Washington Murphy appeared first on 1811/12 Gallia County duplicate Personal Property Tax List. (Chattel List) Henry paid taxes for 1 horse, while Washington was taxed for two horses and four head of cattle. Both men were living in Union Township, Gallia County, Oh. (Later - Union Township, Lawrence Co.) Henry Murphy's family is not listed in Lawrence County after 1830.

Washington Murphy - b 1780 SC and died before 1860 Lawrence Co. (OH Prison Records)

1811-1812 Gallia County, Duplicated Personal Property Tax. The first reference to the Murphy families.

1814 1st of many Court cases began in Gallia County, Ohio, and continued into Lawrence County, with last

Case beginning in 1845 and dealing with property that was sold while Washington was in prison.

1816 Married first @1816 - Polly (white – Irish) son Elliot (b 1817 Union Township, Gallia/Lawrence).

1817 son Elliot born (possible mother's surname?) See Idaho census where he lists mother as Irish.)

1820 census (Both 1820 and 1830 census for Union Township, Lawrence County, OH)

1820 census (Law. Co.) Henry Murphy household. 1 mulatto males 0-14, 1 male 26 to 45, 2 f 0-14, 1 female 45+

(Parents and 3 children under 14 (Washington below is probably brother.)

1830 census – Henry Murphy – 1 son and 3 daughters under 10, 2 daughters 10-23,1 female 24-35, no older family.

1820 census - Polly -white head of household 2 male mulattos 1 under 14 m – 1m 26/44 Union Twp.

(In a mixed household, whites were listed first. Polly, son Elliott, husband Washington.)

1830 census – 1 mulatto-m – 14/23, son Elliott - 1 mulatto m 36/54 Washington - (no females)

1832-3 Washington marries 2nd Rebecca (Trailer) (white) Lawrence Co. Union Twp. (named in a court case)

1833 son Burrel born   (Trailer Court case – Ledger 2nd day Term 1836 image 523/665)

1838 Washington sent to prison for Assault with intent to wound.

1839 Lawrence Co. Court –Journal 3&4 p 226 - Elliott Murphy identified as the son of Washington Murphy

1840 census – Fayette Township, Lawrence Co.(mother) Rebecca white – head of household

-1m (mulatto son) under 10 – Burrell - 1m (mulatto stepson) 24/35 - Elliott

1842 Washington was released from prison. (1838-1842)

1843 daughters born - Eliza Jane - 1843, Elizabeth - 1845, Cynthia – 1848 (per 1850 census).

1848? – Elliot goes West to Oregon Territory (see below)

1850 – Census - Rome Twp. Murphy, Washington 70, Rebecca 30,

Children: Burrel J. 15, Eliza 6, Elizabeth 4, Cynthia 2

1855 – last court case – 1859 – Eliza's marriage – Washington dies.

1859 – marriage – Gallia Co. OH –Eliza Jane Murphy m John Oscar Peters- 24 Feb 1859 (Getaway area)

Apparently, Eliza Jane had one daughter and divorced Peters (see 1897 marriage of Rebecca Bass)

1860 – census – Guyan Twp. Gallia Co. OH Mercerville - (north of Rome Twp. in Lawrence Co.)

Murphy, Rebecca 49 SC (white) mulatto John 27 (Burrel J.) Eliza 17, Elizabeth 15, Cynthia 12,

Mary 9/12 (Mary (Rebecca) daughter belonged to Eliza Jane by J.O. Peters)

1860 – marriage – Lawrence Co. OH - <u>Burrel Murphy</u> m Elizabeth Bass – 30 Jun 1860

1863 – Civil War draft – Burwell Murphy - Decatur Twp. Law. Co. OH

1870 – Burrel in Elizabeth Twp. Wife named Mary? - (Mary <u>Elizabeth</u> Bass?)

1863 – marriage – Lawrence Co. OH - <u>Elizabeth Murphy </u>m Peter Bass 3 Sep 1863 (bro to Elizabeth Bass)

        Elizabeth died prior to 1870 (Peter Bass m 2nd 1870 – a total of 5 wives)

1864 – 15 Aug 1864 – Lawrence Co. <u>Cynthia Ann Murphy</u> m William James Lewis

1864 – 17 Sep 1864 – Lawrence Co. <u>Eliza Ann Murphy</u> (Peters) m Samuel W. Bass

1870 - Rebecca Murphy 57 - living in James Cade household (Symmes Twp Law. Co. #51)

1870 – Mary is probably the Rebecca (age 10) living in the Samuel Bass household (Symmes Twp/ #40)

        Sam m Eliza Jane Murphy 1864 – child Mary 1860 census - child of Eliza Jane Murphy (Peters).

1870 - Cynthia in Fayette Twp. with Reddon Turner Family. #165 (dau. Arraja Ann Murphy b 1869)

1880 – Census – Forrest- Vernon Co. Wisconsin – Murphy, Burryl b 1833 OH w/Elizabeth (Bass) 37 (NC)

        Children: Josephine 19, Nancy 18, Allis 16, Thomas 6 – all born OH – all listed white

 1880 Burryl & Elizabeth Murphy, Samuel and Eliza Jane Bass, Elijah Bass, Jr. all Forrest, Vernon Co. WI

        same Twp. - Elizabeth Bass' brothers – Samuel Bass and Elijah Bass Jr.

1897 – Vernon Co. Wisconsin - Wilson Gordon (b Alabama) m <u>Rebecca Bass</u> (b Law. Co. OH)

   <u>Father – John Peters, Mother – Liza Jane Murphy (married Peters 1859 -Bass 1864 divorced Peters)</u>.

1900 Elizabeth Murphy – widow (alone) #249 Forrest (Bass household widow/Burrel)

        1840- 28 Nov 1902 – bur Revels Cem. Dilly, Vernon Co. Wis. Lived Forrest. Dau. Alice Revels

1900 -   Samuel 1839-1906 & Eliza Jane Bass 1843-1936 -7 ch - #225 Forrest Twp. Buried Vernon Co. WS

        Samuel 1839-1906 – Eliza Jane 1843-1936 (both buried Vernon Co. Wis.)

Forrest, Vernon County, Wisconsin, was a community of free Blacks, freed slaves, and persons of mixed heritage, including white people and Indians: a place of refuge after the 1850 Fugitive Slave Law was passed.

1850 & 1860 Law. Co. - Decatur Twp. -Elijah Bass Sr.- w/Matilda

Figure A46 – 2 Russell Houses - Getaway

The columned home below was one of several owned by the Russell family. The rumor claimed one house had chains and fetters in the basement for capturing and holding runaways. The houses stood about twenty feet above Symmes Creek on a small bluff facing the trail (OH 243) and Symmes Creek. All the homes were brick made locally, probably laid by brick mason William Chinn. Circa-Civil War period.

Demolished

Standing 2022

Figure A47 – Another Russell house. Standing in 2022.

Figure A48 – Eliza Jane Murphy and 2nd husband Samuel Bass

Appendix #2 – Bryant

Figure A49 - Bryant Census Information - 1820-1830-1840 Census – Fayette Twp.

Bryant Census Information – Lawrence County, Ohio

1820 ages – m14-26-45-45+
    f 14-26-45-45+
Fayette Twp.
Briant, Rosanna 0000-2001
Upper Twp. (adjacent)
Briant, John 2110-4010

Fayette Twp.
1830 m 10-24-36-55-100-100+
   f 10-24-36-55-100-100+
Bryan, John
   020100-430100
Roberts, Pleasent
   m Sarah Bryant 1829
 (1830) Rosanna with them
   110000-110010
   Rosanna died 1833

1840 -m20-24-36-55-100-100+
  -f 20-24-36-55-100-100+
Fayette Twp.
Bryant, John 000010-001000
Bryant, George 110000-010000
Bryant, Wm. 201000-110000
Roberts, Pleasant
  w/Bryant 320100-211000
(Sarah Bryant Roberts named on
 1881 land survey of Rosanna's
 with John's sons Wm. & Geo. W.
 indicating Sarah sister to John)

Lynch, Phil 001000-011000
  w/Rosette Bryant dau/John
Reed, William 100100-211000
  w/Nancy Bryant dau/John

Roseanna's children:
 -William Bryant listed as minister in 1880
 -George Washington Bryan was listed as a minister on the 1850 census, William in 1880.
 -Geo. W., & William Bryant with his son Isaac Vinton were Ministers at Macedonia.
 -Sarah Bryant m Pleasant Roberts. His C.W. Roberts minister m Susannah Bryant.
 -Juda Bryant married Jefferson Craddock (a Ward) in 1831. Jeff died before 1840, but a son was born.
The 1850 census shows Judy and their son William living with her brother William Bryant.
Her son, William Portrait (W.P.) Cradic became a Macedonia Minister. He died in Columbus in 1912.

Rosanna Bryant's Family

Rosanna b@1770/5 – 1820 census age 45-65 – (She could have been born by 1755 and died in 1833.)
Rosanna - purchased @1782 by William Bryan
Son JOHN - b@ 1783-85 (father - William Bryan)
John m Susan(?) @1805 (these dates are only guesses from children's ages)
1820 - Both Rosanna and John 'Briant' on 1820 Law. Co. census
****

ROSANNA BRIANT/BRYANT (1755/75-1833) had SON-JOHN (Many family members lived to 80.)
Law. Co. Common Pleas Court Journal 1830-1835 (Genealogytrails.com/Ohio/Lawrence)
12 Mar 1833, the will of Rosanna Bryant (decd) presented to Court, said Court issued a commission to
Marion County, OH to take a disposition of Horatio II. Wheeler (Witness to the signature of Rosanna.)19
Jun 1833 Will of Rosanna Bryant produced by John Bryant, the executor. (No actual will located.)
****

There were two John Bryan/t men in Lawrence County, Ohio, between 1820 and 1850.
One was Black, the son of Rosanna Bryant. John married Susan (?), and they had at least 7 children.
(possibly, one of the girls living with Rosanna in 1820 was his daughter)
John was a farmer and a founder of the Macedonia Church.
JOHN and w/Susan not mentioned after 1841 - dating problem here - lack of documents.
–John b 1782/4 m Susan --   children:
William b @1813 m 1833, Geo. W.(Sr.)b @1817 m 1839 (ages given in 1881survey deed)
Daughters: Sarah 1804 m 1829, - Harriet 1806 m 1838 (maybe Rosanna's)
- Nancy 1810 m 1833, - Juda 1812 m 1831, - Rosetta 1816 m 1833,
- Susannah 1823 m 1839, - Sara Jane 1825-
JOHN w/ SUSAN -DEED 1841-(sold last of Rosanna's property - Bk 8-p493-494 (Index #2)

****

John Bryan (#2) (white) m widow Sarah Frampton Lane in 1827. A Master Tanner, he owned properties in Burlington
, including a riverfront store purchased in 1823. He was Lawrence Co. Auditor from 1835 until 1848 and died in 1850.
(It is possible this John Bryan was also a son of William Bryan. His wife was a Frampton whose father sold all the land
'Fry Lands.' Their home was about where Charlotte Lane runs.) (Both families interacted with Black families.)
The oldest son named William.   (See Hardesty's Atlas p214 and Family Search image FS007900697)

****

CENSUS INFORMATION – (Fayette & Upper are both fragmented townships.)

1820 Census lists Rosanna 'Briant' in Fayette Township, Lawrence County, OH
Age 45 to 65 with two females under fourteen. They may be listed below with John.
1820 John and Susan (unnamed) appear on the 1820 Lawrence County census in Upper Township.
Upper Township adjoins Fayette Township. The household lists seven children.
Susan (w/John) was listed on the 1841 deed for the remainder of Rosanna's property.

1. 1804 Sarah m 1829 to Pleasant Roberts – (Ward) deed indicates she was Rosanna's daughter.
2. 1806 Harriet m 1838 to Henry Smith   - maybe Rosanna's -died by 1860
3. 1810 Nancy m 1833 to William Reed
4. 1812 Juda m 1831 to Jefferson Craddock (Ward) s/Lewis & Winnie (sis to Martha)
5. 1813 William m 1833-Lovenia Bentley, 1847 Elizabeth (?),1851 wid. Martha Craddock Randall
6. 1816 Rosetta m 1833 Phil Lynch (Ward) recognized part of UGRR (His family went to Clinton Co. OH)
7. 1817 George W. m 1839 Cory Ann Cradwick (Ward) dau/Lewis & Winnie (sis to Martha)
8. 1819 Susannah m 1839 to Charles Roberts (Ward - probable son of Pleasant) minister
9. 1825 Sara J. m ------Landscroft – Death Certificate – parents named
Note: Surname spelling variations are numerous. Worst: Craddock/Cradic/Cradwick/Crandolph/etc.

1840 Census -Pleasant Roberts and family (Black) living in Fayette Township, Lawrence Co. OH
By 1860 the Black Roberts owned land in Windsor Township, OH, and were enumerated white.
Sarah Bryant Roberts not recorded after 1881 land survey when Wm. & G.W. listed their age.

1850 Census – Fayette Twp.		1860 Census – Fayette Twp.	
#90 Lynch, Philip	30 VA 1820 (Ward)	#214 Lynch, Philip	45 VA 1815
m Rose(tta) Bryant	30 VA 1820	Rosetta	44 VA 1816
ch May	9 OH 1841		
#93 Bryant, William	36 VA 1815	#288 Bryant, William	45 VA 1815 m 1851
m 1st Lovenia Bentley 1833 d 1840		m 3rd Martha Craddock Randall (wid Wm.)	
ch Geo. W.	15 OH 1835 – CW (1860 #286)	Martha	38 VA 1822
James K./S.	13 OH 1837 – CW	James S.	22 OH 1838 with uncle
Nancy Jane	10 OH 1840	---------	1870 #181
m 2nd Elizabeth------- (m1847 d 1848)		---------	
	26 VA 1824	---------	
ch Rachael	2 VA 1848	Rachel	13 OH 1847
		Nancy	8 OH 1852
(GW – 1870 #185)		Emly F.	5 OH 1855
		Isaac Vinton	4 OH 1855 (minister)
		Lewis Clinton	2 OH 1858
		(1870 # 119)	
#93 Cradick, Judy	38 VA 1812/3 sis to Wm.		
Bryant m Jefferson Craddock 1831 (Ward)		(Craddock = Cradic = Cradwick)	
ch William	16 OH 1834	W.P. Wm. Portrait Cradic – (minister)	
		1880 #277- 1900 Allen OH #526	
		1910 Columbus, OH #608 d 14 Jul 1912	
		m Mariah Anderson (8 children)	
		Bur. Union Cem. Columbus	
#94 Reed, William	50 KY 1800	#263 Reed William	65 VA 1795
m Nancy Bryant	40 VA 1808/10	Nancy Bryant	52 VA 1808
ch Mary	16 OH 1834	----	
Rosetta	12 OH 1838	----	
John	6 OH 1844	John R.	17 OH 1843 - CW
William	5 OH 1845	Wm. H	15 OH 1845
		James H.	11 OH 1849
		Geo. W.	8 OH 1852 ('70 #185)
		Saml. L.	6 OH 1854
#109 Bryant, George (W.) 36 OH (1817) minister		#289 Bryant, Geo. W.	43 VA 1817
m Cory Ann Craddock 30 VA 1820 (Ward)		Carry Ann	41 VA 1819
ch John W.	10 OH 1840 – CW	John W.	20 OH 1840 - CW
Philip (Albert) 8 OH 1842 - CW		Philip A.	18 OH 1842 - CW
Geo. W.	6 OH 1844	Geo. W. Jr.	15 OH 1845 – CW
Lena A.	2 OH 1848	Letha A.	12 OH 1848
		Benjamin	8 OH 1852-1873
		Lucinda	6 OH 1854
		Charles	3 OH 1857
		Dorinda	1 OH 1859
(1870 Winnie Craddock 84 with dau/Cory Ann & GW. Bryant		James S. Bryant 22 OH 1838 nephew	
1776 – 12 Feb 1871 bur. Macedonia)		(1870 #173 – 1880 #263 – 1900 #181 d 1912)	

1830 Fayette Twp.

Roberts, Pleasant – (Ward) wife Hannah – she died 1828 (trip?)

	1830 m - un 10	10-23	36-54	55-99	1830 f - un 10	10-23	36-54	55-99	
Roberts, Pleasant	1	1	1 (b 1788)		1	1		1	(Hannah d/trip) ?
m 1829 Sarah Bryant									
1840	2	1	1 (b 1804)		2	1	1		Sarah dau/Rosanna

1850 Windsor Twp.
     Non-population census only
1860 Windsor Twp
     Family enumerated white
   #119 Roberts, Pleasant   67 VA 1793
         Sarah   55 VA 1805
         Sarah   17 VA 1843

1850 Perry Twp. (Adjacent to Fayette) **1860 Fayette Twp.** **1870 Fayette Twp**

#27 Roberts, Charles
    Charles was son of Pleasants
    m 1839 Susan Bryant - niece to Sarah #291   #163   wagon maker

1850 Perry Twp.				1860 Fayette Twp.			1870 Fayette Twp	
#27 Roberts, Charles	27 VA 1823		Roberts, Charles	36 VA 1824 CW		Roberts, Chas.	60
Susan Bryant	25 OH 1825		Susan	37 OH 1823		Susan	58
Eliza Jane	10 OH 1840		Eliza J.	20 OH 1840		--------	
William	8 OH 1842		Wm. D.	18 OH 1842 CW		--------	
James H.	6 OH 1844		James H.	OH 1844		--------	
Mallissa A.	4 OH 1846		Mellissa	14 OH 1846		--------	
Harriet L.	0/12 OH 1850		--------			--------	
			Alex	8 OH 1852		--------	
			Isaac B.	6 OH 1854		Barton	23
			Clinton	4 OH 1856		Clinton	22
			Wyatt C.	0 OH 1860		Curtis	20
						Ida	12
						Wm. O.	10

Other family members were not located.

2nd left -Cadet Frank Bryant was a s/James R.
gs/William, ggs/John, and gggs/Rosanna Bryant.
1891 *Ironton Register*

Appendix #3 - Ward

PITTSYLVANIA COUNTY, VA – WARD REGISTRATIONS – 1827
Register Numbers 70 – 204: Registration Book pp 29 – 97
Freed by Will of John Ward, Sr. (1826) - probated 20 Nov 1826 Will Book 1 pp 109 -112
Registration certified correct 1 Jan 1827 by Executors John Ward, Jr.(nephew) & Lynch Dillard.

			1830 census Moved to OH County
#70 Lynch, Richard	24 – 5.8 ¼ "	dark mulatto	Clinton
#71 Lynch, Dorcas w/Richard	22 – 5.1 ¼ "	bright complexion	Clinton
#72 Lynch, Rhoda ch/Richard & Dorcas	3 ½ months	-	Clinton
#73 Roberts, Betsey ch/Pleasant &Hannah	17 – 5.4 ¼ "	light complexion	Lawrence
#74 Roberts, Elvy ch/Pleasants & Hannah	16f – 5.3 ¼ "	light complexion	Lawrence
#75 Roberts, Paulina ch/Pleasant & Hann.	14 – 5.0 "	light complexion	Lawrence
#76 Roberts, Laura ch/Pleasant & Hannah	13 – 4.10 ½ "	bright complexion	Lawrence
#77 Roberts, Penelope ch/ Pleasant & Han.	10 – 4.6 ¼ "	light complexion	Lawrence
#78 Roberts, Charles ch/Pleasant & Han.	8 – 4.1 ¼ "	bright complexion	Lawrence
#79 Roberts, John ch/Pleasant & Hannah	3 in Jun. 2.10"	light complexion	Lawrence
#80 Roberts, Pleasant (12 Dec 1826) –	38 – 5.11 ½ "	bright complexion	Lawrence
#81 Roberts, Hannah w/Pleasant	32 – 5.2"	light complexion	Lawrence
#82 Lynch, Peter	23 – 5.11 ½ "	light complexion	Clinton
#83 Ward, Daniel	21 – 5.8"	black man	Not found
#84 Johnson, Benjamin - wife is #195	58 – 5.3"	black man	Lawrence
#85 Johnson, Benjamin (Jr.) s/Benjamin	25 – 5.7 ½ "	black man	Lawrence
#86 Johnson, Jerry s/Benjamin	18 – 5.7 ¾ "	black man	Lawrence
#87 Ward, Harry	30-40 -5.6 ½ "	black man (Henry)	Lawrence
#88 Ward, Lydia w/Harry	45 – 5.4 ½ "	light complexion	Lawrence
#89 Ward, Sarah ch/Harry & Lydia	12 – 4.8 ¼ "	light complexion (Sary)	Lawrence
#90 Ward, Bob ch/Harry & Lydia	9 – 3.7 ¼ "	black (Robert)	Lawrence
#91 Ward, Anderson ch/Harry & Lydia	7 – 3.7 ½ "	black	Lawrence
#92 Ward, Judith ch/Harry & Lydia	3 – 2.9 ¾ "	light complexion	Lawrence
#93 Craddock, Lewis	75 – 5.8"	black	Lawrence
#94 Craddock, Winney w/Lewis	45 – 4.11 ¾ "	bright complexion	Lawrence
#95 Craddock, Jefferson ch/Lewis & Win.	----- 5.3 ¾ "	bright complexion	Lawrence
#96 Craddock, Lucy ch/Lewis & Winney	16 – 5.3"	light complexion	Lawrence
#97 Craddock, Martha ch/Lewis & Win.	10 – 4.3"	light complexion	Lawrence
#98 Craddock, John ch/Lewis & Winney	12 – 4.3 ½ "	light complex. (Jonathan)	Lawrence
#99 Craddock, Cory Ann ch/Lew. & Win.	8 – 3.11"	light complexion	Lawrence
#100 Craddock, Permelia ch/Lew. & Win.	5 – 3.6 ½"	bright complexion	Lawrence
#101 Craddock, Mourning ch/Lew & Win	3 - 3.0"	Light complexion	Lawrence
#102 Craddock, Mary ch/Lewis & Win.	3/12	-	Lawrence
#103 Greenhill, John	75 – 5.2 1/8 "	black man – bald	Lawrence
#104 Greenhill, Sylvia w/John	60 – 5.2 ¾ "	black woman	Lawrence
#105 Randolph, Gilbert	55 – 5.1 ½ "	black man	Not found
#106 Randolph, Biddy w/Gilbert	65-70 – 5.2 ½ "	black woman	Not found
#107 Tolbert, Christopher	65 – 5.6 ¾ "	black man – bald	Gallipolis
#108 Farmer, James	40 – 5.6 ½ "	black man	Not found
#109 Brooks, Holiday	40 – 5.7 ¼ "	black man	Not found
#110 Williams, Jackson	40 – 5.5 ½ "	black man	Not found
#111 Tantarobogus, William	55 – 5.1 ¼ "	black man	Not found

These people will be organized into family units beginning on page 90.

		1830 census or	Moved to OH County
#112 Ward, Samuel	60 – 5.5 ½ "	black/mulatto	Clinton
#113 Ward, Lucy w/Sam	56 – 5.4 ¼ "	black woman	Clinton
#114 Ward, Aaron ch/Sam & Lucy Ward	34 – 5.7 "	black	Clinton
#115 Ward, Handy son/Sam	20 – 5.8 ½ "	light complexion	Clinton
#116 Ward, Charles son/Sam next July	12 - 4.11 ¼ "	light complexion	Clinton
#117 Ward, Mary dau/Sam	22 – 5.6 ¾ "	mulatto	Clinton
#118 Ward, Rachel ch/Sam & Lucy	17 - 5.5 ½ "	black woman	Clinton
#119 Ward, Patsy ch/Sam & Lucy	10 – 4.9 ¼ "	light complexion	Clinton
#120 Ward, Hannah ch/Sam & Lucy	26 – 5.5 ¼ "	black woman	Clinton
#121 Ward, Charles s/Hannah Ward	1 - ---	light complexion	Clinton
#122 Ward, John s/Hannah Ward	11 – 4.8 ¾ "	black boy	Clinton
#123 Ward, Harrison s/Hannah Ward	8 – 4.3 ¾ "	black boy (twin)	Clinton
#124 Ward, Lindy dau/Hannah Ward	8 – 4.0 ½ "	light complexion (twin)	Clinton
#125 Ward, Simon s/Hannah Ward	4 – 3.4 ½ "	black boy	Clinton
#126 Ward, Jack son/Sam Ward	30 – 5.9 ¼ "	mulatto (John)	Clinton
#127 Ward, Christian w/Jack	20 – 5.7 ¼ "	light complexion	Clinton
#128 Ward, Lynch son/Jack	2 – 2.10"	light complexion	Clinton
#129 Ward, James son/Sam Ward	25 – 5.9 "	light complexion	" Not verified
#130 Callaway, Jack	48 – 5.6 ½ "	black man	Lawrence
#131 Callaway, Letty w/Jack	45 – 5.0 "	black	Lawrence
#132 Callaway, Polly dau/Jack	9 – 4.4 ¾ "	light complexion	Lawrence
#133 Allen, Caezar	37 – lost all toes	black man	Gallipolis
#134 Ward, David (25 Dec 1826)	30 - 5.10"	mulatto (favorite)	Clinton
#135 Ward, Nancy (sister to David)	28 – 5.4"	mulatto (favorite)	Clinton
#136 Ward, George s/Nancy	16 – 5.9"	bright mulatto	Clinton
#137 Ward, Joseph s/Nancy	12 – 5.0"	mulatto	Clinton
#138 Ward, Molley (Old Molley ?)	60 – 5.1 "	black woman (mother/Dav & Nan?) Law.	
#139 Ward, Amanda	4 – 3.0"	bright mulatto	Not found
#140 Lynch, Phil	15 – 4.10 ¾ "	light complexion	Clinton/Lawrence
#141 Lynch, Chaney (f)	12 – 5.0 ½ "	light complexion	Clinton
#142 Mundal, Joseph	45 – 5.3 ¾ "	black man	Gallia/Green
#143 Mundal, Critty	35 – 5.6 ½ "	black woman	Gallia
#144 Mundal, Peter ch/Critty	4/12	black	Gallia
#145 Mundal, Eliza ch/Critty	12 – 4.2 ½ "	black girl	Gallia
#146 Mundal, Thomas ch/Critty	9 – 4.3 "	black boy	Gallia
#147 Mundal, Betsey ch/Critty	6 – 4.6 "	light complexion	Gallia
#148 Mundal, Laurenzo ch Critty	5 – 3.11 "	black boy	Gallia
#149 Mundal, Woodson ch/Critty	4 – 3.5 "	black boy	Gallia
#150 Mundal, William ch/Critty	3 – 3.1 ¾ "	black boy	Gallia
#151 Mundal, Doctor ch/Critty	2 – 2.8 "	black boy	Gallia
#152 Mundal, Joseph ch/Critty	18 months	black boy	Gallia
#153 West, Rowland	25 – 5.7	black man (Rolen)	Gallia/Springfield
#154 West, Clary w/Rowland	23 – 5.3 ½ "	black woman	Gallia
#155 West, Otey ch/Clary	5/12	light complexion	Gallia
#156 West, Nancy ch/Clary	7 – 3.11 ¾ "	black girl	Gallia
#157 West, Walker ch/Clary next Mar.	5 – 3.4 "	mulatto boy	Gallia
#158 West, Jincy (f) ch/Clary	2 – 2.9 "	black girl	Gallia
#159 Johnson, Rachel	26 – 5.4 ½ "	black woman	Not found
#160 Johnson, Sophia ch/Rachel	1 ½	mulatto child	Not found
#161 Johnson, George	10 – 4.8 ¾ "	black boy	Not found
#162 Johnson, Annaca	8 – 4.2 ½ "	black girl	Not found

PITTSYLVANIA COUNTY, VA – WARD REGISTRATIONS – 1827 (cont)

		1830 census or	Moved to Ohio County
#163 Ward, Isbel	45 – 5.3 "	black woman	Not found
#164 Ward, Peggy ch/Isbel	21 – 5.4 ¼ "	black girl	Not found
#165 Ward, Viney (f) ch/Isbel	12 – 5.0 "	black girl	Not found
#166 Ward, Peter ch/Isbel	8 – 4.0 ¼ "	light complexion	Not found
#167 Henry, Patsey	75 – 5.1 "	black woman	Not found
#168 Johnson, Charles last Apr.	28 – 5.5 ¾ "	black man	Lawrence
#169 Ward, Simon	26 – 5.9 ½ "	light complexion	Clinton
#170 Ward, Samuel, Jr.	23 – 5.11 ½ "	black man	Clinton
#171 Dudley, Henry	35-40 – 5.7 ¼ "	light complexion	Pike
#172 Adams, David	50 – 6.0 "	mulatto	Highland
#173 Dudley, Sally w/Henry Dudley	33 – 5.4 ½ "	light complexion	Pike
#174 Adams, Milly w/David Adams	48 – 5.6 "	very black woman	Highland
#175 Adams, James ch/Dav. & Milly	10 – 4.6 "	black boy (25 Dec 1826)	Highland
#176 Adams, Mary ch/Dav. & Milly	6 – 3.11 "	bright complexion	Highland
#177 Adams, Milly ch/Dav. & Milly	4 last Jan. 3.5 "	bright complexion	Highland
#178 Adams, Sally ch/Dav. & Milly	2 – 2.10 "	bright complexion	Highland
#179 Jordon, Thomas	12 – 5.0"	bright complexion	Not found
#180 Dudley, Annica ch/Henry & Sal.	19 – 5.5 ¼ "	very bright	Pike
#181 Dudley, Lusey ch/Henry & Sal.	17 – 5.5 ¼ "	light complexion (Lucy)	Pike
#182 Dudley, Aaron ch/Henry & Sal.	16 – 5.2 "	very bright	Pike
#183 Dudley, George ch/Henry & Sal.	13 – 5.1 ¼ "	dark complexion	Pike
#184 Dudley, Mary ch/Henry & Sal.	10 – 4.8 ¼ "	bright complexion	Pike
#185 Dudley, Sam ch/Henry & Sal.	8 – 4.2 ¾ "	bright complexion	Pike
#186 Dudley, John ch/Henry & Sal.	6 – 3.9 ½ "	bright complexion	Pike
#187 Dudley, Hudley ch/Henry & Sal.	4 – 3.4 "	bright complexion	Pike
#188 Dudley, Henry(Jr.) ch/Hen.& Sal.	2 – 2.9 "	white negro-yellow eye	Pike
#189 Dudley, Wm. Green ch/Lucy	2 - ----	bright mulatto	Pike
#190 Powell, William	70 – 4.8 ½ "	black man	Lawrence
#191 Hodges, Ned	70 – 5.7 ¾ "	light complexion	Not found
#192 Ward, Saul	25 – 5.7 ¾ "	light complexion	Not found
#193 Bobbitt, George	40 – 5.5 "	bright complexion	Not found
#194 Shelton, Buck	30 – 5.7 ½ "	black man	Not found
#195 Johnson, Matilda w/Ben #84	31 – 5.3 ¼ "	light complexion	Lawrence
#196 Johnson, Nancy ch/Ben & Matilda	6 weeks old	light complexion	Lawrence

The next 5 children are entered (reputed child of Ben & Matilda Johnson) Rch.

#197 Johnson, Charlotte-Rch/Ben & Mat.	16- 4.11 ¼ "	light complexion	Lawrence
#198 Johnson, Dorcas – Rch/Ben & Mat.	14 – 4.7 "	light complexion	Lawrence
#199 Johnson, Moses – Rch/Ben & Mat.	10 – 2.8 "	light complexion (2 Nov 1826)	"
#200 Johnson, Sucky (f) Rch/Ben & Mat.	5 – 3.4 "	light complexion (Jun 1826)	"
#201 Johnson, Gib Rch/Ben & Mat.	2 - 2.8 "	light complexion	Lawrence
#202 Roberts, Molley	70-75 – 5.4 "	black woman	Lawrence
#203 Tucker, Milly	55 – 5.2 "	bright complexion	not found
#204 Dabney, Cato (states born free)*	21 – 5.6 ¼ "	black	not found

*(complier thinks this was a free person and not a Ward slave. Not found in any of the counties.)

#190 William Powell may be part of the Dudley family. Note: Registration order.
Once these people were grouped by family connection and settlement location, certain patterns appeared.
The census count in several counties does not match the registration information as families combined.
Some un-located were part of extended families that could not be identified by numbers of the earlier census.

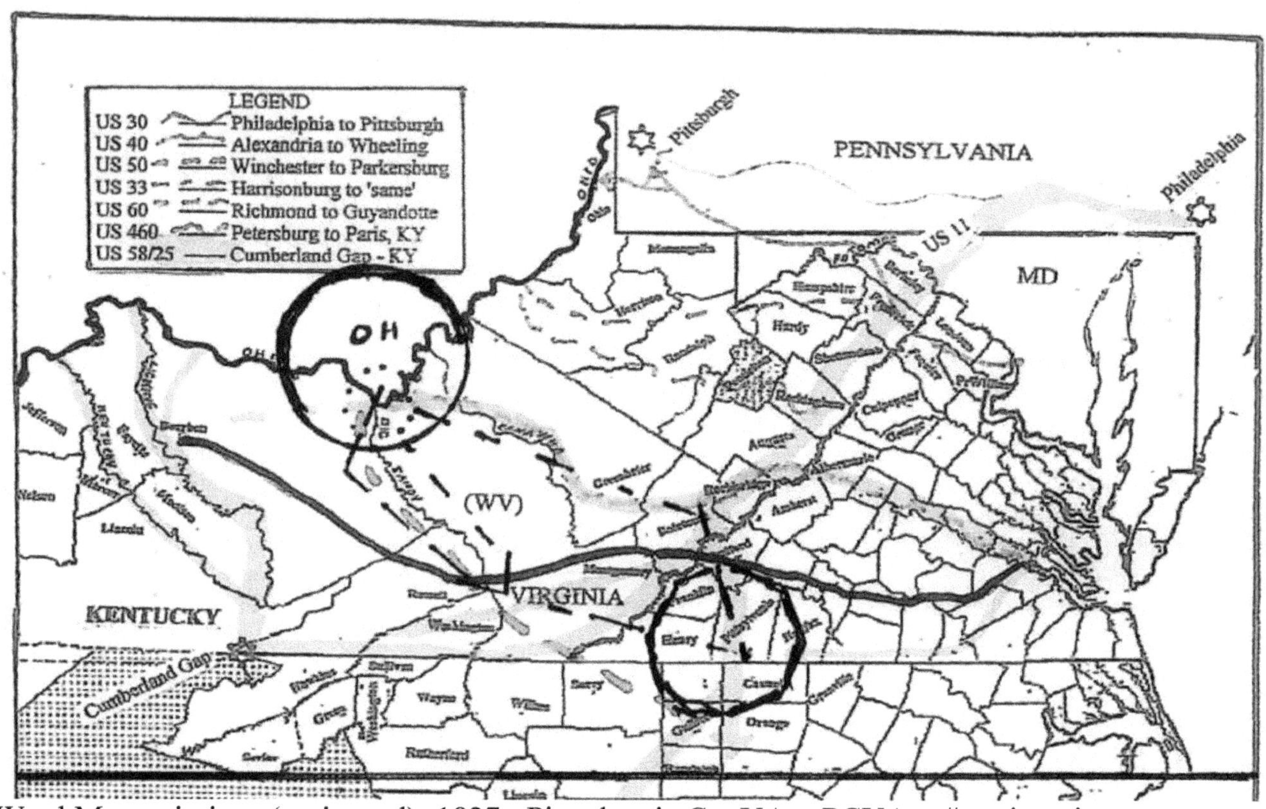

Ward Manumissions (registered) -1827 - Pittsylvania Co. VA = PCVA = # registration
Will - John Ward, Sr. 1826 - of Pittsylvania Co. VA - manumitted 138 individuals - family groups
Clinton (34), Gallia (23), Highland (7+7), Lawrence (48), Pike (12+5), total located 136

Figure 53 – Pittsylvania County, Virginia

Individuals settled in Lawrence County, Ohio (46) Fayette or Union Township. All marriages Lawrence Co. OH = LC.

# PCVA 1827	Name	age 1827 register	known OH location - source 1830 Census
#80	Roberts, Pleasants	38	Lawrence Co. OH m 18 May 39 Sarah Bryant
#81	" Hannah -wife	33	died? " (only 6ch) 3m3f – 1830 Fayette Twp
#73	" Betsey -ch	17	"
#74	" Elvy (f) -ch	16	" m Charles Johnston 26 Feb 1829 LC
#75	" Pauline -ch	14	"
#76	" Laura -ch	13	"
#77	" Penelope -ch	10	"
#78	" Charles -ch	8	" m 28 May 39 Susannah Bryant LC
#79	" John - ch	3 (June)	"
#84	Johnson, Benjamin (Sr.)	58	Lawrence Co. OH did not survive the trip
#85	" Benjamin, Jr. s/Ben 25		
#195	" Matilda Wife (Ben Sr.)	31	" (by registration – wife/Ben Sr.)
#196	" Nancy -ch	6 wks	"
#197	" Charlotte -ch ?	16	" m 4 Oct 1829 William Randall LC
#198	" Dorcas -ch?	14	"
#199	" Moses -ch?	10	"
#200	" Sucky (f) -ch?	5	"
#201	" Gib (m) -ch?	2	" Gabriel (see Matilda's Obit)
#86	" Jerry - s/Ben (Sr.)	18	? not located
#87	Ward, Harry	30-40	(Henry) Lawrence Co. OH - 1830 census
#88	" Lydia - wife	45	" (15 people) - Fayette Twp.
#89	" Sary(Sarah) -ch	12	"
#90	" Bob -ch	9	"
#91	" Anderson -ch	7	"
#92	" Judith -ch	3	"
#93	Craddock, Lewis	75	died on trip ?
#94	" Winney - wife	45	Lawrence Co. OH - 1840 -1850
#95	" Jefferson -ch	?	m 20 Nov 31 Judah Bryant
#96	" Lucy -ch	16	m 27 Feb 1834 Daniel Moses
#97	" Martha -ch	10	(1850) ? m 5 Oct 1834 Wm. Randall (2nd)
#98	(Craddock), John -ch	12	Law. Co.. (Jonathan) 1840-1850
#99	" Cory Ann -ch	8	m 24 Mar 1827- Geo. W. Bryant
#100	" Permilia -ch	5	" (1850)
#101	" Mouring -ch	3	m 22 Aug 1839 Robert Brassfield
#102	Craddock, Mary -ch	3m	Lawrence Co. OH 1830 census & (1850)
#103	Greenhill, John	75	Lawrence Co. OH 1830 census
#104	" Sylvia -wife	60	" (4) Union Twp.
#130	Callaway, Jack	48	(Josiah) Lawrence Co. OH 1830 census -3 Fay.
#131	" Letty -wife	45	" m 2nd-27 Sep 1840 Horace Withers
#132	" Polly -d/Jack	9	"
#137	Ward, Joseph -s/Nancy	12	" also 1850 Law. Co. census
#138	Ward, Molly	60	Lawrence Co. OH 1830 census
#139	Ward, Amanda	4	?
#140	Lynch, Phil	15	1827 Clinton- 1850 Law. m 26 Sep 33 Rosetta Bryant
#168	Johnson, Charles	28	Lawrence Co. OH 1830 m 26 Feb 29 Elvy Roberts #74
#190	Powell, William	70	Lawrence Co. OH 1840 census
#202	Roberts, Molly	70/75	Lawrence Co. OH - 1830 census (3f)

There were 3 John Wards in Pittsylvania Co. VA. John Sr. 1826 (Major John),(made the will) who was a son of John. John 1826 named a nephew, John as his executor. John Sr. 1826 had both a brother (Jeremiah Ward) and a nephew (Sheriff Thomas Ward) living in Cabell County, VA. Nephew (Daniel Ward) in Lawrence Co., OH.

Ward Manumissions registered -1827-Pittsylvania Co. VA = PCVA = # registration 1827

Will - John Ward, Sr. - of Pittsylvania Co. VA -1826-7 - manumitted 138 individuals – family groups
Families settled in these Ohio counties: Clinton (34), Gallia (14), Highland (7), Lawrence (48), Pike (12), lost (23)

CLINTON COUNTY, OH - Clark Twp. and Vernon Twp. Total (34)

1827 manumission number   * head of household

1830 census			1827	1830 census
Clark Township				census says (7) persons
* Lynch, Richard	#70	(7 people)	24	2m under 10 1f under 10
	#71	Dorcas, wife	22	1m 10-23
	#72	Rhoda, ch	3/12	2m 55-100 1f 55-100 who?
	#82	Lynch, Peter	22	probably in Clinton
	#140	Lynch, Phil	15	probably in Clinton, but returns to Law. Co.
	#141	Lynch, Chaney	12(f)	1860 census m to #169 Simon Ward. 1838
*Ward, Samuel	#112		60	(census says 5 people not 13)
	#113	Lucy, wife	56	(registration # out of order)
	#114	Aaron, s/ S&L	34	
	#115	Handy (m) s/ S	20	
	#116	Charles s/ S	12	m Hannah Sipley 20 Aug 1836-Clinton Co.
	#117	Mary dau/S	22	
	#118	Rachel dau/S&L	17	
	#119	Patsy dau/S&L	10	
	#120	Hannah d/S&L	26	
	#121	Charles s/Han.	1 (12m)	
	#122	John s/Hannah	11	
	#123	Harrison s/Han.	8 tw.	
	#124	Lindy d/Han.	8 tw.	
	#125	Simon s/Han.	4	
*Ward, Jack	#126	s/Samuel	30 (John)	census says 2
	#127	Christian, wife	20	
	#128	Lynch s/J&C	2	
*Ward, James	#129	s/Samuel	25	(not on the census as an individual)

*(David and Nancy (brother & sister, children of Old Molley) were listed as favorites receiving $150 each) (Petition
to remain in Pittsylvania was ignored.)*

*Ward, David	#134		30	brother - census say 9 people
	#135	Ward, Nancy	28	sister
	#136	George s/Nan.	16	
	#137	Joseph s/Nan.	12	
	#138	Ward, Molly	60	? Old Molley - also listed in Law. Co. OH
	#139	Ward, Amanda	4	
	#169	Ward, Simon	26	1860 m to #141 Chaney Lynch(Adams Twp.)
	#170	Ward, Samuel, Jr.	23	1830 census Vernon Twp, Clinton Co. OH
	#93	Ward, Daniel	21	not located
	#192	Ward, Saul	25	not located

Are Simon, Samuel, and Daniel siblings of David & Nancy or sons of Samuel Sr.?

Do Saul # 192 and Daniel #83 belong in Lawrence Co. with #87 Harry Ward

listing 9 persons on the census but registered only 6?

<u>GALLIA COUNTY, OH</u> - WARD MANUMISSION   - Total (23)

    # 1827 manumission number   * head of household - 1830 Gallia County Census
                    Ward #   age   Ages not given
Gallipolis Town ____
    *Allan, Ceasar   #133   37 (Ward Reg. # 133)
    *Ward, Kitt Tolbert C. #107   65 (Maybe Ward Registration #107 - Christian Tolbert-65.)
Green Twp.____
    *Munday, Joseph (Probably Ward Reg. # 142 Joseph Mundal 45 with wife and 9 children.
                #143 Critty, wife 35   #148 Laurenzo   5 s/ Critty
                #144 Peter   4m s/Critty #149 Woodson   4 s/ Critty
                #145 Eliza   12 dau/Critty #150 William   3 s/ Critty
                #146 Thomas   9 s/Critty   #151 Doctor   2 s/ Critty
                #147 Betsy   6 dau/Critty #152 Joseph   18m s/ Critty
Springfield Twp____
    *West, Roben   #153   25 (Ward Reg. # 153 Rowland West - 25, wife, & 5 ch.)
                #154 Clary, wife 23
                #155 Otey   5mo s/Clary #157 Walker   5 s/Clary
                #156 Nancy   7 dau/Clary   #158 Jincy   2 dau/Clary
Raccoon Twp.____
    *Johnson, Rachel #159   26
                #160 Sofia   18 mo dau/Rachel
                #161 George   10
                #162 Annaca   8(f)   .
____

<u>HIGHLAND County, OH</u> - Ward Manumission - total (7+7) registration (census 14)
                    Paint Twp, Highland Co. is across the county line from Perry Twp. Pike Co.
                    # 1827 manumission number   * head of household
Possible Paint Twp.   1827   1830 census
    *Adams, David   #172   50   (14 people in Highland Co.)
                #174 Milly, wife 48   1m under 10   -1
                #175 James -ch   10   2m - 10-23   -1
                #176 Mary -ch   6   1m - 36-54
                #177 Milly -ch   4   6f under 10   -3
                #178 Sally -ch   2   1f - 10-23   -1
                                                    1f - 24-35   -1
        maybe #179 Jordan, Thomas   12 (because of register #)   none -36-54

@ Note: 1850 David Adams - living in Paint Twp. Highland Co. OH-wid. b VA – d Apr 1850 aged 76

<u>PIKE COUNTY, OH</u> - WARD MANUMISSION - Total (12) registration (16) census
1830 Pike County census # -numbers in Pittsylvania Register (missing 2 teen boys & 2 teen girls)
Perry Twp.   1827   (16 persons – Pike County)
    *Dudley, Henry   #171   35/40
                #173   Sally, wife   33   #185 Sam   ch 8
                #180   Annica (f)-ch   19   #186 John   ch 6
                #181   Lusey (f) -ch   17 (Lucy) #187 Hudley (m) ch 4
                #182   Aaron   -ch   16   #188 Henry, Jr.   ch 2
                #183   George   -ch   13
                #184   Mary   -ch   10   #189 Wm. Green ch 2 – s/Lucy

Ward Manumissions registered -1827-Pittsylvania Co. VA = PCVA = # registration 1827
Will - John Ward, Sr. - of Pittsylvania Co. VA -1826-7 - manumitted 138 individuals – family groups

LOST	see Ward Registration 1827		
#105 Randolph, Gilbert	#110 Jackson, William	#167 Henry, Patsey	# 203 Tucker, Milly
#105 Randolph Biddy w	#111 Tantarobogus, Wm.	#191 Hodges, Ned	
#108 Farmer, James	#163-166 Ward, Isbel 45 & ch	#193 Bobbitt, Geo.	# 204 Dabney, Cato
#109 Brooks, Holliday	Peggy 21, Viney 12, Peter 8	#194 Shelton, Buck	born free.

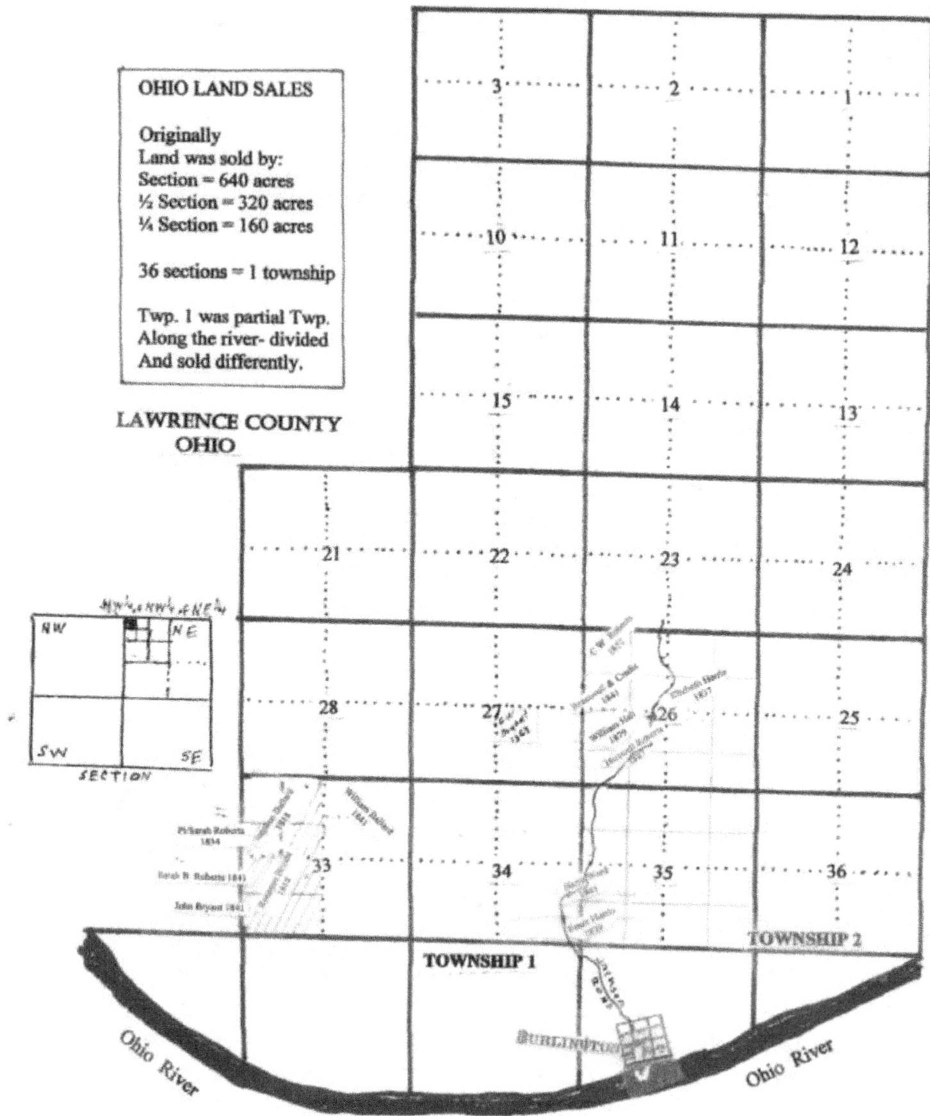

FAYETTE TOWNSHIP - #2 - Sections Numbers
Abstract – 1887 Lake Atlas of Lawrence County, Ohio

Figure A54 – Black Property Sites

Appendix #4 - Marriages

Lawrence County, OH Marriages to 1855 (Book 1817-1843 – digital - ANCESTRY.com) + original settler
before 1820   * = Ward Manumission 1827   (#Twyman 1849 – separate page)
Black or mulatto unless noted – spelling of names was not constant, and dates vary
Rosanna Bryan(t) b @1745/75   John Bryan (1) b@ 1775/80   Ward#   bk 1/pg-

Name		Spouse	Date	Ward#/Notes	Page
Ballard, William R. (wh)	m	+Nancy Reed	29 Jan 1835		
Brassfield, Robert	m	Delia Johnston	27 Jan 1835		p207
Brassfield, Robert	m	*Morning Cradick	22 Aug 1839	#101	p312
Bentley, Lovinia	m	+William Bryant 1st wife	26 Sep 1833	+	p183
Bentley, Permelia	m	*John Craddick	7 Dec 1837	#98 (Jonathan)	p261
Bentley, Rachel	m	William Jones	19 Mar 1835		p210
Brown, Pabner (Dabney)	m	+Biddy Randall	5 Apr 1836	(Abner)	p226
+Bryant, Geo. W. 1817	m	* Cory Ann Cradwick	24 Mar 1839	s/John	p295
Listed minister 1850 census					
+Bryant, Harriet 1806	m	Henry Smith	9 Sep 1838	dau/John ?Rose	p281
+Bryant, Judah 1812	m	*Jefferson Cradwick	20 Nov 1831	dau/John	p150
+Bryant, Nancy 1810	m	William Reed	12 Nov 1833	dau/John	p210
+Bryant, Rosetta 1816	m	*Phil Lynch	26 Sep 1833	dau/John	p183
+Bryant, Sarah 1804	m	*Pleasant Roberts (wid)	18 May 1829	dau/Rosanna	p113
+Bryant. Sara J. 1825	m	------Landcroft	------?--------	dau/John -d 13 Sep 1910 DC	
Bryant, Susanna ?1819	m	Robert S. Scott	18 Oct 1851	(white?)	
+Bryant, Susannah-1823	m	*Charles Roberts	26 May 1839	#78 dau/John	p303
+Bryant, William 1813	m	1st Lovinia Bentley	26 Sep 1833	s/John p183	
+Bryan, William	m	2nd Elizabeth -----	1847/48	s/John	
+Bryant, William	m	3rd Martha Craddock Randall 24 Apr 1851 (wid) #97 s/John			
3rd wife - mother Minister Isaac Vinton Bryant					
Calloway, Frances	m	Nathaniel Harris b1852 by obit –s/ Essex Harris & Elizabeth Roberts			
*Callaway, Letty	m	2nd- Horace Withers	27 Sep 1840	#131 (wid Jack) p339	
Cleetdall, John	m	Nancy Johnson	16 Mar 1836		
*Cradwick, Cory Ann	m	+Geo. W. Bryant	24 Mar 1839	#99	p295
*Cradwick, Jefferson	m	+Judah Bryant	20 Nov 1831	#95	p150
*Craddick, John	m	Permelia Bentley	7 Dec 1837	#98	p261
*Craddock, Lucy	m	Daniel Moss	27 Feb 1834	#96	p190
*Craddick, Martha	m	William Randall	5 Oct 1834	#97	p289
*Cradick, Mourning	m	Robert Brassfield	27 Jan 1839	#101	p207
Gilkerson, John/Jonathan	m	*Pamela Roberts	12 Feb 1829	#75 (Pauline)	p117
Harris, Essex	m	*Elizabeth Roberts	1827/8 obit son (Nathaniel b 1852 d1906)		
*Johnston, Charles	m	*Elvy Roberts	26 Feb 1829	#168 & #74	p115
*Johnston, Charles	m	2nd Rebecca Terry	11 Nov 1832	#168 da/Sylvia	p166
*Johnston, Charles	m	3rd Katherine Thornton	24 May 1840	#168	
*Johnston, Charlotte	m	William Randall	4 Oct 1829	#197	p124
Johnson, Delia	m	Robert Brassfield	27 Jan 1835		p207
*Johnson, Gabriel	m	Ritty Ann Roberson	2 Sep 1849	#201	obit
Johnston, Nancy	m	John Cleetdall	16 Mar 1836		p226
Jones, William R.	m	Rachel Bentley	19 Mar 1835		p210
*Lynch, Phil	m	+Rosetta Bryant	26 Sep 1833	#140 da/John #1 p183	
+Moss, Daniel	m	*Lucy Craddock	27 Feb 1834	#96	p190
+Moss, Eveline	m	+Levi Harris	3 Oct 1854	dauWm. - s/Essex	
+Moss, Lucy	m	#Simon Toms	30 Oct 1851	dau/Wm	
Peters, Mansfield	m	Ellen Payne	29 Apr 1847		
Peters, Shelton	m	Martha Ferguson	17 Dec 1845		

Lawrence County, OH Marriages to 1855 (cont)

+Randall, Biddy	m	Pabner (Abner) Brown	5 Apr 1836	da/Wm.	p226
*Randal, Martha Craddock m		William Bryant #3	24 Apr 1851	#97 both widowed	
Randall, William	m	*Charlotte Johnston	4 Oct 1829	#197	p124
Randall, William	m	2ⁿᵈ *Martha Craddock	5 Oct 1834	#97	p289
+Reed, Nancy	m	Wm. R. Ballard (wh)?	29 Jan 1835		
+Reed William	m	+Nancy Bryant	12 Nov 1833	named dau Rosetta	
Roberts, Elizabeth?	m	Joseph Sammons/Salmons	30 Mar 1826	date too early for Ward	
*Roberts, Elizabeth	m	Essex Harris	1827/28	#73 son's obit	
*Roberts, Elvy	m	*Charles Johnston #2	26 Feb 1829	#74 & #168	p115
*Roberts, Charles	m	+Susannah Bryant	26 May 1839	#78	p303
*Roberts, (John) Hartwell m		Frances Jackson	4 Oct 1849	#79	
*Roberts, (John) Hartwell m		Margaret L. Edwards	14 Nov 1852	#79	
*Roberts, Pamelia	m	John Gilkerson	12 Feb 1829	#75 (Pauline)	p117
*Roberts, Pleasant	m	2ⁿᵈ Sarah Bryant	18 May 1829	#80 (wid)	p113

Appendix #5 – Follow the Census, Deeds, and Taxes

FIRST LAWRENCE COUNTY, OH - BLACKS – 1810 – 1850 - Federal Census
(*) = listed John Ward Manumission   (Lawrence. Co, formed 1817 from Gallia)
1810 Census burned – (Gallia Co. OH tax for 1811 substitute – southern Gallia Co. was Union Township)
            1811 Murphy, Henry
            1811 Murphy, Washington
1820 Census - Lawrence Co. OH   original settler ~

Fayette – ~Briant, Rosanna -- 3		from VA - died 1833 – will
Union - ~Murphy, Henry -- 5 = # in family		(probably from SC – father & son Henry)
Union – ~Murhy, Polly --- 3		Washington from SC & wife Polly
Upper - ~Briant, John -- 9 = #		s/Rosanna - s/ William Bryant

****

Fayette Township		1830	1840	1850
Pg Twp Line		Name	family members	
*314 FA	13	*Johnston, Ben 7	*Johnson, Ben	34 -*Johnston, Gabriel s/Ben/Matilda
				*Johnston, Matilda wife/Ben Sr. 5
				51-*Johnson, Eliza (1826 dau/B& M)
314 FA	14	~Mors, Daniel 6 (Moss)	(1840 in Ross Co.)	da/Eveline Moss m Levi Harris s Essex
		1834 m *Lucy Craddock		
*315 FA	19	*Johnston, Charles 3	*Johnston, Charles 1	
*315 FA	20	*Roberts, Pleasants	*Roberts, Pleasants 10	2nd w Sarah Bryant (sis to John)
			*Roberts, Charles 3	*Roberts, Charles
#315 FA	21	~Bryant, John 11	~Briant, Jno. 3	w/Susan – both gone after 1841
			Bryant, (Wm) 5	Bryant, (Wm.) b 1815 - s/John
			1st w/1833m Bentley 2nd w/Elizabeth? 3rd Martha Craddock Randall	
			Bryant, Geo. 3	Bryant, Geo. b 1817 s/John
				1839 m Cory Ann Craddock
*315 FA	22	*Callaway, Josiah 3	*Calloway, Letty 1 w/Jack -m 2nd Horace Witchers 89	
316 FA	12	~Harris, Essex 4	~Harris, Essex 7	~Harris, Essex 11
			Harris, Timothy 6	
*316 FA	13	*Ward, Henry (Harry) 15	*Ward, Henry 6	*Ward, Henry 2
*316 FA	14	*Roberts, Molloy 3f	Brown, Abner 4	
316 FA	19	~Randle, William 2	Bland, Sam 3	
		m *Charlotte Johnston '29	Miller, Jack 5	90 *Lynch, Phillip (1st to Clinton Co.)
			Sheppard, Emilia 7	m ~Rosetta Bryant 1833 dau/John
		(Craddock, Lewis d 75) w-*Craddock, Winnie 3		*Cradick, Winna 7
			*Craddick. Jonathan 2	*Cradick, Jonathan 2
			*Powel, William 6	
			Brassfield, Robt. 2	Brassfield. Robt. 6 m Craddock

Union Township		1830	1840	1850
*319 UN	11	*Greenhill, John	4	
321 UN	7	~Murphey, Washington	2 wid. Prison	110 Murphy, Washington 70
321 UN	15	~Furguson, Pollay	3	Rebecca 39 – 4 ch
#321 UN	21	~Murphay, Henry	8	
			Murphy, (Rebecca) 2	

Rome Township				
324 RO	26	~Terray, Sylph 8	manumitted	

William Terry manumission issued in Montgomery Co., VA – filed in Lawrence Co. OH 1826.

		Howard. Henry	4
		Howard, Joseph	3
		Perry, Phindly	1
		Grimpton, Jack	8

<u>1850 Lawrence County, OH CENSUS</u> -- Fayette Twp. (Burlington)

~original 1820   Ward manumission 1827 * - age in '27 [ ] - Twyman manumission 1849 @

p435

	13 George Kouns (w)household	
	Chisenhall, William	20m m NC
	Hawks, Caleb	60m m KY
*34	Johnston, Gabriel	26m b VA
	(s/Ben Johnston listed Gib; see Mother's obit)	
	UGRR – barber both Burlington & Ironton	
	Ritty (Robinson) 20f m NC	
	Robison, Mary Ann	9f m OH
51	Burton (w)household	
	*Johnston, Eliza	24f b VA
	sister to Gabe dau/ Ben & Matilda	
89	Witchers, Horice	70m b VA d-106 in 1860
	widower of *Letty Callaway m 27 Sep 1840	
	Patsy (Letty)	75f b VA
*90	Lynch, Phillip	30m b VA
	*140 Lynch, Phil [15](38)	
	~Rose	30f b VA
	(m Rosetta Bryant 26 Sep 1833 dau/John)	
	May	9f m VA
~93	Bryant, William	36m b VA (1815)
	s/John & Susan Briant (1820 census)	
	1st Lovenia Bentley 26 Sep 1833) 2nd Elizabeth 3rd -	
	3rd 1851 Martha CraddockRandalls	
	Elizabeth	26f b VA
	George W.	15m b OH
	James K.	13m b OH
	Nancy Jane	10f b OH
	Rachel	2f b OH
	Cradick, Judy	38f b OH
	–Juda Bryant m Jefferson Cradic 1831 widow 1850	
	William	16m b OH
94	Reed, William	50m m KY
	~Nancy (Bryant) 40f m VA	
	(m Nancy Bryant 12 Nov 1833 – dau/John)	
	Mary	16f m OH
	Rosetta	12f m OH
	John	6m m OH
	William	5m m OH
	James	2m m OH
95	Jones, Joseph	25m m OH
	Temperance	25f m OH
	William H.	1m m OH
102	Jones, Henry	39m m NC
	Matilda	38f m NC
	Martha	16f m NC
	Kesiah	13f m VA
	John R.	9m m VA
	William	6m m OH
	Rebecca	5f m OH

	~109 Bryant, George	36m b OH
	s/John & Susan	
	*Cory Ann	30f b VA
	m Cory Ann Craddock 24 Mar 1839	
	John W.	10m b OH
	Phillip A.	8m b OH
	George W.	6m b OH
	Lena A.	2f b OH
110	Lee, Melton	22m b VA
	Nancy	28f b OH
	Bryan, Sarah J.	24f b OH
	dau/John	
	see deed verification 1884	
119	Bozers, Franklin	5m b VA
	Ellen	7f b VA
	Roberts, Hartwell	22m b OH
	Frances	16f m NC
	Jackson, Willis A.	2m m OH
	Bryant, Susanna	30f b NC (?)
*126	Johnston, Matilda	60f b VA
	Ward # 195 – widow Benjamin	
	Susan	23f b OH
	Jan3	15f b OH
	Catherine	12f b OH
	Abram (boat)	18m b VA
~142	Harris, Essex	63m b VA
	widower m 2nd Elizabeth Roberts da/ Pleats	
	Betsy	35f b OH
	Elizabeth	17f b OH
	m John Shelton 4 Dec 1856	
	Levi	15m b OH
	Pleasants	12m b OH
	Hannah	11f b OH
	Emeretta	9f b OH
	Emely	7f b OH
	Nathaniel	5m b OH
	William A.	3m b OH
	Maria	2f b OH
*142/144	Ward, Harry	45m b VA
	Adaline	19f b OH
*143	Cradick, Jonathan	51m b OH
	#98 s/Lewis & Winna m 7 Dec 1837	
	Pemelia (Bentley)	26f b OH
144	Jones, Reuben	61m b VA
	Margaret	21f b VA
	Scott, Roxa	15f b OH
	Love, Robert	25m b VA
	Nancy	2f b OH

~original 1820   Ward manumission 1827 * age in '27 [ ] - Twyman manumission 1849 @

145	Brown, Dabney (Pabner)	60m b VA
	(m Biddy Randall 5 Apr 1836)	
	Beddy	60f b VA
146	Cooper, James	27m m VA
	Polly	30f m VA
	Martha	12f m VA
	Susan	10f m VA
	James K.	5m m VA
	Charlott T.	5f m VA
147	Hawkins, Charlott	50f m VA
	Margaret	15f m VA
	m Robert Cradwick 6 Jan 1853	
	(5 white children)	
148	Brassfield, Robert	40m b OH – stonemason
	M Mourning Craddock 22 Aug 1839	
	*Morcie	37f b VA
	Mary F.	6f b OH
	Jonathan	5m b OH
	Nancy	4f b OH
	Amanda	3f b OH
*149	Cradick, Winna	67f b VA
	#94 Craddock, Winney (widow Lewis) 45	
	Lucy	39f b VA
	#96 (m Daniel Moss 27 Feb 1834)	
	Martha R.	38f b VA
	#97 (m Wm. Randall 5 Oct 1834 his death by '40)	
	Marsha	32f b VA
	Mary	22f b VA #102
	Sarah	21f b VA
	Robert	18m b VA
	Moss, Eveline	14f b OH (daug. Lucy?)
*	Johnston, Charles	47m b VA
	#168 Johnston, Chas. 28(51)-? s/Winna &Llewis)	
183	Johnson, Jane	55f b NC
188	Box, Andrew	40m m NC
	Abby	40f m NC
	Andrew	17m m NC
	Julia A.	11f m KY
	Allen	8m m KY
	Wilson	5m m KY
	Minta	2f m OH
189	Robison, James	60m m NC
	Anna	40f b NC
	Angeline	16f m NC
	Mary Ann	9f m OH
	Luvicia	7f m OH
	Margaret	6f m OH
	Sherman	3m OH

190	Bryan, Sarah	54f w PA d - 1857
	Sarah Frampton m Wm. H. Lane 1819	
	widow /John Bryan m1827 - died 1850	
	Wm. H.	21m w OH heir
	John M.	20m w OH to CA
	Sarah A.	16f w d 1860
	Isabel	15f w d 1857
	Isaac	13m w– d 1857
@191	Fry, Walker	40m m VA carpenter
	@Charlotte	47f b VA
	@Twyman, Nancy	70f b VA (unk)
	not recorded in any records	
	@Rebecca	26f b VA (Barbara)
	Barbara m Gaunt to norther OH	
	mother Horace and Susan	
	@Horace	13m b VA
	@Susan	4f b VA
@192	Twyman, Noah	70m b VA
	@Winna	75f b VA
	@Charles	50m b VA
	@William	37m b VA
	@Lewis	31m b VA
@193	Twyman, Simon	55m b VA
	@Violet	55f b VA
	@Ambrose	15m b VA
	@Abram	13m b VA
	@John	45m b VA
@194	Twyman, Lurence (Law.)	24m b VA
	@Albert	22m m VA
	@Robert	30m m VA blksm
@196	Twyman, John	49m m VA
	@Maria	42f b VA
	@Nancy	27f b VA
	@Jane	24f b VA
	@Beck	22f b VA
	@Henry	19m m VA
	@Elizabeth	16f b VA
	@Mary	14f b VA
	@Ellen	12f b VA
	@Lucy	9f b VA
	@Percilla	8f b VA
	@Edmund	6m b VA
	@David	3m b VA
	@Julia	10f b VA
	@Eliza	2f b VA
	@Wm.(Traveler)	2m m VA
	@Alex	1m m VA
	(Stephen no info)	
	James	1/12m OH

<u>1850 Lawrence Co. OH CENSUS</u> (cont)

Union Township   Rome Township

p384

55 Dolby, William	19m m NC
Janney	17f m VA
D.A.	8/12 m m OH
56 Peters, Tursy	41m m VA
Julia A.	22f m VA
Emily	21f m VA
Nancy	14f m VA
Norval	12m m VA
Josiah	11m m VA
57 Arnold, Drury	38m m VA
Patsy	12f m VA
May	11f m VA
Lumy	8m m OH
Catherine	4f m OH
Frank	8/12m m OH
83 Messit household- white	
Peters, Esther	35f m VA
Peters, Martha	18f m VA
101 Holton, James	47m m VA
Margaret	40f m VA
Licera	20f m VA
Martha	18f m VA
Minnie	16f m VA
Esther	13f m VA
May E.	10f m VA
Sarah I.	5f VA~
George	3m VA~
Nancy	5/12f OH~
Elizabeth	1/12f OH~ white?
102 Graham household	
Peters, Joshua	9m m VA
138 Smith household	
James, John	31m m VA
149 Peters, Mansfield	24m m VA
Ellen	72f m VA
Thomas	2m m OH
Anna	3/12f m OH
Payn, May	55f m VA m-law
Joseph	22m m VA bro
Phlem	19m m VA bro
159 Peters, Selden	27m m VA
Martha	22f m OH
Ferguson, Seely	51f m VA m-law
Mary	16f m OH sis
Norval	10m m VA bro
164 McCune, Young	65m b VA
Lucy I.	45f b VA

Rome Township

110	Murphy, Washington	70m m VA
	Rebecca	39f w NC
	Burrel	10m m OH
	Eliza J.	6f m OH
	Elizabeth	4f m OH
	Cynthia A.	1f m OH
146	Howard, Joseph H.	38m m NC
	Esley	41f m OH
	Allen	9m m OH
	Phebe	5f m OH
	Mary	3f m OH
	Jane	7/12f m OH
	Howard, Jane	28f m OH
147	Howard, Henry	65m b NC
	Elizabeth	54f b VA
	Alex	14m b VA

****

Figure A56 - 1860 Federal Census of Non-Population – Agriculture – Lawrence Co.

<table>
<tr><td colspan="3"><u>Fayette Township</u> Twyman =@</td><td colspan="3"><u>Union Township</u></td></tr>
<tr><td>Name</td><td>acres</td><td>value</td><td>Name</td><td>acres</td><td>value</td></tr>
<tr><td>Atwood,. Eli
300</td><td>35</td><td>$ 500 minister</td><td>Brooks, Lewis</td><td>60</td><td>$</td></tr>
<tr><td>Bryant, Geo.
300</td><td>40</td><td>400</td><td>Peters, Sheldon</td><td>30</td><td></td></tr>
<tr><td>Bryant, Geo. W.</td><td>107</td><td>2,000 minister</td><td></td><td></td><td></td></tr>
<tr><td>@Fry, Thos. Walker</td><td>403</td><td>3,000 minister</td><td></td><td></td><td></td></tr>
<tr><td colspan="3">Twyman lands in his name - undivided</td><td></td><td></td><td></td></tr>
<tr><td>Harris, Penelope</td><td>16</td><td>200</td><td colspan="3"><u>Washington Township</u></td></tr>
<tr><td>Isley, Edy</td><td>44</td><td>200</td><td></td><td></td><td></td></tr>
<tr><td>@James, Albert
$7,000</td><td>50</td><td>300</td><td>Argo, Solomon</td><td>76</td><td></td></tr>
<tr><td>@James, Lawrence
800</td><td>35</td><td>800</td><td>Stewart, Mary</td><td>3.5</td><td></td></tr>
<tr><td>Johnson, Bellfield</td><td>40</td><td>400</td><td></td><td></td><td></td></tr>
<tr><td>Penn, Charles</td><td>85</td><td>500</td><td></td><td></td><td></td></tr>
<tr><td>Roberts, Charles</td><td>40</td><td>400 minister</td><td></td><td></td><td></td></tr>
<tr><td>Roberts, Jonathan</td><td>45</td><td>600</td><td></td><td></td><td></td></tr>
<tr><td>Shelton, William</td><td>17</td><td>1,000</td><td></td><td></td><td></td></tr>
<tr><td>@Toms, John</td><td>80</td><td>2,000</td><td></td><td></td><td></td></tr>
</table>

People listed on Census of Agriculture not always listed in Census of Population.

<u>1860 Lawrence Co. CENSUS</u> – Black -Original (before 1827)~   Ward * (1827) Twyman # (1849)

Civil War – Co H 5th USCI (United States Colored Infantry or T Troops)

Fayette Township

206 Johnson, Bellfield	33m	m NC 1827 – farmer	268 Kilgore, John	45 m VA 1815	
Mary	25f	m OH 1835	#Rebecca 30 b VA 1830 19 Apr '55		
Brooks M.	7m	m OH 1853	Alexander	11 m VA 1849	
Hamilton	6m	m OH 1854	Cornelia	6 m VA 1855	
Ella G.	4f	m OH 1856	269 Taylor, Noah	70 m VA 1790	
Nancy M.	2f	m OH 1858	#Thomas, Charles	57 b VA 1803 Toms	
Lydia A.	2/12f	m OH 1860	270 Bland, Samuel 94 b VA 1766 whiskey		
Carnut, Tate	20m	m VA 1840 Co H 5th USCI	Mary(Rachel)	54 b VA 1806 x	
212 Witcher, Horace	106m	VA 1754	Bryan, Mary J.	20 w VA 1840	
m *Letty Calloway-widow 26 Mar 1840 (Wither)			273 Rogers, Geo. W.	36 m VA 1824	
214 *Lynch, Philip	45m	m VA 1815 m 26 Sep 1833	Margaret A.	30 m VA 1830	
Rosetta(Bryant)	44f	m VA 1816	John	17 m VA 1843	
Caster, Samatha	12f	m OH 1848	Stephen	14 m VA 1846	
216 Ballard, Elisha household		w	Wm. W.	12 m VA 1848	
McCall, Geo.	50m	b KY 1810	Nancy J.	8 m VA 1852	
255 Chadic, Charles	60m	b VA 1800	Thomas J.	6 m VA 1854	
Elizabeth	40f	m VA 1820	Martha L.	2 m VA 1858	
Goff, Katherine	16f	m VA 1844 (Zoff)	276 Bricefield, Robert	55 b OH 1805	
Charles	14m	m VA 1846	Brassfield m Morning Craddock 22 Aug 1839		
Selanial	12m	m VA 1848	Jonathan	16 b OH 1844	
James	8m	m VA 1852	John Co H 5th USCI-MC		
Duet, Edmund	50m	b KY 1810	Nancy m/Stewart)14 b OH 1846		
259 Dennis, Charles	75m	b NC 1785	Amanda	12 b OH 1848	
260 *Cradic, Robert	27m	b OH	Wilson	9 b OH 1851	
(Craddock - Cradwick s/Winnie & Lewis b/VA)			Wm. B.	6 b OH 1854	
Margaret	26f	b VA	Jefferson	5 b OH 1855	
262 Hanks, Caleb	70m	m PA 1790 (Hawks)	Gustus	4 b OH 1856	
Jane	65f	b NC 1795	Saml. N.	1 b OH 1859	
263 Reed, William	65m	m VA 1795 – farmer	277 Evans, William	42 m VA 1818	
Nancy (Bryant)	52f	m VA 1808	Hayman, Katherine	40 m VA 1820	
John R.	17m	m OH 1843 Co H 5th USCI-MC	McCune, Lucy	30 m VA 1830	
Wm. H.	15m	m OH 1845 farm hand	278 Bill, Wm. C. 25 m NC 1835 carp'ter		
Jas. H.	11m	m OH 1849	Nancy	23 m NC 1837	
Geo. W.	8m	m OH 1852	Hayman, Alex	17 m OH 1843	
Saml. L.	6m	m OH 1854	279 *Cradic, Jonathan	41 m VA 1829	
264 Bailey, Brown	30m	m KY 1830	(Craddock) – Clergy Regular Baptist		
(CW# KIA 1863) Co H 5th USCI (MC)			Pamelia 36 - Bentley 7 Dec'37		
Mary	27f	w TN 1833	280 *Johnson, Charles	56 m VA 1804	
Susannah	10f	m KY 1850	286 ~Bryant, Geo. W.	25 m OH 1835	
Martha S.	6f	m KY 1854	Jane (Cooper)	22 m VA 1838	
Wm.	3m	m OH 1857 CW-#239112	Daniel	1 m OH 1859	
Mary A.	8f	m KY 1852	Bryant, Rachel	12 m OH 1848	
Rose	1f	m OH 1859	288~Bryant, William	45 m VA 1815	
Wallace, Mornan A.	14f	m TN 1846 wife's sis?	3rd w Martha Craddock Randall m 24 Apr 1851		
268 Robertson, Anna	44f	b NC 1816 washwoman	Martha	38 m VA 1822	
Mary	30f	m NC 1830	Rachel 13 m OH 1847 (chElizabeth)		
Margaret	16f	m OH 1844	Nancy 8 m OH 1852 (chMartha)		
Sherman	14m	m OH 1846	Emily F.	5 m OH 1855	
James	19m	m OH 1851	Isaac Vinson	4 m OH 1856	
Armintha	4f	m OH 1856	Lewis C.	2 m OH 1858	
John H.	2m	m OH 1858			

<u>1860 Lawrence Co. CENSUS</u> – Black

Original ~ (before 1827)   Ward * (1827)   Twyman # (1849)   -   marriages Law.Co.

Fayette Township (cont)

289~Bryant, George   43m   m VA 1817 farmer
     m Cory Ann Craddock 24 Mar 1839 – farmer
    *Carry Ann   41f   m VA 1819
    John W.   20m   m OH 1840 Co H 5th USCI (MC)
    Philip A.   18m   m OH 1842 CW?
    George W.   15m   m OH 1845 Co H 5th USCI (MC)
    Letha A.   12f   m OH 1848
    Benjamin   8m   m OH 1852
    d-Aug 1873 cholera on *Fleetwood* – IR
    Lucinda   6f   m OH 1854
    Charles   3m   m OH 1857
    Dorinda   1f   m OH 1859
  Bryant, James R/K   22m   m OH 1838
    (2nd son G.W.per 1850 census)
290 Payne, David   40m   b VA 1820 farmer
    Malinda   50f   b VA 1810
    Maria   17f   b VA 1843
    Harriet   14f   b VA 1847
    Polly   10f   b VA 1850
    Frances   8f   b VA 1852
    Martha J.   3f   b OH 1857
  Payne, William   12m   m VA 1848
291 *Roberts, Charles   38m   m VA 1822 farmer
    CW- Co H 5th USCI (MC)
    ~Susan   37f   m OH 1823
    (Susannah Bryant 26 May 1839- dau/John)
    Emily J.   21f   m OH 1839
    Wm. D.   18m   m OH 1842 Co H 5th USCI (MC)
    James H.   15m   m OH 1845
    Mellissa   13f   m OH 1847
    Harriet L.   10f   m OH 1850
    Alex   8m   m OH 1852
    Isaac B.   6m   m OH 1854
    Clinton   4m   m OH 1856
    Wyatt C.   6/12m   m OH 1859
292 Penn, Charles   57m   - VA 1803
    Salina   52f   - KY 1808 (Sabrina?)
  Turner, John   19m   m KY 1841
    Lovina A.   16f   m KY 1844
    Redington   14m   m KY 1846
    (Reddon Turner - Co H 5th USCI (MC)
    Richard   11m   m KY 1849
  Dalton, Frances   10f   m VA 1850
    William   7m   m OH 1853
    Jane   5f   m OH 1855
293 Justice, Douglas   27m   b VA 1833
    Nancy J.   6f   m OH 1854
    Winfield   4m   m OH 1856
  Hill, Lewis   40m   m VA 1820
    Marie   40f   b KY 1820

295 King, Henry   41 m VA 1819
    Sophia   30 m VA 1830
    Ellen   13 m VA 1847
    Eliza   11 m VA 1849
296 Goff, Henry   80 m VA 1780
297 #Smith, Ambrose 26 m VA 1844
    s/Nancy Twyman Smith - manumitted
    Rosetta   21 m OH 1839
    m 27 May 1860 Rosetta Reed dau/William
head--#Nancy   50 m VA mother
    Polly A.   24 m VA 1836
    Rush   19 m VA 1841
    Lorenzo   18 m VA 1842
    Stephen   16 m VA 1844
    Jane   14 m VA 1846
    Melissa   13 m VA 1847
    Sarah E.   4 m OH 1856
298 Holly, William   40 m VA 1820
    Mary   30 m VA 1830
    Rebecca J.   10 m VA 1850
    Katherine   8 m VA 1852
299 Holley, Leonard   66 m VA 1794
    Clara   53 m VA 1807
    Benjamin   23 m VA 1837
    John s/Benj. 3 m OH 1857
303 Lynn household
    Dolton, John 44 m VA 1816
307 Moore household
    Carnook, Clark   14 m VA 1846
350 Isely, Edey-f-   44 m NC 1805
  Chisenhall, Runnels C. 21 m NC 1839
    H.A.P.   18 m NC 1842
    Sarah A.F.   17 m NC 1843
    C.D.R.S.   14 m NC 1846
    Gilmore, Theodore 2 m OH 1858
357 Wright, James   25 m VA 1835
    Co H 5th USCI (MC) d 1910
    Julia A. (Boggs) 20 m KY 1840
    Alonzo   3 m OH 1857
    Oliver   1 m OH 1859
358 Boggs, Abigail   40 m NC 1820
    Alamander   16 m KY 1844
    Wilson   13 m VA 1847
    Co H 5th USCI
    Arminta   11 m OH 1849
359 Cooper, Robert   30 m VA 1830
    Martha   26 m VA 1834
    Missouri -f- 5 m OH 1855
    James   1 m OH 1859

360 Gainor, Henry	45m	m NC 1815	
Adelia	40f	m NC 1820	
John	18m	m NC 1842	
Susan	15f	m NC 1845	
Samuel	14m	m NC 1846	
Lavina	14f	m NC 1846	
Lavica	10f	m NC 1850	
Betsey	9f	m NC 1851	
Alice	8f	m OH 1852	
361 Cradic, William	25m	m OH 1835 st'boat hand	
Lavica	22f	m VA 1838	
Kilell	3f	m OH 1857	
Perry M.	3 ½	m OH 1850	
362 Jones, Matilda	40f	m NC 1820	
John	18m	m NC 1842	
William	15m	m NC 1845	
George	10m	m NC 1850	
Gabe	7m	m OH 1853	
Hall, William	30m	m VA 1830 st'boat hand	
Kiziah	24f	m NC 1836	
363 Boggs, Andrew	26m	m NC 1834 st'boat labor	
Juda	22f	m VA 1838	
Rosetta	23 f	m OH 1837	
364 Runnels, Mary	45f	m VA 1815	
Americus	30m	m VA 1840 boat hand	
Henry	23m	m VA 1837 Boat hand	
Fourly	17m	m VA 1843	
James	14m	m VA 1846	
Isom	12m	m VA 1848	
Polly	10f	m OH 1850	
365 Love, Robert	37m	m VA 1823 (Cabell,VA)	
Miluge J.	25f	m OH 1835 (Wilgue ?)	
Sally	13f	m OH 1847	
Mary	7f	m OH 1853	
Huranica	6f	m OH 1856	
Josephine	3f	m OH 1857	
Wm. A.	1m	m OH 1859	
372 Atwood,Eli	52m	m NC 1808	
		blacksmith (Minister) [Atwell]	
Nancy	51f	m VA 1809	
William	22m	m VA 1838	
Samuel (G)	20m	m VA 1840 boat hand	
		m Martha Bailey '61- Co K 44th USCI (bur. Gallia)	
Analiza	17f	m VA 1843	
John	15m	m VA 1845	
Margaret	13f	m VA 1847	
Benjamin	12m	m VA 1848	
Eli	10m	m VA 1850	
Henry	6m	m VA 1854	
Robt. Cooper	6m	m VA 1854	
Stewart, Martha A.	20f	m NC 1840	

373 Buffington, Squire	32 m NC 1828	
Nancy	30 m NC 1830	
Jane	7 m NC 1853	
Stewart, Milly	20 m NC 1840	
375 Stewart, William	34 m NC 1826	
	Co E 5th USCI (MC) d 1893	
Ritter – f-	27 m NC 1833	
John W.	19 m NC 1841	
376 Evans, William	24 m NC 1836	
	Co H 5th USCI d 5 Apr 1865	
Emily P.	22 m NC 1838	
James L.	8 - - 1852	
Burvender, (Matt)	18 m NC 1842	
Burvender, Martin	24 m NC 1836	
Nixon, Jacob	55 m NC 1805	
379 Harris, Penelope	40 m VA 1820	
Philip N.	19 m OH 1839	
Chas. W.	15 m OH 1845	
Hartwell	11 m OH 1849	
380 Burvender, Jacob	53 m NC 1807	
Chanty A. -f-	25 m NC 1837	
Thos. F.	6 m NC 1854	
Mary J.	1 m NC 1859	
383 Toms, Simm	65 m VA 1795	
Lucy	47 m VA 1813	
Bricefield, Wilson	9 m OH 1851	
343 Harris, Levi s/Esx	23 m OH 1847	
	Corp. – Co H 5th USCI	
Eveline	22 m OH 1848	
Cecil	2 m OH 1858	
Elly	1 m OH 1859	
*387-383 Toms, Sim 65 b VA 1795- 1864		
(7) Lucy 47 b VA1813-1896		
Buxfield, Wilson 9 b OH 1851		
*398'94 James, Lawrence 37 b VA 1823 d 1886		
(35) Jane	26 m VA 1834	
Camilius R. 8 m OH 1852		
Martha 6 m OH 1854		
Lavina 4 m OH 1856		
Creighton 2 m OH 1858		
Mary E. 3/12 m OH 1860		
Johnson, Matilda 69 m VA 1791 (Ward)		
399'95 James, Albert 35 m VA 1825		
(36) Eliza	36 m VA 1824	
Milly	8 m OH 1852	
Caroline	6 m OH 1854	
	both dau/Wm. Dykes – Albert's brother	
Charlotte	3 m OH 1857	
Luellen	2 m OH 1858	
Hester	1 m OH 1859	

<u>1860 Lawrence Co. CENSUS</u> – Black

        Original ~ (before 1827)   Ward * (1827)   Twyman # (1849)   -   marriages Law.Co.

Fayette Township (cont)

*396 Fry, Thomas W. (11)	50 m VA Cl'yman (Reg.Bapt.)		400 *Toms, Henry	27 b VA 1831-1911	
* 12) Charlotte	57 m VA		(22) Emeline	22 b OH	
* 14) Twiman, Harris	22 m VA (Horace Twyman)		Isaiah	5 b OH	
Burvender Mark	23 b NC		James W.	3 b OH	
Ward, Nancy	80 b VA unk -Who?		Wm. C.	2/12 b OH	
397 Shelton, Edward (Edmund)	30 b VA		Toms, Delilah 5 m OH? dau/Ellen King		
* 25) Ellen	22 b VA d 1878 – '37 cem		Toms, Josephine 3 m OH " "		
Mary J.	4- OH		*41 Smith, William 11 m VA s/Nancy Smith		
*398 Toms, John (Short John)	64 b VA *(16)(d prior 1870)		405 Thacker, Persantin 47 b VA		
* 17) Maria	50 b VA		Dorinda	35 b VA	
* 18) Nancy	3 b VA		Mary	13 b VA	
* 23) Elizabeth	26 b VA		Virginia	8 b VA	
* 27) Priscilla	17 b VA		Levista	5 b VA	
* 38) Edmund	15 b VA farm hand		406 Jackson, William	49 b VA	
* 39) Daniel	12 b VA		*(20) Jane	58 b VA age 34	
* 46) Sarah	9 b OH (Brown)		*(40) Eliza	12 b VA	
399 James, Garland	26 m OH teacher		Luvina	8 b OH	
* 19) Julia (Smith)	20 m VA (dau/Nancy bro Traveler)		Elizabeth	5 b OH	
Frank	4 m OH		James	3 b OH	
			Edward	2/12 b OH	
			457- Hall, Dr. Camillus household		
End Fayette Twp.			Harris, Katherine 22 b OH		

1860 Census - Aid Township   1860 Census – Decatur Township

67 Jackson, Andrew	40 b	VA 1820		1656 Calloway, Ceasar	44 b	VA 1816 miner	
Margaret	23 b	VA 1837		Frances	15 b	OH 1846	
Jane	5 b	VA 1855		Lydia	12 b	OH 1848	
John Henry	2 b	VA 1858		Henry	11 b	OH 1849	
Geo. W.	½ b	VA 1859		Sarah	7 b	OH 1853	
107-Turley, Thomas	60 b	VA 1800		Eliza	3 b	OH 1857	
Rebecca	45 w	VA 1815		1702 Holly household			
John (W.)	22 b	VA 1838		Thomas, James	15 m	OH 1845 miner	
Rush F. m	14 b	VA 1846		1747 Bass, Elijah	49 m	NC 1811	
Lucy A.	12 b	VA 1848		Matilda	59 m	NC 1801	
Polly C.	9 b	VA 1851		Elijah	26 m	NC 1834	
Doctor Hill	8 b	OH 1852***		Samuel	21 m	OH 1839***	
Columbus	5 b	OH 1855		Peter	16 m	OH 1844	
Arabella	1 b	OH 1859		William	12 m	OH 1848	
115- Neal household				End Decatur Twp.			
Poage, James	14 m	KY 1846					
148- Wise household				Mason Twp.			
Evans, John	14 m	VA 1846		NONE			
End Aid Twp.				End Mason Twp.			

1860 Lawrence Co. CENSUS – Black
   Original ~ (before 1827)   Ward * (1827)   Twyman # (1849)   -   marriages Law.Co.

1860 Census – Elizabeth Township (Ironton)

1205-	Hamilton, Joseph	46 b	VA 1814	
	Maria	28 b	VA 1832	
	Jacob	10 b	VA 1850	
	Geo. W.	8 b	OH 1852	
	Margaret J.	1 b	OH 1859	
***	Finley, Jefferson	23 b	OH 1837	
1211-	Finley, Randel	50 b	VA 1810	
	Mary	46 b	VA 1814	
	Joseph W.	23 b	VA 1837	
	Harting	21 b	VA 1839	
	William	17 b	VA 1843	
	James	14 b	VA 1846	
	Anderson	12 b	VA 1848	
	Peter	9 b	VA 1851	
	Sarah Bell	5 b	OH 1855	
	Laura Ann	11/12 b	OH 1859	
	Finley, Samuel	28 b	VA 1832	boatman
1218	McGreggor	15 m	OH 1845	servant
1246-	Sanders, Calvin	32 b	VA 1828	teamster

(Sanders Manumission to Michigan)

	Margaret	24 m		
1256-	Ellison household			
	McGregor, Jessie(f)	17m	OH 1843	servant
1299-	Pollock, Samuel	47 wh	PA 1813	
	Sarah	22 m	VA 1838	servant
	Ann	20 m	VA 1840	servant
	Mary	16 m	VA 1844	servant
	Rebecca	14 m	OH 1846	
	Robert	12 m	OH 1848	
	Anthony	10 m	OH 1850	
	Henrietta	8 m	OH 1852	
	William	2 m	OH 1858	
1305-	Stunson, Henry	28 m	MD 1832	
	Rebecca	22 wh	MD 1838	
1307-	Pollock, James W.	25 m	VA 1835	
	Nancy		19 wh	OH 1841
1384-	Stephenson, Wm.	50 m	MD 1810	
	Margaret	51 m	MD 1809	
	William S.	22 m	VA 1838	
	Thos. K.	18 m	VA 1842	
	Margaret A.	16 m	VA 1844	
	James R.	14 m	VA 1846	
1391-	McGregor, Emily	48 m	PA 1812	
	Elizabeth	22 m	VA 1838	
	Joseph	21 m	VA 1839	
	Danl.	12 m	OH 1848	

End Elizabeth Twp.

1860 Census – Hamilton Township

1085-	Black, James	30 b	KY	
	Mary Ann	25 b	KY	
	Hannah	7 b	KY	
	Sarah	3 b	KY	
	Geo. W.	6/12 b	OH	
	Black, Mathew	22 b	KY	
1087-	Young household			
	Gross, Amanda	14 b	)H	
1107-	Hitt, Clayborne	43 b	KY	
	Adeline	25 b	OH	
	Creighton	2 b	OH	
	Juliet	9/12 b	OH	
	Holt, Squire	10 b	OH	
	Harris, Nathaniel	14 b	OH	
1120-	Taylor, Charles	41 b	KY	boot & shoe
	Elizabeth	26 b	KY	
	Phillis Ann	2 b	KY	
	Sarah H.	8/12 b	KY	
1125-	Burdin, Andrew	27 b	SC	

End Hamilton Twp.

1860 Census - Lawrence Township

508	Nelson, Alex.	35m	VA	
	Louisa	36 m	VA	
	Mary A.	10 m	VA	
	Maria	5 m	OH	
	Joseph	1 m	OH	
	Samuel	1 m	OH	
	Finley, Jefferson	25 wh	VA	
509	Witcher, Robert	31 m	VA	
	Hannah	35 wh	VA	
	Ayers, Daniel	7 wh	VA	
610	Spradlin household			
	Polley, Douglas	57 b	VA	

End Lawrence

<u>1860 Lawrence Co. CENSUS</u> – Black

Original ~ (before 1827)   Ward * (1827)   Twyman # (1849)   - marriages Law.Co.

Ironton (town) 1860 (cont)

7-8	Black, Charlotte	56 b	KY	286-285	Black, Madison	34 m	KY
	Payton	24 b	KY		Maria	30 m	KY
	Ann	21 b	KY		Mary Jane	14 m	KY
	Holt, Ann	31 b	KY		Clarissa	11 m	KY
	Black, Martha	3 b	KY		James	8 m	KY
32-33	Holt, Guilford	30 b	KY		George	4 m	KY
	July Ann	30 b	VA		Alice	3 m	KY
	Everette	2 b	OH		Thomas	3/12 m	OH
	Fannie Bina	8 b	OH	289-288	Hamilton household		
	Laura	7 b	OH		Humphrey, Sarah	16 m	OH
39-40	Thompson house			291-290	Dempsey household		
	Holt, Mary	15 b	KY		Cropland, Charles	28 b	PA
61-62	Bixby house			292-291	Davidson, Elias	44 m	VA
	Beaty, Martha	23 m	VA		Eliza Ann	37 m	VA
98-99	Lewis house				Mary Ann	21 m	VA
	Pogue, Jane	33 m	KY		Hiram K.	18 m	VA
	William	14 m	KY		Margaret E.	14 m	VA
	Harris, E. M. (m)	28 b	KY		Lorenzo Dow	13 m	VA
99-100	Roberts, William	28 b	OH – barber		William K.	8 m	VA
	Martha	20 m	VA		Olivia A.	6 m	VA
	Mary	1/12 b	VA		Martha L.	3 m	VA
	Cooper, James	15 m	VA	301-300	Pogue, Henry	54 b	KY
	Rogers, Ellen	17 b	VA		Perlina	46 b	VA
100-101	Walker, John	29 m	KY – barber		Hannah L.	26 b	VA
	Martha M.	24 m	Miss.		Harry C.	22 b	VA
	Lilly	5/12 m	OH		William H.	21 b	VA
	Bradford, Amanda	12 m	KY		Richard M.	18 b	VA
102-103	Johnson, Lewis W.	48 m	PA		Elias	15 b	VA
	Minerva J.	28 b	KY		James S.	13 b	VA
	John W.	9 b	OH		Amanda	7 b	VA
	Eliza C.	1 b	OH		French A. (m)	4 b	VA
	Ditcher, James	30 b	VA UGRR		Roberts, Lizzie A,	14 b	OH adopted
112-113	Thomas house			438-423	Holt household		
	Scott, Peyton	65 m	VA – merchant		Housen, Allice	15 m	KY
157-157	McCodough house				Velina	7 m	KY
	Clary, Elliza	22 b	NC	450-436	Rodgers household		
165-165	tavern				Pogue, Mary F.	11 m	KY
	Holt, Albert	19 b	KY – porter		Kelly, Frances (f)	19 m	OH servant
	Black, Paten	20 b	KY – servant	452-438	Bolles, household		
	Viney, Sarah	26 m	KY		Toll, Elizabeth	21 b	VA
	Razor, Ann	20 b	KY	575-558	Beverly, K. (f)	48 b	VA wshrw
172-172	Brown, Philly H.	29 m	Mass. – barber		Elizabeth	13 b	VA
	Mary A.	23 m	OH		Bulen (m)	10 b	VA
172-173	William, Joshua	28 m	NC	576-559	Shelton, Elizabeth	48 b	VA
	Mary	20 m	OH		Marie C.	29 b	OH
	John	1 m	OH		Hannah R.	21 b	OH
					Emma R.	19 b	VA
					Amelia	17 b	VA
					Nathaniel	13 b	VA

1860 Lawrence Co. CENSUS - BLACK

Ironton Town (con't)

576-559	Shelton, Elizabeth	48	b VA		577	Johnson, Gabe	35	b VA barber -UGRR
Cont	Wayne, Evangeline	6	b OH			Ritter	30	m NC
	Augustine	3	b OH			Mary Jane	9	b OH
580-563	Henderson, Jefferson	56	b VA			Florida	8	b OH
	Nancy Jane	56	b VA			Samuel	11/12	b OH
	Hesekiah (m)	11	b VA			Robinson, Margaret	17	m OH
	William H.	9	b VA		688	Graham, Solomon	20	b OH barber
	Elijah	6	b VA			Victoria	16	m KY
581-564	Hote, Ebenzer	40	b KY			Webster, Lavina	4	b OH
	Anne	29	b OH		706	Smidt household		
590-570	Smith, Benjamin	30	m KY			James, Frank	101	b KY wood sawyer
	Elizabeth	29	m VA					
	James	12	m VA					
	Edward	9	m VA					
	Anna	9	m VA – adopted					
	Charles	6	m VA					
	Henry	3	m OH			End Ironton		

1860 Census - Perry Township

2-2	Blankenship house				
	Frazior, Mary	17	b	VA – maid	
87-84	Polley, Peyton	58	b	VA	
	Violet	44	m	KY	
	Martha	14	m	KY	
	William H.	8	m	OH	
	James H.	6	m	OH	
90-87	Polley, Huldah(f)	27	m	KY – washrwn	
	Mary	8	m	OH	
	Ann E.	6	m	OH	
	Emariah (f)	4	m	OH	
	Sarah	2	m	OH	
178-174	Johnson house			VT	
	Barnes, Ellen	16	b	VA	

END Perry Township

1860 Census - Rome Township

980	Peters, Mansfield	32	m	VA
	Margaret	28	m	VA Payne
	Thomas	12	m	OH
	Anna D.	9	m	OH
	William	8	m	OH
	Mary	6	m	OH
	Lelia G.	5	m	OH
	Willegmener	3(f)	m	OH
	Judson G.	1	m	OH
	Payne, Mary	62	m	VA in -law
	Fleming	27	m	VA bro

1860 Census – Rome Township

981	Payne, Joseph	33	m VA	
	Nancy	20	m VA	
	California (f)	9	m VA	
	Marshall (m)	3	m OH	
	Fleming (m)	3/12	m OH	
	Peters, Thursey (f)	61	m VA	
		mother-in-law		
982	Terry, Julius (m)	34	m OH	
	Josephine	30	m OH	
	Benjamin	12	m OH	
	Theodore	11	m OH	
	Edward	9	m OH	
	Joseph	8	m OH	
	Nancy	4	m OH	
	Frances (f)	4	m OH	
	Areanna (f)	2	-	

<u>1860 Lawrence Co. CENSUS</u> – Black

Original ~ (before 1827)   Ward * (1827)   Twyman # (1849)   -   marriages Law.Co.

Rome Twp. (cont)

982 Terry, Julius	34	m	OH		1108 Howard, Joseph	46 m NC	
Josephine	30	m	VA		Julia	37 m VA	
Benjamin	12	m	OH		Allen	19 m OH	
Theodore	11	m	OH		Phebe	15 m OH	
Edward	9	m	OH		Mary	12 m OH	
Joseph	8	m	OH		Jane	10 m OH	
Nancy	4	m	OH		Emily	8 m OH	
Francis (f)	4	m	OH		Thursey L.	6 m OH	
Areanna (f)	2	m	OH		Joseph	4 m OH	
995 Murphy, Horatio	36	m	OH		Martha E.	2 m OH	
McBride, Elizabeth	65	m	VA		Shelden (m)	5/12 OH	
Parker, Josephine	17	m	OH		1169 Ligon, Katherine	50 m VA	
1050 Sayre household					John	36 m VA	
Sayre, Mary	24	m	NC			wagon mkr	
					END Rome Twp.		

1860 Census - Union Twp.

629 Kouns house			
Flowers, Anderson	25 m KY –(slave)	728 Arnold, Drury	50 m VA blksmth
713 Ferguson, Seely	60 m VA washerwoman	Emily J.	37 m VA
Allen, Emily	4 m OH	Betsey	18 m VA
715 Peters, Shelden	40 m VA gunsmith	Mary	16 m VA
Martha	35 m OH (Ferguson)	Virginia	13 m OH
Ferguson, Mary	25 m OH sister	Susan	12 m OH
Samuel	7 m OH	Frank	10 m OH
Peters, Norvel (m)	20 m VA brother	Martha	8 m OH
Peters, Jonah	19 m VA brother	Nancy	6 m OH
Ferguson, Charles	1 m OH ch/Mary	William	4 m OH
718 Ferguson, Samson	42 m VA bro/Martha	Ananias (m)	1 m OH
Gincy	32 m VA	827 Brooks, Lewis	50 m VA
Mary J.	18 m VA	Nancy	51 m VA
Joseph S.	16 m OH	John H.	21 m VA
John	12 m OH	Thomas J.	20 m VA
Charlotte A.	7 m OH	William F.	18 m VA
Mahala	4 m OH	Edward	17 m VA
Joanna	2 m OH	Mary A.	16 m VA
John W.	7/12 m OH	Elizabeth	14 m VA
719 Mitchell, John	31 m NC – harness maker	Dorothea	13 m VA
Lucinda	31 m NC	Lewis	11 m VA
Peters, John O. S.	22 - NC?	Martha	9 m VA
		Richard	8 m VA
		Alfred	6 m OH
		Walker	5m OH
		828 French, Frederick	70 m VA
		END Union Township	

<u>1860 Lawrence Co. CENSUS</u> – Black

Original ~ (before 1827)   Ward * (1827)   Twyman # (1849)   -   marriages Law.Co.

1860 Upper Township

767 Housin, William	50(20)	m	KY		899 Honley, William	39 m VA (Houley)	
Isabel	35	m	KY		Elizabeth	27 wh NC	
Gibson, Emma	12	m	KY		Mary	21 m VA	
William	10	m	KY		Booker (m)	18 m VA	
Susan	6	m	KY		Elizabeth	17 m VA	
Florence	3	m	OH		Jerry M.	15 wh VA	
Peter	1	m	OH		John W.	12 wh NC	
Hote, James	17	B	KY		Armina	11 wh NC	
768 Adams household					Lydia	10 wh NC	
Cooper, James	15	m	VA		Martha J.	8 wh NC	
895 Honley, Sarah	37	m	NC widow		Sarah A.	7 wh VA	
(Houley) Eli F.	20	m	VA		Amanda E.	5 wh OH	
John	18	m	VA		George	1 wh OH	
Mary Ann	16	m	NC				
William T.	12	m	VA				
Robert J.	9	m	VA		END Upper Township		

1860 Census - Washington Twp.

-1789	Baker, Abram E.	69 b VA
-1836	Woodson, Barbara	26 b OH widow
	Emmarilla	6 b OH
	Jane	3 b OH
	Nancy Ann	4/12 b OH
-1837	Keals, Mary	27 b OH
	Cornelis	7 b OH
	George W.	1 b OH
-1828	White, Pohna (f)	26 b VA
	Eliza Jane	1 b VA
-1845	Harris, Cornelius	73 m VA
	Nancy	52 wh SC
	Cornelius	17 m TN
	Nancy	6 wh OH
	Marsh, Lewis	26 wh KY
	Harris, Adam	22 m TN – Co D 5th
-1846	Brown, John	27 b VA
	Sarah Ann	18 m TN
-1847	Keal, John	26 b OH
	Telitha	22 m KY
	Nancy Ann	5 m OH
	Wm. I. (J)	4 m OH
	Thomas, John	2 m OH
-1848	Wilkenson, Jupiter	55 b TN
	Amelia	16 m VA
	Joseph	10 m VA

END Washington Twp.

1860 Census – Windsor Twp.

90 Dolby, Sally A.	62 wh VA
William	29 m NC
Virginia	26 m OH
Docia Ann	11 m OH
Joseph	7 m OH
Frances (f)	5 m OH
Wm. W.	1 m OH
Dolby, Nathaniel	19 m OH

END Windsor Township.

END LAWRENCE COUNTY 1860 CENSUS

Appendix #5 - FOLLOW THE DEEDS

All Deeds are in Lawrence County, Ohio, unless noted otherwise.

NOTE: S=South E=East N=North W=West SE=Southeast – etc. Sec=Section Twp=Township R=Range
There are 36 sections in each full township. Township 2 is Fayette(partial) in the 17th Range. (see map A54)
Deeds listed as 33-2-17 = Section (33) – township (2) – range (17)   (Bryant and Briant interchange)

Book/page   Date   Names

Bk 1- p115-116-117 –   1 Jun 1818   (west half)   33-2-17
****   Rosanna Briant sells to Stephen Ballard (price $184 for 92 acres)
....   Tract beginning at a pawpaw bush on the *S line SW 1/4 of Section 33 Township 2 Range 17* (33-2-17-
Fayette Township) thence N89E -85.79 poles to stake N1W -171.58 poles thence S89W -85.79 poles to stake corner
Rosanna Briant thence with her line S1E -171.58 poles to the beginning – 92 acres more or less.
Wit: Abraham Moore   Magistrate: Gabriel Kerr   Rosanna X Briant {seal}
    A. Kerr   Recorded Burlington 1 Jun 1818
****

    Rosanna's original tract was located on Solida Road near the present South Point exit of US 52.
    Rosanna Bryant was possibly 1st Black woman to own and sell land in Southeast Ohio. ¼ section of land was
deeded to her by James William Bryan in 1818. ½ sold in 1818, the remainder sold by son & daughter 1841.
****

Bk 1- p197-198   19 Dec (1817) R LC (recorder Law. Co.)   (west half)   33-2-17
****   The USA government to William Bryant of Gallia County, OH.
....   Wm. Bryant has deposited a Certificate of Registration to the Land Office at Chillicothe for full
        Payment for *SW 1/4 Sec 33 Twp 2 R 17.*
        Sold under the Act to sell US Territory North of Ohio River above the mouth of the Kentucky River.
        Patent, seal and filed - 22 Jul 1817 – Recorded Vol. 22, p 130. Jonah Meigs, Commissioner
        Recorded in the Chillicothe Land Patent -Volume 25, page 104
        William Bryant presented to Law. Co. Court.   Received and recorded 19 Dec (1817) R LC
            (Indication - William Bryan was white, son of James Bryan.)
****

4Bk8-p493-494   23 Feb 1841   33-2-17
    John Bryant & wife Susan $500
    Sell to William Ballard W ½ of SW ¼ Sec 33 T2 R17-Fayette Twp. being 43.33a Signed by X
****

Bk9-p60-61   2 Aug 1841 $80   33-2-17
    Pleasant Roberts and wife Sallie (Roberts m Sarah Bryant ½ brother to John -18 May 1829)
    Sell to William Ballard SW ¼ of NW ¼ Sec 33 Ta R17 – 44a signed Pleasant seal – Sarah X
****

Plate Bk #1p235-236   16 Apr 1881   33-2-17
    Deposition to establish a line of property -
    #1 – Geo. W. Bryant, *son of John Bryant, named in the will of Rosannah Bryant to whom the land was
given and where we now stand.* The original line run by William McKee and Armstrong Dunn with Geo. W. Bryant
as flagman. *John Bryant received the land to the south, and Sallie (Bryant) Roberts received the north part.* Signed
by mark X Geo. W. Bryant, aged 64, has always accepted this line.
    #2 – William Bryant, *son of John Bryant.* William McKee and Armstrong Dunn were chosen to make a
division of the estate, and they selected the bed of a creek as the division line. Reference points being an Elm tree
and a planted stone. John Bryant to receive the south section and Sallie Roberts the part north of the line. *William
states is 68 years old, he has always lived here, and this line has always been accepted.*   Signed by mark X and by
Deputy Law. Co. Surveyor: G.T. Shirkey 16 Apr 1881
    States will of Rosannah Bryant 1833 (unlocated) divided property 33-2-17 between son John Bryant and daughter Sarah Bryant
    Roberts (m Pleasants Roberts 18 May 1829). Also states property given to Rosannah. Court has a notation of the presentation of the will
    By John Bryant. (No actual will found).
Bk 7-p396   5 Mar 1834   (east half)   33-2-17
    USA Government Certificates 2301 & 1955 to William Ballard
    #2301- 44a SWNE & 88a E ½ NW 33-2-17
    #1955 – 441 SW ¼ NE ¼ 33-2-17 (William was the son of Stephen in above deed Bk1-p115)
****

Appendix #5 - FOLLOW THE DEEDS (cont)

Book/page   Date   Names

****

Bk8-p69   Nehemiah Valentine and wife   20 Jun 1839 $200   35-2-17
****   To Essex Harris (colored man) SW ¼ of SW ¼ 35-2-17 – 43.72 a *(Except cord of wood, cabin, and yard in possession of Matilda Johnston to hold for her lifetime)* (Ward – Widow of Ben –mother Gabe)
****

    The community called Macedonia Hill centered on the Church, which was built on 26-2-17. The following deeds try to trace the ownership of the Macedonia Church property, which appears on the 1878 Hardesty Atlas map lying in the NW ¼ of the SW ¼ (26-2-17). Although the Church was reported in existence by 1813, and the present building built in 1849, no deed was issued for the Church building. (Current Lawrence County map shows the Church in the SW ¼ of the NW ¼, but very near ¼ line.)
****

BK 9-p499   William Ballard & wife Harriet   9 Sep 1844   26-2-17
          To William Hayman (Haman)   8a $20 SE corner of SW ¼ of NW ¼
Bk10-p214   Armstrong Dunn & wife Mary   16 Jan 1845 $800   26-2-17
          To William Ballard   (3 parcels on 27-2-17) plus
          SW ¼ of NW ¼ 43.08a(26-2-17) and NW ¼ of NW ¼ 86.16a - Sec. 26 2-17
Bk10-p473   William Ballard & wife Harriet   16 Feb 1847 $20   26-2-17
          To <u>Essex Harris</u>   8a beginning at SE corner lot sold to Hayman NW ¼ 26-2-17
          (Essex Harris m 2nd Pauline/Pamela Roberts, another child of Pleasant Roberts. See below)
Bk12-p470   Smith, Russell and wife Matilda   8 Feb 1841 $150
          To <u>Harry Ward</u>   SW ¼ NW ¼ Sec 35 T2 R17 – 43.72a   35-2-17
Bk12-p486   Beckley, Solomon & wife Laura   10 Aug 1841 $85 -43.08a
          To <u>Robert Brassfield and Jno. Craddock/Cradock/Cradoc</u>   SW ¼ NW ¼ Sec   26-2-17
Bk13-p217   Davidson, Joseph and wife Maria   31 Dec 1847 $125
          To <u>Hartwell Roberts</u>   NE ¼ SW ¼ Sec 26 T 2 R17 – 43.08a (see will 1858)   26-2-17
          (should be part of church site)
Bk14-p469   Hartwell Roberts & wife Frances   9 May 1853   1a   26-2-17
          To Susan Scott in her lifetime and afterward to Malissa A. Jackson
          1 acre being part of the NE ¼ of the SW ¼ (26-2-17) – acre situated on the East line of said lot
          Somewhere near the center of said East line to be a square. (Susannah Bryant m Robert S. Scott
          14 Oct 1851
****

Macedonia Church located in the western ½ section of Section 26-Fayette Twp 2-Range 17   26-2-17
It sits on the line between several deeds at the intersection of the quarters. Jonathan Craddock was a minister for many years. Robert Brassfield married his sister, Morning Craddock. (John) Hartwell Roberts was the younger brother of Charles Roberts and both sons to Pleasants Roberts, all from the Ward manumission except Brasswell. Pleasant Roberts married a 2nd wife, Sarah Bryant, a daughter of Rosanna Bryant, while Charles Roberts married her niece, Susanna Bryant, daughter of John Bryant. Charles was also a minister at Macedonia and listed in the Non-Population Census for Lawrence County. One of the underlined properties should be the site where 1849 Macedonia Church was built, now at the junction of CR 120N and CR 144. Charley Creek Road (CR 144) connects to Solida Road, while CR 120N is Macedonia Road – originally surveyed as the Old Jackson Road to Jackson, Ohio.
    When Hartwell Roberts died in 1858, he willed everything to his brother Charles, named a daughter Kernelia, and had his will witnessed by William Bryant, Philip Lynch, and George W. Bryant.
****

Bk16-113   Robert Brassfield & wife Morman (Mourning Craddock)   9 Jan 1855   26-2-17
          To Fayette Twp. Board of Education – ¼ a for $10 (a square for a schoolhouse) at the top of the ridge and 46 rods east from the west line of SW ¼ of NW ¼ -26-2-17 – Robt. * Brassfield (seal) Mourning signed X
          Where was the school from the Church?

Bk15-p491   James H. Drury and w/Sarah   21 Aug 1852   26-2-17
       To Charles W. Roberts   NE ¼ of NW ¼   43.08a $175
Bk18-p277   Widow Elizabeth Harris (wife/Essex)   10 Feb 1854   26-2-17
       To Andrew Boggs   SW ¼ of NE ¼ - 49.06a $200
       Levi Harris (son) to have use of cabin where he lives until 1 Apr 1854. Andrew Boggs recorded Ander
       Bogs 3 times within deed. Also known as Andrew Box, he was murdered in June 1855 (IR)
Bk18-p345   Widow Elizabeth Harris   20 Mar 1858   26-2-17
       To Auditor of Law. Co. for a tax debt of $.873 mill plus inst. $.235 - total owed $1.72.
       (Boggs died before paying tax. Land sold to Joseph Davidson for taxes.)
Bk18-451   Joseph Davidson   2 Dec 1856   26-2-17
       To Edmund Shelton   NE ¼ of SE ¼   40a $150
Bk20-p75   Joseph Davidson   10 Apr 1860   26-2-17
       To William Craddic   S ½ of SW ¼ of SE ¼   21a $75
Bk36-p426   Jeff Brassfield   17 Jun 1879   26-2-17
       To William Hall   N ½ of SE ¼ of NW ¼   quit claim to 22a $10
Bk36-p426   Wilson Brassfield, Gustus Brassfield,   19 May 1879   26-2-17
       John Brassfield & wife Mary and Nancy Stewart   Quit claim to 22a $45
       To William Hall   N ½ of SW ¼ of NW ¼
       36-426 all children of Robert d 1877 and Mourning Craddock Brassfield d 1859 (see deed 12-486)
       William Hall, born in VA in 1836, does not appear in Law. Co. until the 1880 census. Wife Susan and 2 grandsons living in 26-2-17
       next to Henry King.
Bk40-p220   A church deed
                 Henry King and wife Sophia   28 May 1873   26-2-17
       To Antioch Freewill Baptist Church   1/2a for $1
       Property located in NW ¼ of the NE ¼ - Section 26 Fayette Township (Not Macedonia)
****
                 In 1889, there were four deeds to the trustees of Macedonia Freewill Missionary Baptist Church.
                 Chains and links are surveyor measurements; N 33 E means North 33 degrees East. There seem to be two lots.
Bk 49-p156-157 William Hall & wife Susan   20 Nov 1889   26-2-17
       To George Bryant, Sr., Phillip A. Bryant, and Eli Justice: Trustees of Macedonia 'Baptist' Church:
       For $3 – part of the SE ¼ of the NE ¼ (26-2-17) beginning NE corner of Macedonia graveyard lot
       running 52 feet to a stake, then south 209 feet to a stake, then west 50 feet to graveyard line
       to a place of the beginning being ½ acre.   Signed by mark, both William & Susan Hall
       Wit: Caleb Arthur, J.P.   20 Nov 1889
       Moses Bowser   recorded 20 Dec 1889 recorder P. F. Gillett
Bk49-p157-158 S.V.F. Davidson and wife Neva   6 Dec 1889   26-2-17
       For $1 and vacation of the site formerly held by the Macedonia Missionary Baptist Church -.63acres
       Part of the NW ¼ of the SW ¼ (26-2-17) Beginning stake 5.04 chains West from the corner of
       said quarter then S 12 W 2,98 chains to a stake where a 12-inch hickory bears S 6 W 11 links then S 8.25 E
       1.86 chains to a stake at the forks of the road on top of ridge thence N 66.25 W 2.04 chains to stake thence
       N 8.75 E 1.62 chains to a stake from which a 10-inch white oak bears N 33 E 12 link thence N 17.75 E 2.46
       chains to a stake in the N line of the quarter then E with said line 1.23 chains to the beginning being 63/100
       acre.
       Wit: W. M. Remy, J.P.   signed by seal   S.F.V. Davidson & Neva F. Davidson
       Henry Dillon   received to record 17 Dec 1889 3:30 PM
                                                 Recorded 20 Dec 1889 recorder, P. F. Gillett
Bk 49-p159   William Hall and wife Susan M.   23 Nov 1889   26-2-17
       To Trustees of the Macedonia Baptist Church for receipt   of $1 for 1 acre
       Following estate in Fayette Township, Law. Co. OH: a part of the SE ¼ of the NW ¼ beginning at
       a stake on the N side of the road leading to Buffalo Creek and each of the schoolhouse lots: thence
       E 3.155 chains to a stake on the hillside, thence N 3.165 chains over top of the ridge to the beginning
       containing 1 acre.
       Wit: Caleb Arthur J.P.   signed by mark William Hall & Susan M. Hall
       Henry Hall

Bk49-p160-161   Trustees of Macedonia Missionary Baptist Church   26-2-17
    To S.F.V. Davidson   6 Dec 1889 $1 - ½ acre
    Part of NW ¼ of the SW ¼ (26-2-17) Beginning at the NE corner of the said lot at a stake & stone.
    Thence S with the E line of the said lot 300 links to a stone, thence W 166.20 links to a stone
    thence N 300 links to a stone in the North line of said lot, thence 166 .66 links to the place of the
    beginning and containing one half (½) acre.
    Trustees: G.W. Bryant, Sr., Phillip Harris, and P. A. Bryant. – And signed by them 6 Dec 1889.
    Wit: W. M. Remy J.P   Received 17 Dec 1889 3:30 PM
    Henry Dillon   Recorded 21 Dec 1889 P.F. Gillett
****

Additional deeds of interest.

Bk12-p481   Gabriel Johnson and wife Ritter   17 Aug 1850   (price $55)   lot 27
    from John M. Bryan (2nd son of John) Burlington lot 27
****

IRONTON BEGAN 1849 – THE COUNTY COURT MOVED 1852 - See Burlington lots map
****
Bk14-p439-440   Gabriel Johnson & wife Ritter   27 Jun 1853 $200
    To Wm. H. Bryan – Burlington lot 8   lot 8
    (Gabe Johnson – Ward manumission, a barber and active in UGRR - moved to Ironton.)
Bk18-p384   (reference Bk3-p252 – 1823)
    Wm. H. Bryan and wife Romanie M.   12 May 1858   (price $300)
    To Stephen Wilson – 1/3 undivided share of the following property:
    Beginning at stake on the bank of the Ohio River at the corner of Solomon Beckley North along the line of
Wm. Burton heirs 65.76 poles to corner of Wm. C. Johnson (see 3-252) 5a -1 rod 37 poles more or less (lot 6?)
Bk18-p535   (reference Bk3-p252 - 1823)   15 Jun 1858   (price $300)
    John M. Bryan of San Francisco, CA
    To Stephen Wilson 1 equal, undivided share of 5a near Solomon Beckley (Wilson now has 3/3)
      These 2 deeds for 1/3 indicate that sister Sarah has died.
    <u>Solomon Beckley and Stephen Wilson interact with the Black community in several deeds.</u>
Bk21-p237
    Charles R. Denny   23 May 1863   (price $50)
    To Geo. W. Bryant (s/William/grs/John/ggrs/Rosanna) NW ¼ of SE ¼ -Sec 27 Twp 2 R 17
    Except 8a sold to John Jones off South part AND Except 10a now reserved off North part 27-2-17

    Question: Was John Bryan, who married widow Sara Frampton Lane in 1827, kin to William Bryan, who manumitted Rosanna Bryant? John was white and served as Lawrence County Auditor from 1835-1848, but he and his family seem to be connected to the Bryants. In addition, the Frampton family was also involved with the Black community by selling land to the '37. In 1824 (white), John Bryan purchased lots at the Burlington boat ramp, where he built a store called S. Bryan and Co. (after Sara – why?) He was also a master tanner who took apprentices. Both these businesses would have allowed him to hire Blacks who collected information. Perhaps Bryan passed on information gathered from rivermen or provided references to Captains about available Black workers.

    Bryan died in early 1850 and was buried at Greenlawn. His oldest son, Wm. H. Bryan, took over the business and made extensive land purchases when the county seat was moved. His mother, a sister, and a brother died within months of each other in 1857; another brother moved to California, dying in 1867, and his last sister died in Ashland in 1860. An interesting fact showed Wm. H. and sister Sarah Bryan Davidson sold S. Bryan and Co. in 1858 to Stephen Wilson, a partner and another person connected to the Bryants. Wm H. Bryan survived the Civil War and moved to Indiana, where he worked as a clerk and died in 1901.

Figure A57 - Lawrence County Taxes – 1820 -1850 – Property & Personal

Property Tax	parcel	location	acres	value	dates
Bryant, Rosanna	17-2-33	Solida Creek	92	$141	1820 thru 1833 (her death)
		Fayette Twp. (Jct. US 52)			
Bryant, William	17-2-33	same			1820
Murphy. Henry	16-1-23	Bradrick	83	$108	1828-1829
		Indian Guyan Creek-great bend			

Personal Property   (first list located is for 1826) h=horse $40   c=cow $8

1832 all Blacks listed 'colored'

Fayette Township	1826	1827	1828	1829	1830	1831	1832	1833	1834	1835
Bryan, Rose Ann	1h-1c	1h-1c	1h-2c	1h-1c	1h-1c	1h-1c	1h-1c			
Bryan, John	----2c	----2c	1h-1c	1h-1c	2h-2c	1h-1c			1h-3c	1h-5c
*Calaway, Jack							1h-1c			
*Greenhill, John (2)							-2c			1h
Harris, Essex										1h
*Johnston, Benja. (4)		(blk. man)	1h-2c	1h-1c		1h				
*Johnston, Matilda										1h
Moss, Daniel							1h	1h		
Reed, William		1h----	1h blk.1h		1h-1c			1h		1h-2c
*Roberts, Pleasant (4)		1h-2c	2h-1c		1h-1c	1h		2h-1c	2h-3c	
*Ward, Harry (2)		1h-1c	1h-1c							

Bryan, Rose Ann = Bryant, Rosanna

Personal Property   (first list located is for 1826) h=horse $40   c=cow $8

Union Township	1826	1827	1828	1829	1830	1831	1832	1833	1834	1835

1836 1837 1838

Murphy, Henry	----3c									
*Greenhill, John (2)			1h-3c	1h-N	1h-blk					
Moss, Daniel				1h						
Reed, Wm			1h-2c							

*Ward manumission – each person over 15 received $20 cash   # in ( ) = number in family over 15
2 people paid for horse – another bought 2 cows (horse to plow -cow for food)
~ N= Negro – blk= Black (as recorded)

Jobs held by Blacks in Lawrence County where information could be gathered:

Riverboat men (several)	household domestics – mostly women
Whiskey maker – Sam Bland	cooks – private & hotels – Matilda Johnson
Wooden ware – Billy Haman	Fortune Teller – Aunt Edith Chisendall
Tanner's assistant	sellers of eggs & produce – Brooks family
Wood cutters	porters – boats & hotels
Charcoal makers	barbers – Gabe Johnson
Furnace workers	seasonal farm labor – general labor
Wagon drivers	blacksmith – Drury Arnold, Sheldon Peters
Coopers	masons – brick makers

Information from the census and numerous *Lawrence Register* articles.

****

Underground Stations North of Lawrence County operated by Blacks
listed by Siebert (noted Pike & Scioto counties were hostile areas.)

Jackson County	Gallia County	Gallia County	Vinton County
Berlin Crossroads	(Rio Grande)	B-Caliph James	B-Gabriel Jarrett
B-Noah Nooks(Brooks)	B-Joseph Cousins	B-Wm. P. Ellison	B-Gillam Hocks
B- John Chavis	(Morgan-Bethel Ch)		
	B- Howell James & wife Martha		

Appendix #6 - Twyman Manumission – "The Burlington 37"

The Twyman manumission did not occur until 1849, many years after the founding of Macedonia Church and the creation of a UGRR. However, these people were important to both the Church and Lawrence County. The land purchased in their name created a 'Black' corridor from the Ohio River to the Ohio Jackson Road near the Macedonia Hill settlement. The leader of the Twyman manumission was Reverend Thomas Walker Fry. The man quickly joined the Church and was part of Macedonia and the Providence Association for about fifty years. Finally, the arrival of the Twyman group usually called "The Burlington 37" enlarged the Black Community and increased its importance through land purchases.

Information about the manumitted Twyman slaves has been gathered from many sources.

Twyman sources - Madison County Court House, Madison, VA

County records and personal family interviews.

'37' sources   Lawrence County Court House, Ironton, OH

County records, newspaper articles, and personal interviews.

Reference for the chart on page -----------

1) Will Madison Co. VA Vol. 9-157 (d 8 Feb 1849) names "37."

(4 did not come) the census lists 39 – all sources indicate (46)

Also, 2 remained on other plantations.

2) Deeds Lawrence Co. OH, Vol. 12-137-8 (2) (1849) – Vol. 12-315-6 (1850)

3) Lawrence Co. OH, Vol. 12-343-4 (1850)

4) Lawrence County, OH, Vol.12 (signatures) (1850)

5)1850, 1860, 1870, 1880, 1900 Lawrence Co. Ohio census

6) Lawrence Co. OH Common Pleas 22 – 608-626 (1870)

(The deeds in the suit say Furgerson instead of Twyman – clerk's error.)

1850 deed made in March – Census taken in July of 1850

The reference numbers in the following charts notate each family member, then used with each source of information to identify the individual.

These documents provide materials to identify the manumitted slaves, locate their position in the families, find their importance to the community, and determine what portion of the property they received.

Madison County Records

1848-1849 records pertaining to the will and manumission

1849 - $2,000 spent to support invalid Joe

$10,000 allowed for the removal of slaves, to purchase homes, and provide provisions

1849, Oct. 25 - executors paid for transporting slaves to OH

As of 1868, trustee account - $11,760 spent to support Jenny, Amanda, and France Ann (Alburne)

(reading of the will and bequeaths would indicate family)

Location and information about these women page 136.

Lawrence Co. OH deeds

31 Oct 1849   Bk12-137 - 15 Mar. 1850 12-315 (deed to all)

15 Mar 1850 Bk12-343 signatures of all adults (with child's relationship) for delivery of estate

1870 – land divided - suits - William Smith vs. Maria Toms, et, al

No. 756 Common Pleas (CP) Lawrence Co. OH Vol. 22- 608-636

Reverse claims, genealogy and percent of the claim, maps of final division

Figure A58 – A Twyman Plantation
This estate was called Edgewood when the Twyman slaves lived there prior to 1849.
Members of the Twyman family owned about 10,000 acres in Madison County, VA.

Madison County, Virginia, in the rolling eastern foothills of the Blue Ridge Mountains, was the home to various members of the William Twyman family. William, Sr. owned land in the area before the county was created from Culpepper County in 1793, and his son William, Jr. raised his family in Madison County. This family controlled many acres of prime agricultural land, and many of the family plantations were a thousand acres or more.

The Twyman's were also slaveholders along with their in-laws and many of their neighbors. The county population in 1850 was about 8,500, of whom 4,700 were slaves.

Three sons of William Twyman, Jr. were alive in 1849, and they owned slaves as follows: Anthony - 33, James - 40, and Travis - 11. Anthony's four sons owned 107 slaves among themselves. These numbers do not reflect the slaves controlled by their sisters.

Lawrence Co. OH Deed 12-137-138   31 Oct 1849 (copied as deed written & no punctuation)

      Isaac Frampton and wife Jane of Wayne Co. VA
      To Simeon, Violet, and others

Know all men by these presents that Isaac Frampton and Jane Frampton, wife of said Isaac Frampton of the county of Wayne and state of Virginia in consideration for the sum of *six thousand dollars* to us in hand paid by Simeon, Violet, Abraham, Ambrose, Walker, Charlotte, Barbara, Horace, Susan, Short John, Maria, Jane, Beck, Henry, Elizabeth, Mary Ann, Ellen, Lucy Ann, Persilla, Eleanor, Edmund, Daniel, Cilla (daughter of said Jane), Alexander (son of said Beck), Nancy, Julia, William (son of said Nancy) Charles, William, Lewis, Washington, Lawrence, Albert, Yellow John, Bob, Noah and Winna during their natural lives and then to their heirs, forever, for the following premises situate in the County of Lawrence and the state of Ohio and in the township of Fayette and described as follows: The East part of fractional section No. 2 in Range No. 17 and Township No. 1. Beginning at a stake on the Ohio two hundred and forty-three poles easterly by the said river from the South West corner of the said fractional section at the South East corner of Barton's heirs land thence running North 69 degrees East one hundred and thirty-three and two thirds poles to a stake the South West corner of land formerly owned by Yager now owned by George Kouns, thence due North along said Koun's line to the back line of the said fractional section to a stake, thence West on the said back line to such a point as will by running due South therefrom intersect the stake of place of beginning, thence from said point South to said first mentioned stake, the place of beginning. Excepting and reserving out of the about granted premises the following parcels of land heretofore sold and surveyed by William Lynd to wit: 5 ½ acres to Elijah Frampton. Also, 6 acres, 2 rods, and 1 pole to William C. Johnson, the above two described tracts are taken from the South West corner of said tract = containing one hundred and fifty-four acres more or less. Also, the South East quarter of the North West Quarter of Section 35 Township 2 of Range 17 saving and excepting one acre out of the North West corner sold to Arty Carter and one acre sold to Abner Johnson off the West side of said tract. Also, one acre of the same side was sold to Anna Robinson, containing forty-*one* acres more or less. Also subject to a life lease heretofore grant to Samuel Blankenship and wife for about 15 acres on said lot. Also, part of the South West quarter of the North East quarter of Section 35 Township 2 of Range 17 being all that part of the said quarter section that lies South of the top of the ridge: commencing at the corner of the said Isaac Frampton and (   ) Randall the center corner of Section 35, thence North with the West line of the said quarter to the top of the ridge about 35 rods to a stake about one rod West of a Black Locust 12 inches in diameter, thence Easterly along the top of said ridge flowing the marked or blazed trees with the meander of the top of said ridge till it strikes the East line of the said quarter about 10 rods North of the South East corner thereof to a Hickory tree 8 inches in diameter, thence South to the said South East corner of the said quarter, thence West along South line of the said quarter to the place of beginning containing by estimation twenty acres more or less. Also, the West half of the South West quarter of Section 35 Township 2 Range 17 contained 87 acres and 14/100. Also, the South East half of the South West quarter of Section 35 Township 2 Range 17 contained 88 acres and 72/100. Also, the South West quarter of the South West quarter of Section 35 Township 2 Range 17 contained 43 acres and 22/100. Also, the East half of the North West quarter of the South West quarter of Section 35 Township 2 Range 17 contained 23 acres and 86/100. To have and to hold said premises with the appurtenances unto the said Simeon, Violet, Abraham, Ambrose, Walker, Charlotte, Barbara, Horace, Susan, Short John, Mariah, Jane, Beck, Henry, Elizabeth, Mary Ann, Ellen, Lucy Ann, Persilla, Eleanor, Edmund, Daniel, Cilla (daughter of said Jane), Alexander (son of said Beck), Nancy, Julia, William (son of said Nancy), Charles, William, Lewis, Washington, Lawrence, Albert, Yellow John, Bob, Noah and Winna during their natural lives and then to their heirs forever. And said Isaac Frampton for himself and his heirs does hereby covenant with the said Simeon, Violet, Abraham, Ambrose, Walker, Charlotte, Barbara, Horace, Susan, Short John, Mariah, Jane, Beck, Henry, Elizabeth, Mary Ann, Ellen, Lucy Ann, Persilla, Eleanor, Edmund, Daniel, Cilla (daughter of said Jane), Alexander (son of said Beck), Nancy, Julia, William (son of said Nancy) Charles, William, Lewis, Washington, Lawrence, Albert, Yellow John, Bob, Noah and Winna, and their heirs and assigns that he is lawfully seized of the premises aforesaid that the premises are free and clear from all encumbrances whatever and that he will forever Warrant and defend the same with appurtenance unto the said Simeon, Violet, Abraham, Ambrose, Walker, Charlotte, Barbara, Horace, Susan, Short John, Mariah, Jane, Beck, Henry, Elizabeth, Mary Ann, Ellen, Lucy Ann, Persilla, Eleanor, Edmund, Daniel, Cilla (daughter of said Jane), Alexander (son of said Beck), Nancy, Julia, William (son of said Nancy) Charles, William, Lewis, Washington, Lawrence, Albert, Yellow John, Bob, Noah, Winna and their heirs and assigns against the lawful claims of all persons whatsoever. In testimony whereof, the said Isaac Frampton and Jane Frampton have hereunto set their hand and seals this 31st day of October in the Year of Our Lord one thousand eight hundred and forty-nine.

Executed in the presence of Elias Nigh & J.M. Bryan   Isaac Frampton (seal)

154a less 5 ½ and 6+ acre = 143 ½ a - 41a less 1a & 1a & 1a = 38a - 20a plus = 20a
87 14/100a plus = 87 14/100a - 88 72/100a = 88 72/100a - 43 22/100a = 43 12/100a
23 86/100a = 23 86/100a   total 444 20/100 more or less for $6,000 or $13.50 per acre

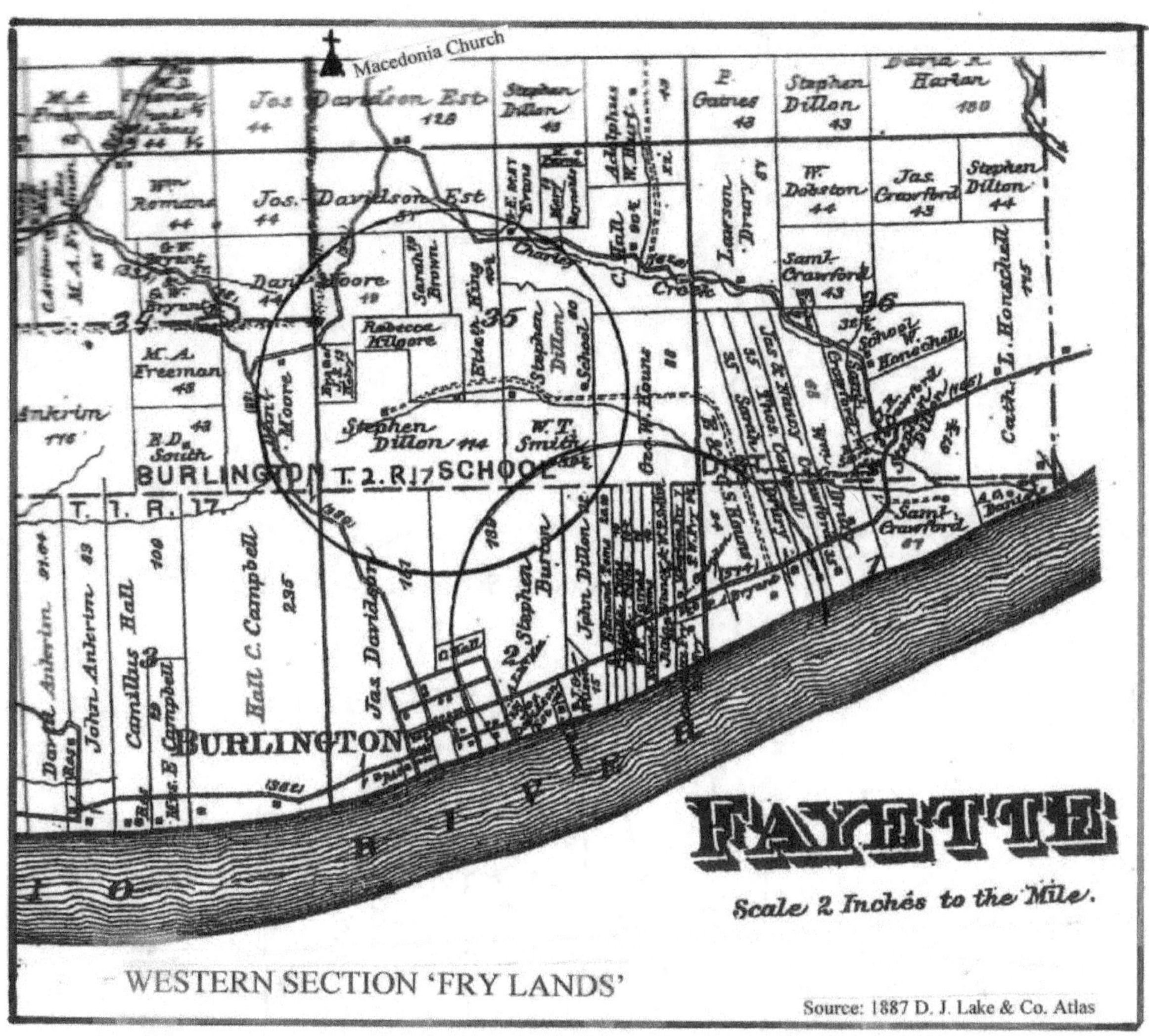

Figure A59 - Location 'Fry Lands' of "THE BURLINGTON 37"
Designation in Lawrence County Deed Books

Figure - A60 - Eastern Section –' Fry Lands'

Eastern section – Sybene Curve on old US 52

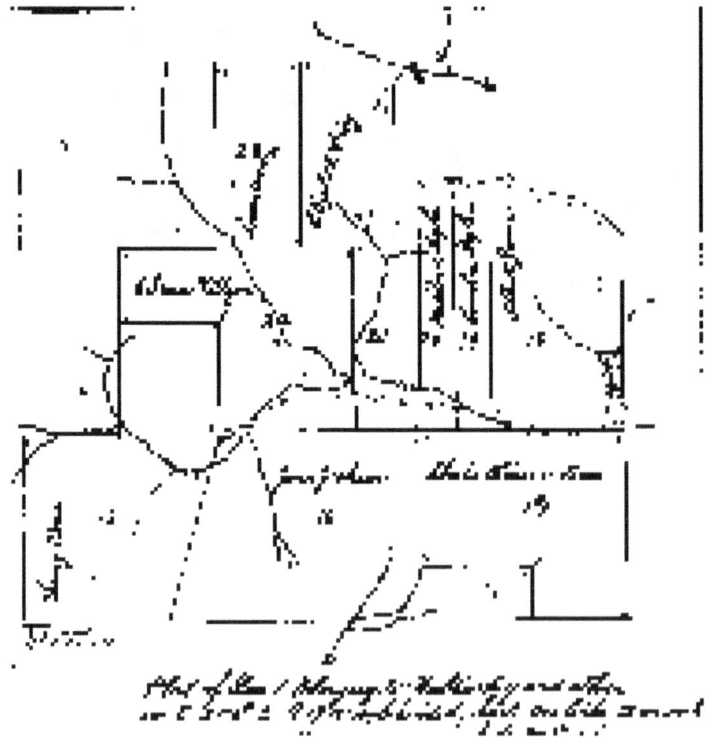

Figure - A61 Fry Lands -Center portion of land along old US 52 includes a school lot

TWYMAN MANUMISSION – Receipt and Signatures of all adult slaves.
Deed 12-343-344   Lawrence County, OH   15 March 1850
  Anthony Furguson (*Twyman*) & William W. Furguson (*Twyman*) receipt from
  Simeon & Violet and others   [name entered incorrectly by county clerk]

We the undersigned persons emancipated slaves of the 1st section of the will of the late James Furguson (*Twyman*) of Madison County and state of Virginia including Noah and Winney who have desired their freedom to whom was bequeathed by said will in our own right and in the right of our descendants hereinafter named with their increase, the sum of eleven thousand dollars to his executors Anthony and William H. Furguson (*Twyman*) herein named to be by them paid out and expended in removing and locating the *undersigned and our children* & c named in said will in some free state of the United States of America as will more fully appear by reference to the 9th section of said will in the way of furnishing us with land and other property to wit: land provisions for one year tools & c for which we in our own right and in right of our descendent or increase do hereby acknowledge that we have received of the executors Anthony and William H. Furguson (*Twyman*) through the hands of William H. Furguson (*Twyman*) the sum of twenty six hundred and sixty nine dollars in full of the eleven thousand dollars legacies & c. in outfit, in removing us to the state of Ohio in expenses in removing us out, in purchase of land, tools and provision for one year. Now we Simon and Violet in our own right and in the right of Abram and Ambrose, Walker and Charlotte in our own right, Barbara in my own right and in right of Horace and Susan infants, Short John and Maria his wife in our own right and in right of our children Jane, Beck, Henry, Elizabeth, Mary Ann, Ellen, Lucy Ann, Priscilla, Eleanor, Edmund and Daniel infants, and for our grandchildren James infant child and Beck infant child, Nancy in my own right in right of my children Julia and William, Charles in my own right, William in my own right, Lewis in my own right, Laurence in my own right, Albert in my own right, Yellow John in my own right, Bob in my own right, Noah and Winney in our right *and the parents of the aforesaid* in right of their children and grandchildren from since the 31st day of October 1849 if any, do acknowledge the above receipt of the said executors of James Furguson (*Twyman*), deceased, through the hands of William H. Furguson (*Twyman*) one of the said executors and we the aforesaid do acquit the said executors of the said James Furguson (*Twyman*) deceased of the above consideration and sum of money named above coming to us legatees under the will of the said James Furguson (*Twyman*) deceased. Given under our hand and seals this 15th day of March in the year of our Lord one thousand eight hundred and fifty.

1850(23 signatures)

Barbara her - mark (seal)	Nancy her x mark (seal)	Beck her + mark ( )
Walker his * mark (seal)	Charles his x mark (seal)	Henry his x mark ( )
Charlotte her + mark (seal)	William his + mark (seal)	Elizabeth X mark ( )
Simeon his + mark (seal)	Lewis his 7 mark (seal)	Mary Ann X mark ( )
Violet her x mark (seal)	Lawrence his F mark (seal)	Ellen her + mark( )
Short John his x mark (seal)	Albert his + mark (seal)	Bob his + mark ( )
Maria her + mark (seal)	Yellow John his + mark (seal)	Noah his -\ mark( )
	Jane her + mark (seal)	Winney her x mark( )

ALL SIGNED BY MARK - (adult James 30) of will not listed - Washington 34) of will does not sign
  Numbers refer to listing in will – same used throughout the study.
In their own and for their children: 5) Noah & 6) Winney TWYMAN– parents of all

7) Simon & 8) Violet	*16) Short John & 17) Maria Toms*		18) Nancy –Smith	
Twyman	20) Jane	27) Perscilla	19) Julia	31) Wm. Dykes
9) Abram	40) *Eliza*	28) Eleanor (?)	43) Wm. T.	33) Bob James
10) Ambrose	21) Beck	38) Edmund inf		34) missing "
11) Walker & 12) Charlotte	42) *Alexander*	39) Daniel inf		35 Lawrence "
Fry	22) Henry	gr Children		36) Albert "
13) Barbara Gaunt	23)Elizabeth	44) Beck inf		37) Yellow John
14) Horace	24) Mary Ann	45) James inf		Twyman
15) Susan	25) Ellen	29) Charles Thomas		46) Sarah Brown
	26) Lucy Ann	32) Lewis Twyman		inf

Lawrence Co. OH Deed 12-315-316   15 Mar 1850
Isaac Frampton and wife Jane of Wayne Co. VA #2 (#1 in the first section)
To Barbary, Walker, and others --NOTE: County clerk wrote <u>Furguson</u> instead of Twyman in this deed also.
Know all men by these presents that Isaac Frampton and Jane Frampton, wife of said Isaac Frampton of the county of Wayne and state of Virginia in consideration for the sum of fifteen hundred dollars to us in hand paid by Barbara, Walker, Charlotte, Simeon, Violet, Short John, Maria, Nancy, Charles, William, Lewis, Lawrence, Albert, Yellow John, Jane, Beck, Henry, Elizabeth, Mary Ann, Ellen, Bob, Noah and Winney of the County of Lawrence and the state of Ohio (*being emancipated slaves of James <u>Furguson </u>late of Madison County and State of Virginia deceased*) have bargained and sold and do hereby grant sell and convey unto the said Barbara, Walker, Charlotte, Simeon, Violet, Short John, Maria, Nancy, Charles, William, Lewis, Lawrence, Albert, Yellow John, Jane, Beck, Henry, Elizabeth, Mary Ann, Ellen, Bob, Noah and Winney emancipated slaves as afore mentioned during their natural lives with the remainder unto their children and their heirs and assigns forever, the following premises situate in the County of Lawrence and the state of Ohio and in Fayette Township and described as follows: The North East quarter of the North West quarter of Section 36 Township 2 Range 17 containing 43 acres more or less. Also, the West half of the South East quarter of Section 36 Township 2 Range 17, except five acres more or less, taken off the North West corner of said half of said quarter section conveyed by John Crawford to George Kouns containing 80 acres more or less. To have and to hold said premises with the appurtenances unto the said Barbara, Walker, Charlotte, Simeon, Violet, Short John, Maria, Nancy, Charles, William, Lewis, Lawrence, Albert, Yellow John, Jane, Beck, Henry, Elizabeth, Mary Ann, Ellen, Bob, Noah and Winney during their natural lives with remainder to their children and their heirs and assigns forever and the said Isaac Frampton for himself and heirs doth hereby covenant with the said grantees, their children and assigns that he is lawfully seized of the premises aforesaid; That the premises are free and clear from all encumbrances whatsoever: and that he will forever Warrant and defend the same with appurtenances unto the said Barbara, Walker, Charlotte, Simeon, Violet, Short John, Maria, Nancy, Charles, William, Lewis, Lawrence, Albert, Yellow John, Jane, Beck, Henry, Elizabeth, Mary Ann, Ellen, Bob, Noah and Winney during their natural lives with the remainder to their children and their heirs and assigns against the lawful claims of all persons whatsoever. In testimony whereof said Isaac Frampton and Jane Frampton have hereunto set their hands and seals this 15th day of March in the year of our Lord one thousand eight hundred and fifty.

Executed in the presence of Elias Nigh	Isaac Frampton (seal)
John Bryan	Jane Frampton (seal)
118 acres for $1500 - $12.70 per acre - total acres 444 + 118 = 562	$7,500 = $13.35 per acre

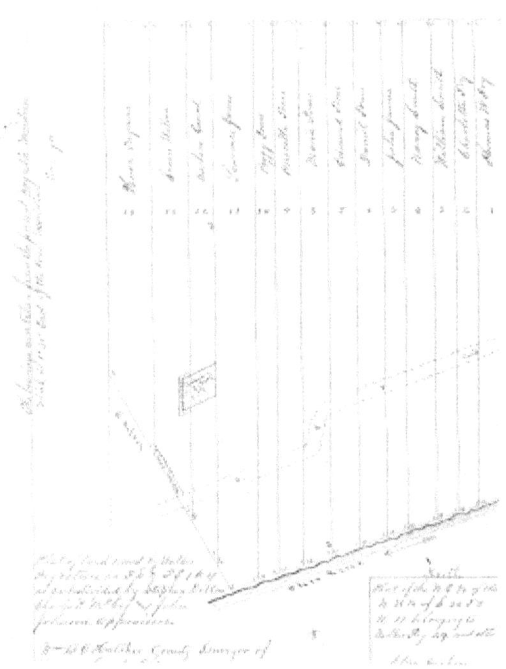

Figure - A59 - Charlotte Lane west to Wal-Mart Way

Family Groups

1850 Lawrence Co. Census p447-448 Fayette Twp. (Burlington) (all born in Virginia)

Household   (# is taken from Twyman Will)

          (* not in the will)   Notes   died   "37" cem
                                                                                                   cemetery

194

11)	Fry, Walker	40 m M	Carpenter (minister /reg. Baptist)			
12)	Fry, Charlotte	47 f B				
*	*Twyman, Nancy	70 f B	(possibly the mother of Charlotte and Marie – sister to Winney)			
13)	*Twyman, Rebecca (Barbara) 26 f B		should be Barbara (m/Gaunt) to Huron Co. OH d+1872			
14)	Twyman, Horace	13 m B	s/Barbara – in MO 1872 back to Lawrence Co. OH			
15)	Twyman, Susan	4 f B	dau/Barbara –returned to Lawrence took the name, Wilson m Gordon			

195

5)	Twyman, Noah	70 m B	farmer	father of all	1858	cem
6)	Twyman, Winna	75 f B		mother of all	1852	cem
29)	Twyman, Charles	50 m B	farmer	Charles Thomas	after 1880	
31)	Twyman, William	37 m B	farmer	William Dykes	1853	cem
32)	Twyman, Lewis	31 m B	farmer		1856	cem

196

7)	Twyman, Simon	55 m B	farmer		1864	cem
8)	Twyman, Violet	50 f B			1850	cem
9)	Twyman, Ambrose	15 m B			1860	cem
10)	Twyman, Abram	13 m B			1860	cem
37)	Twyman, John (Yellow John) 45 m B		farmer	(brother to Simon)	prior 1860	cem

197

35)	Twyman, Laurence	24 m B	farmer	Lawrence James	1886 dc	
36)	Twyman, Albert	22 m M	laborer	Albert James	after 1900	
33)	Twyman, Robert	30 m M		Robert James	1850	
	xxx			Washington James (escaped d 1849)		

198

16)	Toms, John (Short John)	49 m B	farmer	parents of 22-36	1864	cem
17)	Toms, Maria	42 f B		(daughter Noah & Winnie)	1915	cem
18)	*Toms, Nancy	27 f B	ch J &M (Smith-mother/Wm. "Traveler")			
20)	Toms, Jane	24 f B	ch J & M m William Jackson			
21)	*Toms, Beck (Rebecca)	22 f B	ch J & M m John Kilgore		1896	
22)	Toms, Henry	19 m B laborer	ch J & M		1911 dc	cem
23)	Toms, Elizabeth	16 f B	ch J & M m ------King			
24)	Toms, Mary (Ann)	14 f B	ch J & M		1857	
25)	Toms, Ellen	12 f B	ch J & M m Edmund Shelton		1878	cem
26)	Toms, Lucy (Ann)	9 f B	ch J & M		1858	
27)	Toms, Percilla	8 f B	ch J & M			
38)	*Toms, Edmund	6 m B	ch J & M			
39)	*Toms, David (Daniel)	3 m B	ch J & M		1917	cem
19)	Toms, Julia (Smith)	10 f B	gr ch (daughter /Nancy) m Garland James			
40)	*Toms, Eliza	2 f B	gr ch (daughter /Jane)			
41)	*Toms, William	2 m B	(not listed anywhere else)			
42)	*Toms, Alex	1 m B	(son /Beck)			
* 43)	*Wm. Traveler s/Nancy	9/12 B	not on census son /Nancy (see 35?)		1931	cem

Not on the census pages: Barbara (probably #4 Rebecca 26), Washington, James, Eleanor, (children)William (Traveler), Beck, James, Sarah(19 in 1870 – born after arrival in OH)?)

<u>1860 Census - Lawrence County, OH – Fayette Township</u> -*will - # share

<u>268</u>	Kilgore, John	43 b VA farm	
* 21)	Rebecca	34 b VA	
* 42)	Alexander	11b VA	
	Cornelia	6 b OH	
269 Taylor, Noah			
* 29)	Thomas, Charles	57 b VA - d after 1880	
*<u>383</u> Toms, Simm (7)		65 b VA - d 1864	
	Lucy (2nd wife)	47 b VA -d 23 Sep 1896	
	Buxfield, Wilson	9 b OH	
*<u>395</u> James, Albert (36)		35 m VA farmer d after 1900	
	Eliza	36 m VA (died prior to 1870)	
	Milly	8 m OH (dau/William Dykes)	
	Caroline	6 m OH (dau/William Dykes)	
	Charlotte	3 m OH	
	Luellen	2 m OH	
	Hester	1 m OH	
<u>397</u> Shelton, Edward		30 b VA farm hand (Edmund)	
* 25)	Ellen	22 b VA d 1878 cem	
	Mary J.	4 b OH	
399 James, Garland		26 m OH teacher	
*19)	Julia (Smith)	20 m VA (daug/Nancy Smith)	
	Frank	4 m VA	
*<u>400</u> Toms, Henry (22)		27 b VA farmer	
	Emeline	22 b OH	
	Isaiah	5 b OH	
	James W.	3 b OH	
	Wm. C.	2/12 b OH	
	Toms, Delilah	5 m OH (?dau/Ellen King)	
	Toms, Josephine	3 m OH (?dau/Ellen King)	
* 41) Smith, William		11 m VA (s/Nancy Smith)	

*<u>394</u> James, Lawrence (35)		37 b VA d 1886
	Jane	26 m VA
	Camilius R.	8 m OH
	Martha	6 m OH
	Lavina	4 m OH
	Creighton	2 m OH
	Mary E.	3/12 m OH
	Johnson, Matilda	69 m VA (Ward)
	widow/Ben. Mother to Gabe	
*<u>396</u> Fry, Thomas W. (11)		50 m VA Reg. Bapt
(12) Charlotte		57 m VA
(14)Twiman, Harris(Horace)		22 m VA Twyman
	Burvender, Mark	23 m NC
	Ward, Nancy	80 b VA (who ?)
*<u>398</u> Toms, (Short) John (16)		64 b VA d (–1869)
*17)	Maria	50 b VA
*18)	Nancy	3 b VA
*23)	Elizabeth	26 b VA
*27)	Priscilla	17 b VA
*38)	Edmund	15 b VA farm hand
*39)	Daniel	12 b VA
*46)	Sarah	9 m OH Brown
406 Jackson, William		49 b VA boat hand
*20)	Jane	58 b VA aged 34
*40)	Eliza	12 b VA
	Luvina	8 b OH
	Elizabeth	5 b OH
	James	3 b OH
	Edward	2/12 b OH

<u>Marriages from Lawrence County Marriage Books</u>

		Spouse	date	book
James, Lawrence	to	Jane Johnson	5 Jan 1851	4-184
Toms, Simon	to	Lucy Moss	30 Oct 1851	4-198
Tomes, Jane	to	William Jackson 1	4 Jun 1852	4-217
Toms, Rebecca	to	John Kilgore	19 Apr 1855	5-130
Toms, Ellen	to	Edward Shelton	27 Dec 1855	5-185
James, Albert	to	Jane Johnson	5 Jan 1851	5-186
Smith, Julia	to	Garland D. James	11 Nov 1856	5-192
Sarah Mariah Toms 18)	to	Squire Burvender 21	29 May 1861	19(wid/Ambrose)
Elizabeth Thoms 18	to	Daniel King 21	5 Nov 1863	8-87
Julia James (2nd)	to	Lemuel Holmes	19 Nov 1874	11-115 (Smith)
Susan Wilson	to	Isaiah Gordon	27 Jan 1876	12-93(1875-84)
Tomes, Isaiah	to	Nancy Argo	9 Jun 1881	13-179 (s/Henry)
Tomes, Daniel	to	Maria Toney	22 Dec 1881	13-259
Gordon, Barbara	to	Wm. Henry Reynolds	2 May 1901	19-597
Gordon, Iona	to	Owen Pleasant, Sr.	22 Oct 1901	19-111
Pleasant, Owen, Jr.	to	(Emajean) Boggs	5 Mar 1935	37-11

Owen descended from the '37' through Thomas Walker Fry's granddaughter Susan Gordon.
Emajean also descended from the original '37' through William "Traveler" Smith.
Several of these marriages were preformed by Reverends Jonathan Cradic,
Wm. P. Cradic and Thomas Walker Fry.

Figure A63 – '37' Marriages

<u>1870 Census - Fayette Township</u>   *named will/received share   Macedonia member 1884   x

#	Name	Age	Race	Birth	Notes					
#67-67	Hall, Camillus		white - physician		(active in UGRR)					
*	Toms, Prescilla	24 f	(W)	VA-single	domestic					
*	Smith, William	21 m	(W)	VA	domestic (Traveler)					x
*#104	Toms, Maria	59f	B	VA						x
*	Nancy	40f	B	VA						
*	Edmund	25m	B	VA						x
*	Daniel	22m	B	VA	widower					
*	Ellen	23f	B	(KY)	(wife/Edmund)					
	Wm. W.	8/12m	B	OH	ch/Ed & El - d 9 Dec 1888 Louisa,KY					
(*)	Brown, Sarah	20f	B	OH						
	Adda	5/12f	B	OH						
*#105	Frey, Thomas	60m	B	VA	(Fry)					x
*	Charlotte	67f	B	VA						
*#106	James, Lawrence	47m	B	VA						x
	Jane	38f	B	OH	Mary	10f	B	OH		
	Cornelius	18m	B	OH	Barbara	8f	B	OH		
	Martha	16f	B	OH	Emma	7f	B	OH		
	Novina	15f	B	OH	Sarah	4f	B	OH	x	
	Creighton	12m	B	OH	Wilanna	2f	B	OH		
	Johnson, Matilda	75f	B	VA (a Ward)						
#118	Harris, Levi				s/Essex & Elizabeth Bryant Harris					x
*	Toms, Lucy	58f	B	VA keeping house	(2nd w/Simon) d 23 Sep 1896					
#121	Shelton, Edmund	40m	B	VA						
*	Ellen	32f	B	OH(VA)						
	Mary	13f	B	OH						
	James	1m	B	OH						
#135	King, Daniel	50m	B	VA	Josephine	12f	B	OH		
*	Elizabeth	36f	B	VA	Nancy	5f	B	OH		
	Delilah	15f	B	OH	Ernest	5/12m	B	OH		
#140	Kilgore, John	49m	B	VA	d 21 May 1882 aged 80.4.17					
*	Rebecca	42f	B	VA	d 30 Jul 1896 aged 65					
*	Alexander	24m	B	VA						
	Cornelia	16f	B	OH						
	Mary	10f	B	OH	d 18 Dec 1879 aged 18.11.15					
	Thomas	6m	B	OH	d 15 Nov 1912					
	Lydia	3f	B	OH	d 19 Sep 1879 aged 12.7.0					
#142	Jackson, William	62m	B	VA						x
*	Jane	41f	B	VA						
	Lurana	19f	B	OH						
	Elizabeth	17f	B	OH						
	James	13m	B	OH						
	Edward	10m	B	OH						
	John	7m	B	OH	d 5 Oct 1883 aged 21					
	Alice	4f	B	OH						
	Charles	1m	B	OH	d 10 Mar 1871					
*#143	James, Albert	44m	B	VA						
*	Mildred	18f	B	OH	(daughter *William Dykes)					
*	Caroline	16f	B	OH	(daughter *William Dykes)					
	Lottie	12f	B	OH						
	Luella	11f	B	OH						
	Hester	10f	B	OH						
	James	8/12m	B	OH						
*#148	Thom, Henry	37m	B	VA	d 1 Feb 1911 age 82					x
	Emeline	35f	B	VA	d 19 Apr 1902					
	Isaiah	15m	B	OH						
	James	13m	B	OH						
	William	10m	B	OH						
	Timothy	8m	B	OH	d 24 Feb 1881					
	Camillus	5m	B	OH	d Oct 1890 Cincinnati					

#1	Hall, Camillius	67	Dr.			
*	Toms, Priscilla	35f B	servant	VA	d 22 Aug 1890 age 49	
#19	Roberts, Alexander					
*	Shelton, Ellen	42f B	servant	VA	d prior 1900 - widow Edmund	
*#51	Toms, Edmund	36m B		VA		x
	Ellen	30f B		VA		
	William	10m B		OH		x
	Wattshedd	1m		OH	d 23 Jun 1890 - 11.6.10	
*	Daniel w/Mariah	31m B	VA brother/Edmund		d 20 Jan 1917 aged 68	x x
*#52	Smith, William	31m B		VA (Traveler)	d Aug 1931	x
	Mary	23f				
*	Nancy	51f		VA Mother		
	Walter	3	(Traveler lived OH & WV – another child Ernest Boggs			
	James F.	1	-information from granddaughter Imogene Boggs Pleasants)			
*#54	Fry, Thomas W.	70m B		VA	d 15 Dec 1898	x
*	Charlotte	77f B		VA	d 6 Nov 1892	
*	Twyman, Horace	39m B	grandson	VA (s/Barbara)	d 9 Jul 1912 – 76.4.5	
	Susan	35f B	granddau.	VA (?) (first wife, Horace ?)		
	Edith H(G.).	4f				
	Alexander	1m				
	Maud	2/12f b March				
#55	Gordon, Isaiah	26m B				
*	Susan	33f B		VA (Wilson-dau. /Barbara- Walker & Charlotte))		
	Mercer (Iona)	3f		d 1928 (m/Pleasant)		
	Barbara	1/12f b Apr.		(m/Reynolds)		
#82	King, Daniel	60m B		VA		
*	Elizabeth	46f B		VA		
	Nancy	15f B	dau.	OH		
	Ernest	10m B	son	OH		
#84	Brown, Richard	31m B				x
*	Sarah F.	29f B		OH	(born after census 1850)	
	Adeth S.	10f B		OH		
	Edgar	7m B		OH		
	James	5m B		OH		
	George	2m B		OH		
*#85	James, Albert	50m B		VA		
	Hester	20f B	dau	OH		
	James F.	11m B	grandson	OH		
	Ellwood	7m B	grandson	OH		
	Francis	6f B	granddau.	OH		
	Elizabeth	3f B	granddau.	OH		
# 87	Killgore, John	68m B			d 21 May 1882 – 80.4.17	
*	Rebecca	50f B		VA	d 30 Jul 1896 aged 65	
	Alexander	31m B	stepson	VA	(Rebecca's son)	
	Walker	15m B		OH	d 15 Nov 1912	
*90	Toms, Henry	49m B		VA	d 1 Feb 1911 – 82.0.0	x
	Emaline	42f B		VA	d 19 Apr 1902	
	Timothy	18m B		OH	d 24 Feb 1881	
	Camilus	15m B		OH	d Oct 1890 Cincinnati	
	Julia	7f B		OH	d 14 Jul 1883 – 10.11.11	
	Reny	2m B		OH		
	Unnamed	4/12m B May		OH		

#91	Jackson, William	79m B		VA		x
*	Jane	50f B		VA		
	Wm. J.	23m B		OH		
	John Thomas	18m B		OH		
	Alice	16f B		OH		
*#92	Thomas, Charles	75m B		VA	d after 1880	
#116-113	Boggs, (Henderson)	47m B				
	(Juditte) 43f B					
	Roberta	23f M	dau			
	Boggs, Ernest	5m M	grandson		(son of Traveler Smith)	
	Boggs, Ellwood	2m M	grandson			

1880 Lawrence County Census – Upper Twp. - Ironton

Ironton-Dist.4 : pg 195B	James, Lawrence	58		x
	Jane	48		
	Barbara	18		
	Sarah	14		x
	Anna	12		

1900 Census Lawrence Co. OH – Fayette Twp.   *will or received a share

			Born		died	
*#4	Toms, Wm. E.(Edmund)	55m B	Apr 1845	VA m 31yr.		x
	Ellen	53f B	Aug 1847	VA		
#6	Gordon, Isaiah	47m B	Aug 1853			
*	Susan	53f B	Feb 1847	VA m 1876	18 Jun 1941	
	Iona	22f B	Jan 1878	m – Bk 19-111	26 Feb 1928	
	Barbara	20f B	Apr 1880			
	Herman C.	2m B	Apr 1898		grandson/Iona	

(Susan Wilson Gordon, mother of Iona Gordon, mother of Owen Pleasant)
(Barbara, mother of Susan Spencer – long-time teacher in Burlington)

*#9	Twyman, Horace	61m B	Nov 1839	VA	9 Jul 1912-76.4.5	
	Gussie	24f B	Jan 1875	IL dau.		
	Alexander	20m B	Oct 1879	OH son		
	Maude	20f B	Mar 1880	OH dau		
	Charlotte	19f B	May 1881	OH dau		
	Jasper	18m B	Nov 1882	OH son		
	Moses	17m B	Jan 1883	OH son		
	Cora	16f B	May 1884	OH dau		
*#10	Toms, Daniel	53m B	Mar 1847 VA	m 15 yr.	20 Jan 1917 – 68	x
	Mariah	57f B	Oct 1842	WV	1 Sep 1915	x
	Mayo, Mary	34f B	Mar 1861	dau		
	" Clarence	11m B	Jul 1889	grandson		
	" Eugene	4m B	Mar 1896	grandson		
#116-121	Kilgore, Thomas W.	36m B	Jul 1864	son/John & Rebecca		
	Margaret	28f B	Jan 1872			
	Kilgore, Alexander	51m B	May 1849	son of Rebecca		
*#117-122	Toms, Henry	71m B	Oct 1828		1 Feb 1911- 80.4.17	x
	Emeline	60f B	Jan 1840		19 Apr 1902	
	Howard	20m B	May 1880			
*#126-131	Smith, William	51m B	May 1849	(Traveler) 9 Aug 1931		x
	Mary K. 44f B		Apr 1856			
	James F. 21m B		Feb 1879			
	Lloyd	7m B	Jun 1893			

(Traveler died in WV but was buried in "37 Cemetery".) Source: Susan Wilson Gordon and Owen Pleasant
****

<u>Cabell County, WV 1910 Census</u>   <u>1920 Cabell County Census</u>

*#--	Smith, William	61m	B	#1616 Smith, William	71m B d Aug 1931
	Mary K.	54f	B	Mary K.	64f B
	James E.	30m	B	Lloyd	26m B
	Lloyd	16m		(across the Ohio River from Lawrence Co. OH)

<u>Huntington City Directory – Cabell County, WV -(Guyandotte was absorbed by Huntington)</u>

1910	Layne, Nelson B.	plaster		3rd & Richmond, Guyandotte
	Wife -Nettie(Maud)	laundress at WV Asylum	(dau. Horace Twyman)
1910	Smith, Wm. T.	carpenter	(Traveler)	1513 9th Ave.
1910	Smith, James. F.	laborer	(s/Traveler)	215 12th
1910	Twyman, Alexander	helper	(s/Horace)	Short St. Guyandotte
1916	Lane, Nelson (Maud)	plaster	(dau/Horace)	313 Richmond, Guyandotte
1916	Lane, Wm. A. (Gussie E.) laborer	(dau/Horace)	305 Richmond, Guyandotte
1920	Twyman, Cora	domestic	(dau/Horace)	1210 8th St.
1920	Twyman, Alexander C. (Cleopatra)	(s/Horace)	421 Water St. Guyandotte
1920	Smith, Wm. T. and (Mary K.)	(Traveler)	1502 9th Ave.
1920	Smith, James F. (Maggie) contractor	(s/Traveler)	1011 8th St.
1926	Twyman, Alexander C. (Violet) machine helper C & O		421 Water St. Guyandotte
1930	Layne, Hugh & Cora B.	(dau/Horace)	218 Staunton, Guyandotte
1930	Smith, Wm. T. (Mary K.)	(Traveler)	1502 9th Ave.
1930	Smith, James F. contractor	(s/Traveler)	714 11th Ave.
1930	Smith, James F., Jr.	superintendent	(gr s ")	R 714 11th Ave.
1930	Smith, Lloyd (Ada)	teacher Douglass	(s/Traveler)	513 9th Ave
1930	Twyman, Alexander C. (Violet)	(s/Horace)	421 Water St. Guyandotte
1940	Layne, Cora (widow/Hugh)	(dau/Horace)	419 Water St. Guyandotte
1940	Twyman, Alexander C. (Violet)	(s/Horace)	421 Water St. Guyandotte
1949	Twyman, Alexander C. (Violet M.)	(s/Horace)	406 Richmond St. Guy.

Figure A64 - Aunt Susan's Porch 1902

Appendix 6 - TWYMAN   -   Property Division

<u>Common Pleas-Complete Record 22-p608-634 – 1870 - Division of property with maps</u>

Originally 9 land plots, only 2 deeds were written in the name of all slaves for a total of 562 acres

In order to divide the property into individual plots, the court had to decide on each share

This document is long and complicated. The following is an abstract of its contents.

Abstracts from the said document: 19 Sept 1870 division in 36 shares (the first suit was for 35 shares)

p608 William Smith vs. Maria Tomas et al. (reads Ulana Toms)

      for division of property E part Sec.2 Twp. 1 Range 19 (see Deed 12-137)

p609	Maria Toms	1/20	plus part as the widow of John Toms 1/35
	Charles Thomas	1/20	
	Thomas W. Fry	1/20	
	Mildred Dykes	1/40	age 18 daughter of William Dykes
	Caroline Dykes	1/40	age 16 daughter of William Dykes
	Maria Busvender	1/35	with husband Squire - widow of Ambrose Toms
	Lucy Toms	1/35	2nd wife of Simon
	Alexander Kilgore	1/35	s/Beck
	Eliza Jackson	1/35	(called Cilla) married Henry Woodfin
	Susan Wilson	1/35	(in Huron County, OH in 1870 – returned m Gordon)
	Charlotte Fry	1/35	and husband Thomas W. Fry
	Albert James	2- 1/35	
	Lawrence	2- 1/35	
	Barbara Gaunt	1/35	and husband Moses of Huron Co. OH *below
	Horace Twyman	1/35	(in St. Louis, Missouri in 1870 – returned)
	Julia James	1/35	Julia Smith (Nancy) m Garland James- Kanawha Co.
	Rebecca Toms Killgore	13/350	(Beck) and husband, John Killgore
	Jane Toms Jackson	13/350	and husband, William Jackson
	Elizabeth Toms King	13/350	and husband, Daniel King
	Ellen Toms Shelton	13/350	and husband, Edmund Shelton
	Henry Toms	13/350	
	Edmund Toms	13/350	
	Priscilla Toms	13/350	
	Daniel Toms	13/350	
	Nancy Smith	13/350	
	Sarah Toms Brown	3/350	husband Richard Brown – tenants in common

1/35 of Short John Toms decd. Devised To:

Rebecca Killgore	Priscilla Toms
Jane Jackson	Daniel Toms
Elizabeth King	Nancy Smith
Ellen Shelton	Sarah Brown
Henry Toms	dower to (wife) Maria Toms
Edmund Toms	

P610 2nd suit Nancy Smith vs. Maria Toms et al

      Another division listing all names above

*Barbara Gaunt's deed of sale 1872 states husband Moses Gaunt, formerly 'McCormack.' There is a will reference in Cabell Co. WV Will Book 1-pg 265 from James McCormack of Clark Co. VA to his children in Cabell Co. "To son George – slaves Jenny & Moses for $500." This could be Moses McCormack Gaunt.

<u>P614 cross petition Thomas Walker Fry, Albert James, and Lawrence James</u>

      Answer William and Nancy Smith (same names as above)

Slaves of James Twyman of Madison Co. VA manumitted 1 Aug. 1848 and given $10,000 to purchase land are as follows:

Maria Toms	Eliza Jackson	Barbara Gaunt
Charles Thomas	Susan Wilson	Horace Twyman
Alexander Kilgore	Charlotte Fry	Julia James
Rebecca Kilgore	Jane Jackson	Elizabeth King
Ellen Shelton	Henry Toms	Edmund Toms
Priscilla Toms	Daniel Toms	

And deceased: (by 1870)

Simeon	Abraham Lewis	Bob	Lucy Ann	
Violet	Noah	William	Washington	Mary Ann
Ambrose	Winnie	Short John	Yellow John	

Page 614 Portion of grantees omitted (from the will or 15 Mar. 1850 deed)

Washington James, decd.	Eliza d/Jane Jackson	Horace
William Smith s/Nancy	Daniel Toms	Susan
Julia	Edward (Edmund) Toms	Lucy Ann
Alexander s/Beck Killgore	Abraham Twyman d 1860	Priscilla

Page 616 Explanation of partition

Mother Violet died in 1850, leaving heirs sons Ambrose and Abraham

Ambrose died in 1860, leaving father, Simeon as heir, Ambrose's widow Maria who married Squire
        Burvender and his brother Abraham who also died in 1860

Simeon died in 1864, leaving 2nd wife Lucy entitled to a life estate
        and Simeon's brother (Short) John sole heir

Noah died in 1858, leaving (son?) Walker residing in Madison Co. VA

Winnie died in 1854, leaving children:

| Charles | Walker | grandchildren: Mildred Dykes |
| Maria | Lewis | Charlotte Dykes |

Robert (Bob) James died in 1850, leaving brothers Lawrence and Albert

Washington James died in 1849, leaving brothers Robert and Albert

Short John Toms died in 1864, leaving wife Maria

children:	Nancy Smith	Elizabeth King	Daniel Toms
	Jane Jackson	Ellen Shelton	Sarah Toms
	Rebecca Killgore	Pricilla Toms	
	Henry Toms	Edmund Toms	

Yellow John (Twyman) died, leaving sister Peggy in Madison Co. VA

William Dykes died in 1853, leaving children Mildred and Caroline

Lewis (Twyman) died in 1856
        leaving brothers Charles, Thomas Walker Fry, sister Maria Toms
        (and Mildred and Caroline Dikes, children of his *mother*, Mildred Dikes) ?

Mary Ann Toms died in 1857, leaving brothers & sisters

Nancy	Rebecca(Beck)	Ellen	Edmund
Jane	Henry	Lucy Ann	Daniel
Julia	Elizabeth Priscilla	Sarah	

Lucy Ann died in 1858, leaving the same heirs as Mary Ann

Maria Burvender is entitled to 2/36 (Widow of Ambrose Toms)

Page 617-620 division and proportion   Note: first division is 1/35. This is 1/36 of 562 acres

Family division is complicated. Please use the numbers provided in the will.

Note: 1870 property value considered in the division. The amount divided is 544 acres, not 562 acres.

	Lot - (2nd number see page 5 chart)	final portion	acreage	
1)	(11) Thomas W. Fry	1/24	lot #1 - 10.98a	
2)	(12) Charlotte (Fry)	1/36	lot #2 - 7.13a	
3)	(43) William Smith	1/36	lot #3 - 7.57a	
4)	(18) Nancy Smith	1/36	lot #4 - 9.90a	
5)	(19) Julia (Smith)James	1/36	lot #5 - 7.50a	
6)	(39) Daniel Toms	13/360	lot #6 - 9.92a	
7)	(38) Edmund Toms	13/360	lot #7 - 9.90a	
8)	(17) Maria Toms	1/24	lot #8 - 11.49a	
9)	(27) Priscilla Toms	13/360	lot #9 - 9.98a	
10)	---- Peggy Toms	1/36 Madison Co. VA	lot #10 - 7.57a	(not in will)
11)	(35) Lawrence James	1/18	lot #11 - 15.45a	
12)	(13) Barbara Gaunt	1/36	lot #12 - 10.43a	
13)	(15) Susan Wilson	1/36	lot #13 - 11.90a	
14)	(14) Horace Twyman	1/36	lot #14 - 12.62a	
15)	(22) Henry Toms	13/360	lot #15 - 53.98a	
16)	(20) Jane Jackson	13/360	lot #16 - 60.11a	
17)	(29) Charles Thomas	1/24	lot #17 - 39.51a	
18)	(36) Albert James	1/18	lot #18 - 37.16a	
19)	---- Caroline Dykes	1/48	lot #19 - 11.45a dau/Wm.	

21)	(23) Elizabeth King	13/360		lot #21 - 42.24a
22)	(21) Rebecca Killgore	13/360		lot #22 - 40.59a
23)	(46) Sarah Brown	1/120		lot #23 - 19.16a
24)	---- Maria Burvender	1/24	- life estate	lot #24 - 13.19a wid/Ambros
	½ vested in Albert & Lawrence James & ½ to Toms (11 ch & grch)			
25)	(42) Alexander Kilgore	1/36		lot #25 - 9.21a
26)	--- Walker Toms	1/36 Madison Co. VA		lot #26 - 9.59a (not in will)
27)	--- Lucy Toms	5/72	- life estate	lot #27 - 26.15a 2nd w/Simon
28)	(25) Ellen Shelton	13/360		lot #28 - 27.40a
29)	(23) Eliza Jackson	1/36	School House	lot #29 - .99a
	(7) Simeon Twyman	deceased		
	(8) Violet Twyman	d		
	(10) Abraham Twyman	d		
	(9) Ambrose Twyman	d		
	(5) Noah Toms	d		
	(6) Winnie Toms	d		
	(31) William Dykes	d		
	(32) Lewis Twyman	d		
	(33) Robert James	d		Graveyard .8a
	(34) Washington James	d		located lots 12 & 13
	(16) Short John Toms	d		
	(24) Mary Ann Toms	d		
	(26) Lucy Ann Toms	d		
	(37) Yellow John Twyman	d		

Note: No reference was made to adult James of will or child Eleanor on the census.

Property division is only divided into 29 portions (due to deaths) - Maps pp 10, 12, 14, and p 46.

FROM THE COMPLETE RECORD #22
pp608-634 - Common Pleas Court, Lawrence Co, Ohio
There are several additions to the complete record that are not included in the newspaper notices.

p608 Wm. & Nancy Smith vs. Maria Toms et al. -   Judge Jus. P. Plyley Seventh Judicial City of Ironton
   William Smith vs. Ulana Toms et al. (Maria)[*]   There are several petitions and counter petitions.
           (2nd number is from a petition filed by Nancy Smith, which follows William's petition.)

p609 ---are tenants in common with your petitioner in the said premises and have the legal right to and are seized in
   fee simple in said premises in such proportion as follows: (all parts say undivided) Ulana (Maria) Toms 1/20(7/88),
   Charles Thomas 1/20(7/88), Thomas W. Fry 1/20(7/88), Mildred Dikes and Caroline Dikes 1/40(7/176) each,
   (Maria)Burvender and husband Squire Burvender 3/35(1/22), Lucy Toms 1/35(1/22), Alexander Killgore 1/35, Eliza
   Jackson 1/35, Susan Wilson 1/35, Charlotte Fry and her husband Thomas W. Fry 1/35(1/22), Albert James 2/35(3/44),
   Lawrence 2/35, Barbara Gaunt and husband Moses Gaunt 1/35(1/22), Horace Twyman 1/35, Julia James 1/35,
   Rebecca Killgore and husband John Killgore 13/350(3/55), Jane Jackson and husband William 13/350(3/55),
   Elizabeth King and husband David King 13/350(3/55), Ellen Shelton and husband Edmund 13/350(3/55), Henry
   Toms 13/350(3/55), Edmund Tom13/350(1/110), Priscilla Toms 13/350(1/110), Daniel Toms 13/350(1/110), Nancy
   Smith 13/350(3/55), Sarah Brown and husband Richard Brown 3/350(1/110), and further Ulana (Maria) Toms is
   widow of John Toms decd, who died seized of 1/35(1/22) part which descended to Rebecca Killgore, Jane Jackson,
   Elizabeth King, Ellen Shelton, Henry Toms, Edmund Toms, Priscilla Toms, Daniel Toms, Nancy Smith, and Sarah
   Brown and Ulana (Maria) Toms are entitled to dower, said 1/35.

p614   Cross petition by Thomas Walker Fry, Albert James, and Lawrence James (and all others named before)
   PLUS – and also together with Simon, Violet, Abraham, Ambrose, Noah, Winnie, William, Lewis, Bob, Washington,
   Short John, Mary Ann, Lucy Ann, and Yellow John now deceased, the bondsmen and bondswomen, or slaves of one
   James Twyman of Madison County, VA, decd. Manumitted by his will on 1 August 1848 and bequeathed $10,000 to
   purchase real estate, tools, provisions, and clothing.

p615   Either by mistake of the person who drafted the deed or of the recorder of Lawrence County, a portion of the
   Grantees who were entitled to an interest in the real estate were left out and omitted, viz: Washington, William, son of
   Nancy, now known as William Smith, Julia, Alexander, son of Beck, now known as Alexander Killgore, Eliza,
   daughter of Jane, Daniel, Edward, Abraham, Ambrose, Horace, Susan, Lucy Ann, and Priscilla. (all the children)

p621 Surveyors do lay out land as follows:

 Albert James and Lawrence contiguous. Thomas W. Fry, Charlotte Fry, Horace Twyman, Barbara Gaunt and Susan Wilson contiguous, Rebecca Killgore and Alexander Kilgore contiguous

 Jane Jackson and Eliza Jackson contiguous

 Nancy Smith, William Smith, Julia James, Daniel Toms, Edmond Toms, Priscilla Toms and Sarah Brown contiguous

*Suit says Ulana, not Maria.

IRONTON REGISTER

IRONTON	September 15, 1870	OHIO

LEGAL NOTICE

Dated 10th day December 1870 A.D.

Walker Toms, son of "Noah" Toms dec'd, one of the emancipated slaves of James Twyman, dec'd of Madison County, Virginia and "Peggy" whose name is unknown, sister to "Yellow" John, dec'd, also one of the emancipated slaves of James Twyman, will take notice that a petition has been filed against them and other parties in interest by William Smith and Nancy Smith in the Court of Common Pleas of the County of Lawrence and state of Ohio, in which said William and Nancy Smith demand partition of the following described real estate: situated in the County of Lawrence and State of Ohio, and in Fayette Township, and described as follows: The northeast quarter of the northwest quarter of Section No.36 township No.2 range No.17 containing forty-three acres more or less; also the west half of the southwest quarter of Section No.36 township No.2 range 17 except five acres more or less taken off the northwest corner of said half of said quarter section conveyed by John Crawford to George Kouns, containing eighty acres more or less, also the real estate situate in the County of Lawrence and State of Ohio and the township of Fayette and described as follows: the east part of the fractional section No.2 in Range 19 (17) township No.1 beginning at a stake on the Ohio, two hundred and forty-three poles easterly by the said river from the southwest corner of said fractional section at the southeast corner of Burton's heirs land, thence running north 69*, east one hundred and thirty-three and two thirds poles to a stake, the southwest corner of land formerly owned by Yeager, now owned by George Kouns thence due north along said Kouns's line to the back line of said fractional section to a stake, thence west on said back line to such a point as will by running due south therefrom intersect the stake or place of beginning; , thence from said point south to said first mentioned stake the place of the beginning; excepting and reserving out of the above granted premises the following parcels of land heretofor sold and conveyed by William Lynd to wit: 5 ½ acres to Elijah Frampton, also 6 acres, 2 rods, 1 pole to William C. Johnson – the above described tracts are taken from the southwest corner of said tract , containing one hundred and fifty-four acres more or less. Also, the southeast quarter of the northwest quarter of section 35, township 2, range 17, saving and excepting one acre out of the northwest corner sold to Arty Carter, and one acre sold to Abner Johnson; also, one acre of the same side sold to Anna Robinson; containing forty-one acres more or less. Also part of the southwest quarter of the northeast quarter of section 35, township 2, of range 17, being all that part of the said quarter section which lies south of the top of the ridge, commencing at the corner of said Isaac Frampton and O.O.B. Randall the center corner of section 35, thence north with the west line of the said quarter to the top of the ridge about 35 rods, to a stake about one rod west of a black locust 12 inches in diameter, thence easterly along the top of the said ridge, following the marked or blazed trees with the meanders of the top of said ridge till it strikes the east line of the said quarter about ten rods north of the southeast corner thereof to a hickory tree 8 inches in diameter, thence south to the said southeast corner of the said quarter, thence west along the south line of the said quarter to the place of beginning, containing by estimation twenty acres more or less. Also, the west half of the southwest quarter section 35, township 2, of range 17, containing eighty-seven acres and fourteen-one-hundredths. Also, the southeast half of the southwest quarter of section 35, township 2, range 17, containing eighty-eight acres and seventy-two one-hundredths. Also, the southwest quarter of section 35, township 2, range 17, containing forty-three and twenty-two one-hundredths. Also, the east half of the northwest quarter of the southwest quarter of section 35, township 2, range 17, containing twenty-three acres and eighty-six one-hundredths. And that the next term of said Court demand for partition will be made.

 ENOCHS & CHERRINGTON

Dec15t6 Att'ys for PetitionPARTITION OF PROPERTY LAWRENCE COUNTY COURT OF COMMON PLEAS

The County Court petition required the court to divide the property and required that legal notice of partition be published in the newspaper. Several articles were published (with the same information). Below are the facsimiles of those articles. They show relationships and indicate how the property was finally partitioned.

IRONTON REGISTER

IRONTON   September 22, 1870 A.D.   OHIO

Legal Notice
Dated September 20, 1870 A.D.

Maria Toms, who is sometimes called "Maria," Charles Thomas, who is sometimes called "Charles," Thomas W. Fry, who is sometimes called "Walker," Mildred Dikes, Caroline Dikes, Maria Buvender and her husband Squire Buvender, Albert James, who is sometimes called "James," Lawrence James, who is sometimes called "Lawrence," Charlotte Fry, who is sometimes called "Charlotte," Lucy Toms, Sarah Brown, formerly Sarah Toms and her husband Richard Brown with whom she has since intermarried, Daniel Toms, who is sometimes called "Daniel," Edmund Toms, who is sometimes called "Edmund," Priscilla Toms, who is sometimes called "Persilla," Henry Toms, who is sometimes called "Henry," Ellen Shelton, formerly Ellen Toms, and
sometimes called "Ellen," and her husband, Edmund Shelton, with whom she has since intermarried, Elizabeth King, formerly Elizabeth Toms, and sometimes called "Elizabeth," and her husband Daniel King, Jane Jackson, formerly Jane Toms, and sometimes called "Jane," and her husband William Jackson, with whom she has since intermarried, Rebecca Killgore, formerly Rebecca Toms, and sometimes called "Beck," and her husband John Killgore, with whom she has since intermarried, all of Lawrence County, Ohio; and Barbara Gaunt, who is sometimes called "Barbara, " and her husband Moses Gaunt, both of Huron County, Ohio, will take notice that a petition was filed against them on the 19th of September, A.D. 1870, in the Court of Common Pleas within and for the county of Lawrence, Ohio, by Nancy Smith, who is sometimes called "Nancy," and is now pending, wherein said Nancy Smith demands partition of the following real estate, situated in the county of Lawrence and State of Ohio, and in Fayette township and described as follows: The Northeast quarter of the northwest quarter of Section No.36 township No.2 range No.17 containing forty-three acres more or less; also the west half of the southwest quarter of Section No.36 township No.2 range 17 except five acres more or less taken off the northwest corner of said half of said quarter section conveyed by John Crawford to George Kouns, containing eighty acres more or less, and that the dower of said Maria Toms, widow of John Toms, deceased, in one undivided twenty-second part thereof, be assigned; and that at the next term of said Court the said Nancy Smith would apply for an order that partition may be made of said premises. Dated this 20th day of September A.D. 1870, NANCY SMITH
  By Enochs & Cherrington, her attys. Sep22t6

     There were other notices.

159

Figure A65 - Charlotte, Walker & Susan @1892

Thomas Walker Fry shown with his wife Charlotte and granddaughter Susan. Walker was forty when he came to Lawrence County and in the prime of his life. The leader of 'the 37', he was also a noted preacher, a hedge doctor, a carpenter, a broom maker, and involved in the UGRR. Prior to 1892

Figure A66 - Susan Gordon with grandchildren

Susan Wilson Gordon holding Owen Pleasant and daughter Iona Gordon Pleasant holding Chester Pleasant, Helen Pleasant standing @ 1916 (Owen was 90 in 2003)

Figure 67 – Aunt Susan and Traveler

AGED NEGRESS, NEAR 90, IS LAST SURVIVING MEMBER OF ORIGINAL '37' BAND

16 August 1931

'Aunt' Susan Gordon Lives in Modest Little Cottage in Burlington, Where Original Colony of Freed Slaves Was Formed Before Civil War

The death of William "Traveller" Smith, well known Negro resident of Huntington, who died here several days ago, thinned the ranks of the original "37" a little band of freed slaves who migrated from Virginia and established a colony in Lawrence county, Ohio in 1848, to one surviving member, "Aunt" Susie Gordon, now nearly 90 years old.

"Aunt" Susan, who lives with her husband, himself nearing the century mark in years, in a modest little cottage in the original settlement at Burlington, made the trip by wagon from Madison county, Va., to Lawrence county when she was two years old, while "Little Traveller" Smith was born en route and won the sobriquet of "Little Traveller," a name which followed him throughout his long life in this section.

The aged Negress, idol of a half-dozen great-grandchildren who live near her in the Burlington settlement, "is as sharp as a tack" and remembers many incidents of the early lives of the "freemen" in their homes, across the river from Dixie.

The 37 slaves, including "Aunt" Susan and "Little Traveller" after he was born, were given their freedom by James Twyman, wealthy plantation owner in Madison county, Va., in a will he signed in August, 1848.

The last will and testament, a portion of which will be included in this story, stipulated that funds would be provided for the purchase of property in one of the free states of the Union for each of the 37 freemen. When it occurred to him that the freed slaves might be cheated by dishonest people, Mr. Twyman sent an agent to Lawrence county and later completed negotiations for the purchase of the property in what is now Burlington, a short distance west of Chesapeake.

After the land had been bought, the 37 Negro men and women left the plantation of their former master, "amid much singing and happiness at receiving their emancipation," for their new homes in Ohio.

The slave referred to in the will as "Nancy" was the mother of "Traveller" Smith.

In the journey north in wagons, drawn by horses provided by their master, the freemen were led by Walker Fry, the slave referred to in the will as "Walker," who had been a foreman on the Twyman plantation. After the journey had been completed and the little settlement had taken a definite form, Walker Fry served as common counsellor for all his companions and, according to a story related by "Aunt" Susan and younger members of the present-day colony at Burlington was active in the "underground" railway system, which enabled many runaway slaves to enter Ohio and begin new lives in the free states of the Union.

Walker's wife, Charlotte, was "Aunt" Susan's grandmother, she related yesterday.

Scores of Negro citizens in Huntington and other sections nearby are descendants of the original "37," and are closely related but they are not sure to what extent because of the dearth of adequate records kept during their bondages in Virginia.

James Jackson, of Huntington, is the son of the slave named "Jane" in the will of the Virginia planter, according to "Aunt" Susan's account of the original colony.

"Traveller" Smith died at his home, 1502 Ninth avenue, a week ago. He is the father of Lloyd Smith, a member of the faculty of Douglass high school, who furnished a copy of the will liberating his forefathers. Another brother is W. A. Smith, of Wilberforce university, Ohio.

"Traveller" moved to Huntington from Burlington, 23 years ago.

Susan Twyman Wilson Gordon
1846-1942 aged 94

The ranks of the original "37," a band of freed Negro slaves which established a colony at Burlington, Ohio, near Chesapeake, shortly before the middle of the last century, have been thinned to one surviving member "Aunt" Susan Gordon, upper right, as the result of the death of William "Traveller" Smith, of Huntington, week ago; shown in the upper left are "Aunt" Susan and four of her great-grandchildren; lower left is "Traveller" Smith, who was born enroute to Lawrence county, Ohio from Madison county, Va. and won the sobriquet of "Little Traveller;" and lower right, seated are Charlotte Fry and her husband, Walker Fry, the original leader of the little band of freemen after they settled at Burlington.

1870	Transfer of property by Court from "37" to individuals - after property division				
	Book	Grantor	Grantee	amount	price
1871	26-262	Kilgore, John &	Steven Dillon	heirs	(Rebecca)
		Daniel King		Simon	(Elizabeth)
1871	26-434	James, Albert	Steven Dillon		
1871	26-435	James, Lawrence & Jane	"	dower	
		Toms, Edmund & Ellen		Maria Burvender	
		Brown, Richard & Sarah		and	(Sarah)
		Toms, Henry & Emaline		Lucy Toms	
1871	28-560	Kilgore, Alexander Samuel Crawford		9a /lot 25	$225
1871	28-613	Toms, Daniel	Samuel Crawford	39a	$35
1871	29-262	Twyman, Simon heirs	Samuel Crawford	dower	(Troyman)
1871	29-353	Shelton, Edmund Samuel Crawford dower			(Ellen)
1872	29-386	Jackson, William Samuel Crawford dower			$35 (Jane)
1872	29-434	James, Albert	Stephen Dillon		
1872	29-435	Twyman, Simon heirs	Stephen Dillon	lots 24/27$360	
1872	29-550	Burvender, Squire Stephen Dillon		(Maria widow Ambrose)	
1872	30-13	Gaunt, Barbara	John Dillon	10a (of Huron County, OH) $350	
1872	30-14	Wilson, Susan	John Dillon	10a (of Huron County, OH) $300	
1872	30-334	Toms, Priscilla &			
		Nancy Smith	Stephen Dillon	dower	
1874	32-574	Twyman, Simon heirs	sheriff	4/5a	$150(Troyman)
1875	33-346	Twyman, Horace	John Dillon	12 ½ a	(of St. Louis, MO) $400
1875	33-416	Twyman, Horace	John Dillon	1/8 a	(of St. Louis, MO)
1876	33-633	Woodfin, Henry	Winston Dobston	lot 29/Fry Lands	(Eliza – dau/ Jane Toms)

Figure A68 - The Three Twyman Women

Who were Jenny, Amanda, and Frances Ann and what happened to them?

As of 1868 trustee account Twyman Estate:

$11,760 spent to support Jenny, Amanda, and France Ann (Alburne)

Jenny was Amanda's mother. Amanda was consort of James Twyman and gave him two children. Francis Ann was Twyman's daughter whom he sent to boarding school in Philadelphia and allowed her to keep some of his accounts. These three women were to receive the lion's share of the Twyman Estate, but that never happened. In June of 1850 less than a year after James Twyman death, Frances Ann married in Chillicothe, Ohio to Thomas Alburne, then the women settled in Fairfield County, Ohio (near Lancaster).

A funny thing happened on the way to the reading of the will. James Twyman's relatives discovered Amanda was pregnant with another child by James. The Twyman brothers and sisters quickly started lawsuits and blocked transfer of property. The oldest brother, and administrator, probably suggested the women take the cash money and leave as quickly as possible.

Amanda's son, James Charles Twyman, was born in late 1849 in Virginia and was enumerated in his sister's household in Fairfield County in 1850 with both Amanda (Twiner -35) and Jenny (Jane Pain - 70). By 1860 both Jenny and Amanda (1852) were dead, and James C. was living with sister, but his name had changed from Twyman to Lepscum. He was apprenticed to a blacksmith in Floyd County, IN, became an inventor and died in Clinton County, Missouri in 1911. His death certificate named his parents.

Frances Ann's husband died before 1880. That year widow Frances Alburn was living on High Street in Columbus, OH. She died in 1886 and was buried in Green Lawn Cemetery. Her death certificate named her parents.

Appendix #7 - Churches and Ministers

(There is no proof for these early ministers except location and opportunity.)
Macedonia Church Minutes exist from 1884-1896. Many of the names are listed.

Date	Minister	Birth		Service period	listed business
(1808-1813)	John Bryant	@1785 VA s/Rosannah		1808-1841	farmer
(1808-1813)	Essex Harris	@1787 VA		1808-1850	m 2nd Eliz. Roberts
1820	William Reed	1800		1820-1855	m Nancy Bryant
1827	Jonathan Cradic	1815 VA (Ward 1827)		Tri-state area 1880+	minister
	Cradic = Craddick = Craddock = Crandolph – etc.				
1830	Jefferson Cradick	1800 (Ward)		1830-1833	
1835	Wm. Bryant	1815 VA s/John		1835- after 1884	
1840	Geo. W. Bryant	1817 VA s/John		1840-1912	
1845	Chas. W. Roberts	1819 VA (Ward)		1845- after 1884	
1849	Thos. Walker Fry	1810 (Twyman '37)		1849-1898	carpenter/minister
1850	Henry King	1816		1850-	
	W. P. Cradick	1835 s/Jefferson		1856-1884+	
	W.T. Smith	1849 (Twyman '37)		1875- after 1930	
	I.V. Bryant	1856 s/Wm.		1880- after 1930	
1856	Macedonia	Fayette Twp.		W. Bryant, J. Cradic, T. W. Fry, C.W. Roberts,	
		Lawrence Co. OH		W.P. Cradic (all manumitted)	
1857	Macedonia	Lawrence Co. OH		Wm. Bryant, J. Craddoc, T. W. Fry, W.P. Craddoc	

Macedonia – manumissions:

G. W. Bryant – son of John – grandson Rosanna Bryant
W. (William) Bryant – son of John - grandson Rosanna Bryant 1818
I.V. Bryant – son of William (above)
J. (Jefferson) & (his son) W. P Cradic – (Ward 1827) m Juda Bryant
C. W. Roberts - (Ward 1827) m Susanna Bryant
Thomas Walker Fry – Twyman Manumission 1849
W.T. Smith (Traveler) Twyman

Born from 2 manumissions
s/William Bryant & Martha Craddock
Macedonia member ordained at Macedonia
Regional minister KY, OH, WV
Noted educator, speaker, and author
Pastor at Huntington 1st Baptist 16 years.
WV Department of Arts, Culture & History

ISAAC VINTON BRYANT

Figure A69

1884 Church Minutes (Ministers listed as Elder or Brother in 'Macedonia Minutes')
A copy of "Macedonia Church Minutes" exists for 1884-1896.

S. Atwell	William Bryant	C. W. Roberts (secretary)
N. Barnett	J. J. Cradic	Esrel Roberts (financial clerk)
Geo. Bryant	T. W. Fry	W. T. Smith (secretary
I.V. Bryant	Philip Harris	(possibly more)

A Partial Church Membership List from the 1884 Church Minutes

Original members added additional marriages.

Arnold, Emily	Hall, Gev.	Roberts, A.C.
Atwell, Saml.	Hall, Henry	Roberts, Barton
Banks, Boston	Hanks, George	Roberts, C.W.
Barnett, N.	Harris, John	Roberts, Ersel
Bascom, Nelson	Harris, Levi	Roberts, Curt
Bennett, Moses	Harris, L.B.	Roberts, Lottie
Boggs, Andrew	Harris, Philip	Robinson, Belle
Boggs, Juda	Hill, Charley	Robinson, Hurbert
Botts, T.R.	Hill, Lizzie	Shelton, Aaron
Brassfield, John	Hill, Susan	Smith, Blanche
Brasfield, Martha	Hill, Will	Smith, Dick
Brook, Bent	Heath, George	Smith, Henry
Brooks, Moses	Hogg, Bent	Smith, V.T.
Brown, P.	Hogg, Moses	Smith, Wm.T.
Brown, R.	Holms, Fannie	Sturgeon, Thos.
Bryant, Albert	Hoston, C.	Toms, Daniel
Bryant, Ann	Howard, Mary	Toms, Edmund
Bryant, George, Jr.	Jackson, Henry	Toms, Henry
Bryant, George, Sr.	Jackson, William	Toms, Maria
Bryant, I.V.	James, Lawrence	Toms, Nancy
Bryant, Malissa	James, Sarah	Toms, Redmond
Bryant, Nancy	Johnson, (Elder)	Toms, W.E.
Bryant, P.A.	Jones, Gabe	Toney, Mary
Bryant, S.	Justice, Eli	Turner, Gerturde
Bryant, Wesley	Lane, Sarah	Vinson, I.V.
Bryant, William	Mayo, Jacob	Wagoner, Mickey
Burvender, Nieca	Mayo, Wes	Wellman, Jane
Claughton, Alice	McCormic, Jas.	Wellman, Millard
Cornute, Other	Mullin, Dug	Wray, George
Cornute, Vola	Mullin, Floyd	Wary, Mill
Cradic, J. J.	Mullin, Polley	
Dobson, Maggie	Mullin, Sarah	Several of the young
Dolby, Lily	Mullin, Scott	people were called for
Dolton, Nancy	Penn, David	attending 'Play Parties"
Fry, T.W.	Penn, Nely	for dancing, and for
	Polley, Minnie	playing the banjo.

Figure A70 – 1884 Macedonia Members

Information from the Providence Anti-slavery Baptist Association

PROVIDENCE ANTI-SLAVERY BAPTIST ASSOCIATION OF OHIO
Providence Association materials of the American Baptist - held by the Samuel Colgate Historical Library,
Colgate Rochester Divinity School, Rochester, NY. (Recently moved to North Carolina.)
(pg 802) – page number in Baptist research materials

1835

Churches	Location	Messengers
Providence	Milton Twp. Jackson Co. OH (near Wellston)	Thomas Parker, Francis Champlain, James Saddler
Mt. Zion	(Jackson County)	Sartin McCommis, John Cron, Peter Kingry
Chester	Meigs	Dea. Thomas Everton, Lewis Chase
Union (1819)	Washington Twp. Lawrence Co. Greenfield Twp. Gallia Co.	Elder James B. Stewart, William Stewart, Richard Stewart (POKE PATCH)
Paint Creek	Gallipolis, Gallia Co. OH	Elder Gabriel Hargo (Called the Blind Minister)
Mt. Pleasant (white)	Mason Twp. Lawrence Co. OH (2nd 775 X with Greasy Ridge)	Elder Jacob Ward, Elder Jesse Corn, Jeptha Massy, Silas Shewmate, Wm. Corn

Poke Patch was a free community of mixed settlers, including Black, Indian, Mulatto, and White persons.
The Union Church located in Lawrence also had families from Gallia and Jackson counties.

1856 – 22 Anniversary – **PROVIDENCE ANTI-SLAVERY ASSOCIATION** – of Regular Baptists
(pg) 806   Paint Creek Church, Gallipolis, Ohio * 21-24 August 1856

Church	Location	Messengers
Providence	not represented	
Union	Lawrence Co./Gallia Co.	R. Beverly, J. Coker, H. Liggans
Paint Creek	Gallipolis	H.M. Williams, J. Jones, J. W. Couzens, J.T. Berry, L. Holmes, Jr.
Macedonia	*Fayette Twp. Lawrence Co.*	*W. Bryant, J. Cradic, T. W. Fry, C.W. Roberts, W.P. Cradic*

William Bryant, Jonathan Cradic, Thos. Walker Fry, Charles W. Roberts, William Portrait Cradic.

Church	Location	Messengers
Bethel	Morgan Twp. Gallia Co.	Wm. C. James, J. Elison, J. Couzens, H. James, G. D. James
Zion	Jackson Co.	B. Jones, F. Bryant, R. Carter, R. Jones, J. Jones
Franklin	Jackson Co.	Kendel Lee
2nd Baptist	Columbus, OH	A. Lewis, T.N. Stewart, D. Jones, L. Scott
Sharon	Jackson Co.	D. Raglin, Wiley Dolby, S.P Newman, J.L. Smith and James L. Smith
Wilmington	Clinton Co. OH	Benjamin Jackson
New Hope	Springfield Twp. Gallia Co.	H. McDaniel, A. Bunch, A. Dabner
Shiloh	Portsmouth, OH	Wm. Cook, W. Dickerson
Lebanon	Warren Co. OH	B. Jackson
Calvin Center	Cass County, Michigan	William Stewart (Chain Lake Church)

 [Association resolved to have Union Meetings with each of the churches and recorded the locations.]

Many of the ministers and elders of 1856-57 came from families represented in either the
Macedonia Church or Union Church - compared with census records.

1857 - 23 Anniversary – **PROVIDENCE ANTI-SLAVERY ASSOCIATION** – of Regular Baptists
(pg 827)   New Hope Church, Springfield Twp. Gallia Co. OH * August 19-23, 1857

Providence	not represented	
Union	Lawrence Co.	Jno. J. Stewart, Wm. Chavous, R. Beverly
Paint Creek	Gallipolis	H. Williams, Jr., Jas. W. Couzens, Jos. Jones, A. Ward, Jr., O. Viney
Macedonia	*Lawrence Co. OH*	*Wm. Bryant, J. Craddoc, T. W. Fry, W.P. Craddoc*
Bethel	Morgan Twp. Gallia Co.	Wm. C. James, O. James, H. James, S. Jones, G. D. James and F. James
Zion	Jackson Co.	J. Jones, R. Jones, F. Bryant, T. Wingo
Franklin	Jackson Co.	Kendel Lee
2nd Baptist	Columbus, OH	J. Johnson, T.N. Stewart, J. Jones, J. Goens, A. Alestock (see below Cass Co. MI)
Sharon	Jackson Co.	J.L. Smith, James L. Smith, S. P. Newman, R. Raglin
Wilmington	Clinton Co. OH	B. Jackson
New Hope	Springfield Twp. Gallia Co.	R. Carter, H. McDonald, G. McDonald, A. Bunch, Wm. Viney
Shiloh	Portsmouth, OH	Wm. Cook, W. Dickerson
Calvin Center	Cass County, Michigan	William Stewart (Chain Lake Church)
Salem		Jos. Cousons, S. Ford, Sr., P. Gillmore, Thomas Ford, S. Ford, Jr.
Lebanon	Warren Co. OH	B. Jackson

Lawrence Co. Bryant, Craddoc, and Fry (all from manumissions)
Cass County, MI Halestock (married into the Sanders manumission)
Shiloh Church of Portsmouth – Pastor Jonathan Craddoc, (Ward Manumission) Wilson Dickerson, Wm. H. Cook
Officers & address: Moderator: Elder Wm. Stewart – Brownsville, Cass Co. MI, (raised in Poke Patch area)
Clerk: Eld. Henry Williams, Jr. Gallipolis, Missionary: Wm. C. James – Pine Grove, Gallia Co.

Missionaries Reports –

Elder William C. James
Traveled 1645 miles, preached 158 sermons, held
5 protracted meetings, 16 funerals, 8 Lord's Prayers,
26 baptisms, and organized one Church.

Visits made		funds received
Union	5	$10.61
Paint Creek	5	11.61
Macedonia	3	11.08
Zion	4	11.44
Bethel	5	11.28
Franklin	3	5.45
Sharon	4	13.88
New Hope	3	7.37
Wilmington	1	1.97
Shiloh	3	6.06
Salem	5	9.43
Received of 14 destitute places and friends		20.00
	Total	$120.18
Deductions for horse & expenses		69.64
	Balance	$50.54

Henry Williams, Jr.
Since August 1856 traveled 1233 miles,
preached 109 sermons, and assisted in
constituting one Church.

Visits made		funds received
Paint Creek	10	$ 6.51
Bethel	6	6.32
Zion	1	1.09
New Hope	9	5.24
Macedonia	1	2.05
Salem	1	.33
Received of friends		13.88
	Total	$35.42
	Expenses	15.17
	Balance	$20.25

Balance was due association---

Appendix #8 – Stewart and 'Clan' Problems

John M. Hall (Grandson of Richard M. Stewart's daughter Sarah – wrote a letter in the 1890s.)
Family history:
1) Edward Ned Stewart came from British - King William Island.
    1a) Only one King William Island in the world. It is north of Arctic Circle.
2)"His son" John Peterson Stewart was an Indian (Ocean) prince – Hindu or East Indian.
    2a) More likely – American Indian from King William Co. VA – NE Richmond.
    Between Pamunkey River & York River.
3)John Peterson Stewart - Arrived in Newport News, VA 1800.
    3a) not necessarily from overseas. Newport News founded in 1896!!
    Only all children reported born in Powhatan, Co. VA – 6 before 1800.
Ancestry claims:
Edward Ned Stewart (1721-1801) m Frances Dungey – (1707-1840) King William County, VA
    3) Maybe - puts the family in King William County.
    4) Ned is a nickname for Edward.
    5) None of the sons are named Ned or Edward in the next 3 generations, James – Richard.
    6) Frances (his wife) is supposed to live to 133!!!
    7)Edward Ned dies in Powhatan Co. VA 1801 – probably.

The next part is mostly correct – some proven
About the time Ned Stewart died, numerous slave revolts erupted across the Tidewater Region. Many slaves were captured and put to death, but the rebellions resulted in numerous strict laws which affected all people of color. The frightened white community saw little difference in the people. Life for free-born Blacks became quite difficult, and families began to move west.
    John Peterson Stewart was born in 1757 in King William County, VA – no proof
    Married 1st Dinah --about 1775-9 (from Sierra Leon Africa) – maybe -only proof age of 1st born (1780)
    Married 2nd Frances Dungey - 7 Jan 1801   recorded Powhatan Co. marriages
    All children are born in Powhatan Co. VA   maybe
    1810 Powhatan census has a John Stewart - household of 26 people – free non-white – plus 3 white
    By 1810 John Peterson Stewart was supposed to be in White Co. TN – did not leave until 1810 - census
    1817 death of John Peterson Stewart in White Co. TN - with will

The following children were all born in Powhatan Co., VA (west of Richmond on US 60)
    To 1st wife (Dinah ------- from Sierra Leon, Africa) possibly first 6 ch hers
        Ancestry ages wrong order   By tax lists – Thomas is #1, James B. #2
        Also, Thomas named exec. of will- James not –(ages guessed by census) - Tax list more accurate
    John P. Stewart was born in 1857 King Wm. Co. VA – died 1817 White Co. TN
    Children:
1780-1818 Thomas m Margaret Crowder both d White, TN   correct order (her father local TN official)
1783-1852 James B. m Francis Dungey   d Gallia, OH   minister
1785-1823 John m Polly Carter –   d Wyandot, OH   minister
1786-1821 Elisha m Lucy Creacy 1803   d White, TN
1792-1860 Elizabeth m Peter Coker   d Cass - 1st wife died - 2nd wife, Cass Co.
1798-1858 William (Rev.) m Mary Dungey d Cass   minister

    To 2nd wife Frances Dungy   All children listed in 1817 will – Susannah afterthought in will
1800-1885 Richard W. m Barbara Creacy   d Cass   minister
1801-1860 Susanna m Dungy   d Gallia age 50 in 1850 Gallia dies before 1860?
1802-1854 Littleberry m Mary Woods   d Gallia
1806-1846 Rebecca m James S. Bowen   d Gallia
1808-1870 Mariah m James Crandolph   d Gallia- b maybe 1810 (mother waiting for the birth to leave VA?)
All To Tennessee in 1810 – John Peterson Stewart d 1817 – White Co. TN (age @ 53)

Information proven by census and tax information

John Peterson & Frances Dungy Stewart - children ages 1810 who went to TN – (8 later to OH)

s – Thomas (30) stayed in Powhatan (Tax Lists) until 1816 – went to TN when father got sick –
Thomas d TN 1818

s – James B. (27) headed west on James River and Kanawha Turnpike (US 60) after 1813 and
was in Gallipolis, OH, by 1818 when his son John was born. James B. preached at the opening of
Union Church in 1819 and moved to Greenfield Township before 1830.

s- John (25) went to NW Ohio to convert the Indians – d 1823 in northern Ohio

s- Elisha 24, (m-Lucy Creasy - d1821 White Co. TN) (Lucy to Gallia Co. OH by 1830)

Other ch-Elizabeth 18, William 12, Susannah 11, Richard 10, Littleberry 8, Rebecca 4, Mariah 2.

The Stewart family was living in Powhattan County, VA, in 1810 when the Federal Census
enumerated the John P. Stewart household with 29 persons in the household. The group was
enumerated as three whites and 26 Free 'non-white,' perhaps they had already gathered for the trip
to Tennessee. Apparently, the family chose White County, TN, because the Crowder family from
Powhatan already lived and were county officials. Soon after their arrival, the oldest son Thomas
Stewart married Margaret Crowder.

White County, TN

The Stewart family was taxed with families Brown, Coker, Dungey, Goins, Harris, and Rickman.

All appeared on at least one White Co. Tax List: Tax information is not consistent.

John (P.) Stewart appeared on TN Tax Lists in 1811, 1812, 1813

Elisha Stewart (son) was listed in 1811 and 1813

William Stewart (son) was listed in 1826 – age 18.

(Cornelius Harris) -A relative who moved to Gallia was listed in 1823.)

From White County, TN, family to Gallia County, OH, to join son/brother James B. Stewart.

With the deaths of John P. in 1817, Thomas in 1818, Elisha in 1821, and James in 1823, the
oldest surviving son of the family was the second born, James B. Stewart. He had migrated with
his wife Frances Dungy to Ohio in 1818 instead of going to Tennessee. He was responsible for the
extended family, and by 1830 all had moved to Gallia County, where most settled in Greenfield
Township bordering Lawrence County.

Test   Jacob A. Lane, Clerk
White County Court.

      In the name of God Amen. I, John Stewart of the County of White
and State of Tennessee being sick and weakly in body but of sound mind
and perfect memory, do make and ordain this my last will and testament
in manner and form as follows viz: First, and in the first place, I give
my body to the dust from whence it came to be buried in decent Christian
burial at the discretion of my executors, and my soul to almighty god
who first gave it to me, and as touching my

P 79   worldly estate which it has pleased god to bless me with I dis-
pose of it the following manner. First I give and bequeath unto my be-
loved wife Francis Stewart, my plantation, my two servants Dafnay and
Randal my roan horse, my bay mare and my sorrel mare my stock of cattle
sheep and hogs, my waggon and farming tools together with all my household and kitchen furniture, during her natural life and further I will
that my stud horse my gray mare my bay colt and my brown filly be sole,
giving a suitable credit by taking bond and sufficient security and when
the money is collected I give and bequeath it to my children viz: Thomas
Stewart, James Stewart Elisha Stewart John Stewart Elisabeth Cocker,
William Stewart Richard Stewart Litterberry Stewart Rebekah Stewart and
Mariah Stewart, also my daughter Susanna Dangy to be equally divided
amongst each of them and such of them as is of age to take their part as
quick as it is collected and my executors to keep the balance in their
hands, as those which are under age rises to age they must give them their
part and I also will that at the decease of my wife that my servants be
continued with my children, and the one or ones that keep them pay the
rest their part of the value of said servants or else their part of the
yearly hire of them also the other property given to my wife at her death,
to be sold and the money divided among the above mentioned names equally.
In conformation this my last will and testament. I constitute my friends
Joseph Upchurch Thomas Stewart and Elisha Stewart my sole executors to
this my Last will and Testament.   In witness whereof I hereunto set my
hand and seal this twenty fifth day of March one thousand eight hundred
and seventeen

                                    His
                         John   X   Stewart (Seal)
                                   Mark

Figure A71 – John Stewart – Will 1817 – White County, TN

John Peterson Stewart died in 1817- TN and left a will, naming all children.   d 1817
Son Thomas is named executor – he died in 1818 in TN.   d 1818
Son Elisha also named executor – he died in 1821 in TN.   d 1821
Son John J.   died in 1823 NW Ohio.   d 1823
Sisters (or ½ sisters) Susannah married before 1817 to (William) Dungy

      Elizabeth married Peter Cocker in 1821.

Widow Frances Dungey Stewart remained in White Co. TN at least to 1826 tax.

Other family information claims (the first Frances Dungy – wife of John Peterson Stewart) was also mother to Richard Dungey who m Nancy Penn in Gallia Co. OH. He lived in White, TN, Gallia, OH, and Cass, MI near the extended family.

The six younger unmarried children moved to Gallia County, OH, by 1830.

They married in Gallia Co., and most moved again to Cass County, MI

Gallia County, Ohio Census all for Greenfield Township

1830	Name	household	1840	Name	household	1850	Name	household	
	Stewart, James B. –	8		Stewart, James B.	5		missionary – Ag. Census		(Rev.)
	Stewart, Littleberry –	5		Stewart, Littleberry	1		Gallipolis – river? d 1854		
	Stewart, Lucy (wid-Elisha)	9		Stewart, Francis (widow)	4 -----		w/Grandson – James M.		
	Stewart, Maria - un-mar	1-------	m James Crandoph		4		Crandolph, James	9	
	Stewart, Richard	8					Stewart, Richard	8 (Rev.)	
	Stewart, William	5					Stewart, William	2 (Rev.)	
	Dungee, Elizabeth	2		Dungey, William (?)	3		Dungy, Susannah (wid)	2	
	Dungee, Richard /w/Penn	8		Dungey, Richard	11		Dungey, Richard	7	
	Pleasants, Mathew (TN)	4		Stewart, Rachel (?)	11		Mathews, Pleasant	3	

Coker, Peter & Elizabeth in TN	most ch in Highland Co. OH	living w/son Toliver in KS

What happened to Littleberry Stewart? In 1840, aged 38 and unmarried, he was living in Gallipolis. In 1847 he may have married Mary Wood, but by 1854, he was dead. Was his death the reason the rest of the family moved? Stewarts were better educated than most, and they claimed land, although the farms were small. They were people of property and making a good living for the time and place. Why did everyone move?

United States Agriculture Census 1850 – Greenfield Township, Gallia County, Ohio.
Land owned by Iron Master Campbell who sold small lots to workers.

Bowen, James S.	25a	Stewart, John J.	24a	Stewart, William	60a	Stewart, Richard	60a
Dungey, William	25a	Stewart, Mary	30a	Stewart, Wm. A.	20a	Stewart, Richard M.	26a
Crandolph, James	20a	Dungey, Richard	66a	Stewart. James M.	20a	Stewart, Richard W.	12a

Figure A72 - Gallia County, OH – Land and People

An excellent repository of Stewart Family information is held by the Bonine Research Library, Cass County, MI, part of the Underground Railroad Society of Cass County – www.urscc.org

Appendix #9 – Freedom Trail
The Poke Patch Station of the Underground Railroad and its Conductors

Wilbur Siebert gathered the information for his book: *The Underground Railroad in Ohio* almost fifty years after events took place. Even then, few people were willing to provide information about the stations and conductors. Lawrence County trails began at the Ohio River near the early communities of Quakers Bottom and Burlington on the east side of the county. After 1850, trails lead north from the fledgling town of Ironton.

Reports given by Siebert show both Quakers Bottom (Proctorville) and Ironton had safe houses, hidden rooms, and numerous people looking for runaways. Abolitionists existed among the mostly New England Iron Masters and their wives. Methodist and Presbyterian ministers, their congregations, and Quaker families against slavery shared their expertise with runaways.

However, little information talks about the Burlington area, where a select group of young Black men served as ministers, worked on the river, and participated in other occupations that met the public. These men and their families also worked the Underground Railroad. The following information has been collected over many years and by many individuals.

The following Burlington information was given in the *Ironton Register* in 1890 by John G. Wilson s/Stephen Wilson – both lived near Macedonia Hill and supported Blacks.

Burlington
B-Bryant, G. W. (Macedonia minister)	W – Rev. Jacob Cumming
B-Bryant, William minister	W – Dr. Camillius Hall
B-Cradic, W. P. minister	W – Presbyterian Rev. Gamaliel Beamen
B-Lynch, Philip - whistler	W – Methodist Stephen Wilson
B-Johnson, Gabe-barber – both in Burlington and Ironton	

Quakers Bottom/Proctorville – East Lawrence County adjacent to Cabell County, VA. Begun in late 1790s.
B – Lewis Brooks   W- *H.E. Adams * C.M.Pease *Isaac Miller (Jesse Baldwin)   (Charles Wilgus)
    *J. Kimball   * A.S. Proctor*Judge Wes Reckard   (William Russell)
    * All signed an abolition amendment 28 Feb 1856 – *Ironton Register*

Ironton
numerous Iron Master abolitionists	Conductors
W- Campbell, John	B-Ditcher, James 'The Red Fox'
W- Kelly – wife & servants	B-Gabe Johnson – barber & porter
W- Peters, John	- Matilda Johnson – cook Clark Hotel
Poke Patch – major station (safe houses)	Leading conductors (ran the trails)
B-Holly, Benjamin	
B-Stewart Brothers and sisters (# = ch of John P. Stewart)	
Jacob & John (s/William)	B-Old man Crandolph -James m Mariah Stewart
James B. ch #2 – minister, 1st sermon at Union	B - Mathews, Pleasant – Susan
Isaac & Thomas (s/James B.)	B - all the Stewart sons
William (Union Baptist minister) (ch #6)	------ (Led family to Cass County.)

B-Coker, Peter m -Elizabeth Stewart (ch # 5) and their sons – Tolliver Coker
B-Chavis, Wm. m Francis Stewart (da/Richard ch #7)
B-Crandolph, James m to Mariah Stewart (ch #10)   B (Cratoff-Cradock) at Olive Furnace
W-Iron Master Stafford at Gallia Furnace   (later'Black' manager - James Stewart)
W-Gallia Methodist Church   B- Clawa, Jacob at Buckhorn Furnace
W-Seeley at Buckhorn Furnace

When the Civil War arrived, many of Lawrence County's Black sons joined the Union forces. Company H 5th United States Colored Infantry had sons and cousins of the Bryant siblings. William Bryant's sons: Geo. W. and James K., Geo. W., Sr.'s sons G.W, Jr., John W., and Philip: Nancy Bryant Reed's sons: John P. and William A., and Susanna Bryant Roberts' husband and son, Charles W. & W.D.

There was a Union recruiting office at Ironton, OH. Many joined because relatives joined. At least forty-five young Black men from Lawrence County served with Co. H. 5th USCI and other units during the Civil War. M = Macedonia

Bailey, Brown	Co H 5th USCI – KIA 29 Sep 1863	-M	Howard, Allen	Co C 88th USCI	
Bass, Peter	Co E 23rd OH Inf		Isley, Armstead	Co A 5th USCI d 22 Dec'65	
Boggs, Andrew	Co. I 18th OH Inf	-M	Jones, John R.	Co H 5th USCI	
Boggs, Wilson	Co H 5th USCI	-M	King, Charles	Co H 5th USCI	-M
Brassfield, John	Co H 5th USCI	-M	McKeels. Daniel	Co 17th USCI	
Brooks, W.F.	Co H 5th USCI		Payne, Americus	Co H 27th USCI d 5 Sep'64	
Bryant, Albert	Co 21th OH – d 17 Jun 1865	-M	Pogue, Wm. H.	Co B 4th USCI	
Bryant, Geo.W.	Co H 5th USCI - s/ Wm.	-M	Reed, John P.	Co H 5th USCI – bro.	-M
Bryant, G.W.	Co H 5th USCI - s/ GW	-M	Reed, Wm. A.	Co H 5th USCI – bro.	-M
Bryant, James K.	Co 22nd OH - s/Wm.	-M	Roberts, Wm. D.	Co H 5th USCI	-M
Bryant, John W.	Co H 5th USCI - s/GW	-M	Sheldon, Aaron	Co H 5th USCI	
Bryant, Philip A.	Co 18th OH - s/GW	-M	Smith, Benjamin	Co H 5th USCI	
Burvender, Mark	Co F 5th USCI - d 5 Oct 1864	-M	Smith, J. Rush	Co K 44th USCI	
Cornute, Clark	Co H 5th USCI	-M	Stephenson, Wm. S.	Co E 5th USCI	
Cornute, Tate	Co H 5th USCI	-M	Stewart, William	Co E 5th USCI	
Chisenhall, Wilk.	Co D 5th USCI	-M	Toms, Edmund	Co H 5th USCI	-M/B
Cradic, Robert	Co 27th OH	-M	Turley, John	Co 13th H Art	
Cradic, Wm. P.	Co 25th OH	-M	Turner, Reddon	Co H 5th USCI	-M
Crossland, Chas.	Co A 4th USCI		Walker, John	Co 14th KY Inf	
Evans, John	Co 27th USCI		Wyatt, Robert	Co H 27th USCI	
Evans, William	Co H 5th USCI		Wright, James	Co 27th USCI	-M
Finley, James	Co G 27th USCI – d Apr 1865				
Finley, Jefferson	Co B 227th USCI		Powell, Thos.	Co C 9th H Art	
Haman, Alex.	Co D 5th USCI		Roberts, C. W.	Co. H 5th USCI	-M
Hargo, Aaron	Co C 4th USCI – d 15 Mar 1865				
Harris, Adam	Co D 5th USCI		There were others.		
Harris, Levi R.	Co H 5th USCI – s/Essex	-M			
Hill, Lewis	Co E 5th USCI				

Figure A73 - Civil War Soldiers Lawrence County

Figure A74 - Macedonia Cemetery

Macedonia Freewill Cemetery – Early Member Burials   *Bryant family
                a = after b = before

Brassfield, John	1844-1902 – CW – Co H 5th USCI - s/Robert & Morning Craddock Brassfield
Brassfield, Mourning	1824-1859 m/Robert – (a Ward) dau/Lewis & Winnie Craddock
Brassfield, Robert	1798-1877 m/Mourning Craddock
*Bryant, Cory Ann	1819-1876 m/Geo.W. Bryant – (a Ward) dau/Lewis & Winnie Craddock
*Bryant, Geo. W.	1817-1912 m Cory Ann Craddock - minister
*Bryant, John - minister	1788-a1844 m Susan--- s/Rosanna Bryant
*Bryant, John W.	1844-a1910 s/Geo. W. – CW- Co H 5th USCI (1910 cook in Ironton)
*Bryant, Lovenia	1815-1840 m Wm. Bryant 1st wife- daug/Bentley – d childbirth/Nancy
*Bryant, Lavinia	1844----- m John W. Bryant – dau/Randolph
*Bryant, Philip *Albert*	1841-1901 s/Geo. W. Bryant – CW 18th OH
*Bryant, Rosanna	(1776)-1833 – will - original settler -mother of John
Cradic, Robert	1829-1878 s/Lewis & Winnie Craddock
Cradic, Winnie	1776-1871 (a Ward) m Lewis Craddock
*Harris, Essex -minister	1797-b1854 deed m Elizabeth Roberts (a Ward) dau/Pleasant & Hannah Roberts
Harris, P. N.	1841-1913 s/Timothy & Neverta Roberts Harris
Johnson, Bellfield	1827-1916 b NC m Mary Reed, sister to John Reed
*Johnson, Mary	1834-1871 Reed m Bellfield Johnson dau/Wm. & Nancy Bryant Reed
Johnson, Matilda	1795-1871 (a Ward) w/Ben. Sr. mother to Gabe (died in Scioto Co. bur. Ironton)
*Landcroft, Sarah J.	1825-1910 youngest ch/John & Susan Bryant
*Reed, John P.	1843-1872 – CW Co H 5th USCI s/Wm. & Nancy Bryant Reed
*Reed, Nancy	1810-1870 m William Reed – dau/John & Susan Bryant
*Reed, William	1795-a1860 m Nancy Bryant
*Roberts, Charles W.	1821-a1884 church- m Susanna Bryant s/Pl. & Han. Roberts (Ward) minister Co H 5th USCI
*Robert, Pleasant	1789-a1881 (a Ward) w/Hannah – widow by 1828 – 2nd m Sarah Bryant
*Roberts, Sarah	1804-a1881 m Pleasant Roberts - 2nd wife dau/Rosanna Bryant
*Roberts, Susan	1819-1886 m Chas. W. Roberts dau/John & Susan Bryant
*Roberts, William D.	1841- a1880 s/C.W. & Susanna Co H 5th USCI
Shelton, Ellen	1844-1878 Ellen Toms (a Twyman) dau/John & Maria Toms - m Edmund Shelton
Shelton, Edmund	-------1872 m Ellen Toms

Why Cass County, Michigan?

Cass County, MI, is located just across the state line from Elkhart, IN. It had a group of Quaker settlers, but it was not very close to the Canadian crossing point. Why did so many Blacks head for that section of Michigan? Possibly because of an event that happened in 1847. Cass County made national news and was partially responsible for the passage of the Fugitive Slave Law of 1850.

The event was termed 'THE KENTUCKY RAID.' A group of slaves managed to escape from north central Kentucky, just south of Cincinnati, around Easter in 1847. After about three weeks of hard travel, the group arrived in Cass County and took jobs on the numerous Quaker farms in the area. The Kentucky slaveholders who had lost slaves sent a spy to locate the runaways, and by late summer, the location of every escaped slave was known. With this information, the slave owners went North to get their property. Suddenly, the slaveholders appeared near Vandalia and proceeded to capture the fugitives.

The local population turned out in force to stop the raid, but before the violence occurred, all parties agreed to appear in court. The local judge refused to hear the case, and a neighboring official (a staunch abolitionist) agreed to sit on the bench in a few days. While waiting for the Judge, all parties were taken to the local jail. A funny thing happened, the lock on the Black cells would not close, and all the Blacks slipped out during the night and made their way to Canada.

The Court, led by local abolitionists, ruled against the Kentuckians because they did not carry proof of ownership with them. After getting that information and appealing, the Judge found a few other problems besides the slaves being free in Canada. The case made national headlines. Everyone who heard about the Kentucky Raid knew Cass County was a safe place for Blacks to settle.

Several other events connected the Tri-state area of this study with Cass County. In 1849, Sampson Sanders, from Cabell County, VA/VW across the Ohio River from Lawrence County, manumitted all his slaves and sent them to Cass County, MI. One of those freed slaves, Calvin Sanders, decided to return to Lawrence County in 1850. After finding work at the Iron Furnaces, he spent the rest of his life in Lawrence while telling other workers Cass County was safe.

In the early 1850s, railroads were built in many parts of Ohio, and some of the first served the Iron Region of Lawrence County. It was soon possible to take trains to Fort Wayne, IN, and points north. About this time, Reverend William Stewart of Union Baptist Church made one of many trips to Cass County. By 1856 he was preaching in Union Church and attending Association meetings in Lawrence County, OH, while accepting members into Chain Lake Baptist Church in Cass County, where he claimed to live. Records are unclear about which Stewart's relative was the first to settle in Cass County, but he certainly told the rest of the family it would be a good place to live.

The precarious state of the UGRR in Lawrence/Gallia caused by the new Fugitive Slave Law of 1850 probably convinced the many members of the Stewart 'Clan' that it was time to seek a safer place to live. That new law created professional 'slave catchers' who did not bother to determine if a person was born free, nor did they need any reason to declare a dark-skinned person an escaped slave.

Gallia/Lawrence Settlers to Cass County, MI

Minister Richard Stewart (brother to Elder James B. Stewart) moved his wife Barbara Crecy Stewart and several married children, first to Logan Co., OH, then to Cass County, MI, about 1858. He was following his nephew, Minister William Stewart (son of James B.), who had moved to Cass County by 1856 but continued preaching in Lawrence County, OH, at the Union Baptist Church. William traveled to Cass Co., MI, to accept members to Chain Lake Church in Calvin Township, who arrived from Poke Patch and the Gallia Co. area.

Interrelated families: Stewart m Chavous, Coker, Creacy Dungey, Harris, Hughes, Mathews, Rickman, etc. Many of these families lived in White Co., TN, and Powhatan Co., VA, first.

NOTE: MACEDONIA WAS THE FIRST BLACK BAPTIST CHURCH IN OHIO, MEMBERS OF THAT CHURCH AND UNION CHURCH MOVED TO CASS COUNTY, MICHIGAN, WHERE THE FIRST BLACK BAPTIST CHURCH IN MICHIGAN WAS ESTABLISHED.

Lawrence Co. OH – Washington /Decatur Twps.
Gallia County OH – Greenfield Twp.

Cass Co. MI – Calvin Twp. – Penn Twp.
– Pokagon Twp. - Porter

1850 Census- Lawrence or Gallia	Law. Co./Gallia – OH Township	Cass Co. MI 1860 Census – Cass
Artis, George (Chaves home) w/Ellen	#2117 Greenfield	'60 Calvin Twp. Non-population
Artiss, Jane	?in Calvin	#628 Calvin Twp.
Artis, William w/R.E.		#655 Calvin Twp.
Beverly, Reuben, w/Mary	#93 Washington Twp.	#747 Calvin Twp.
Brown, D.	#82 Washington Twp.	#1778 Porter Twp.
Brown, Henry (Jesse's home) w/Martha	#2198 Greenfield Twp.	#714 Calvin '80 Calvin #172
Brown, John -w/Louisa J.	#2188 Greenfield Twp.	#788 Calvin Twp. Louisa d @'60
Brown, Richard-w/Martha	#2195 Greenfield Twp.	#714 Pokagon Twp.
Calaway, Cal w/May	#163 Decatur Twp.	1880 Calvin Twp.
Chavis, Isham, w/Agnes (57&54)	#2105 Greenfield Twp.	(died?)
Chavous, Wm. w/Frances Stewart(R&B)	#88 Washington Twp.	#702 Calvin Twp.

Coker, Elisha w/Susanna Harris (s/Peter)*	#2187 Greenfield Twp.	#736 Calvin Twp.- Chain Lake
Coker, Elizabeth Stewart (mother)	1850 Highland Co. OH	1860 Sub. Index Calvin Twp.
Coker, James w/Delilah Harris (s/Peter)	#2192 Greenfield Twp.	#774 Calvin Twp.
Coker, John w/Mary Richman (s/Peter)	#2191 Greenfield Twp.	#775 Calvin Twp.
Coker, Michael w/Sarah Hugh (s/Peter)	#2183 Greenfield Twp.	#729-'60 Calvin Twp. Non-pop
Coker, Thomas w/Agnes Newman	#2199 Greenfield Twp.	#114 Greenfield Twp.
Coker, William w/Deliah		#732 Calvin Twp.
Dungy, A. w/C.		#777 Calvin Twp.
Dungay, John R.		#715 Calvin Twp
Dunge/Dunga, Richard w/Nancy Penn	#2204 Greenfield Twp.	'60 Gallia, '70 #289 Calvin Twp
Dungy, Susanna (50-VA) wid & s/Wm.	#2215 Greenfield Twp.	1880 Wm. Calvin Twp.
Dungey, William,(Sr.-Buck) w/Lucinda	#2185 Greenfield Twp.	#746 Calvin Twp.
Dungey, William, Jr. w/Martha Hughes	#2184 Greenfield Twp.	#742 Calvin Twp.
Hall, Sarah Stewart (daug./Richard)	#2219 Greenfield Twp.	#229 Calvin Twp. (w/bro. J.M.R.)
Hawks, Samuel w/Matilda		#737 Calvin Twp.
Hughs, Olmstead/Armstead	#2182 Greenfield Twp.	#710 Calvin Twp.
Mathews, Esther A.	#2217 Greenfield Twp.	
Mathews, Henry	only non-population	#781 Calvin Twp.
Mathews, James w/R.	"	#660 Calvin Twp.
Mathews, James w/Susan	"	#814 Calvin Twp.
Mathews, John w/Martha	#2186 Greenfield Twp.	#814 Calvin Twp.
Mathews, William w/Phebe J.		#722 Calvin Twp.
Mathews, Pleasant & w/Susannah	#2200 Greenfield Twp.	Chain Lake Cemetery
Rickman, Uriah w/Sarah Ann Dungey	#2209 Greenfield Twp.	#713 Calvin Twp. (Uriah d 1858)
Scott, William w/Sarah	#114 Decatur Twp.	#765 Calvin Twp.
Seaton, William	#2218 Greenfield Twp.	Chain Lake Cemetery
Stewart, B. W. w/Mary		#655 Calvin Twp.
Stewart, James M. w/Mary J. Stewart	#2207 Greenfield Twp.	#778 Calvin Twp.
*Stewart, John J. w/Eliza Ann Harris	#2208 Greenfield Twp.	#773 Calvin - Chain Lake Cem.
Stewart, J.M.R. w/F.J. (s/Richard)	#2219 Greenfield Twp.	#229 Calvin Twp.
Stewart, Isaac Perry w/Marinda Dungey	-- (s/James B.) --	#743 Calvin Twp – Chain Lake
Stewart, Littleberry w/Martha?Wood)	Gallia 1840 (Chain Lake)	'60 Calvin Twp. Non-population
Stewart, Mary (33-OH)	#2193 Greenfield Twp.	
*Stewart, Richard - w/Barbara Creasy	#2219 Greenfield Twp.	#351 Penn Twp. -Chain Lake Cem.
Stewart, Richard M. w/Lucinda Mathews	#2216 Greenfield Twp.	Chain Lake Cemetery
Stewart. Richard W. w/Nancy Dungy	#2190 Greenfield Twp	'70 Calvin Twp. – Chain Lake
Stewart, Thomas w/Nancy Rickman	-- (s/James B.)?	#770 Calvin Twp. (also b TN)
Stewart, Wm. A. w/Amanda. Mathews	#2201 Greenfield Twp.	Chain Lake Cemetery
Stewart, William w/Mary Dungey	#2203 Greenfield Twp. Minister	'70 & '80 Mary with Richard W.
Baptist Assoc. shows in both places	Wm. preaching Cass '56, '57	d 1882 Calvin (a son)

Peter Coker m/Elizabeth Stewart (da/John P. & Francis Dungey Stewart – bro. Richd., Wm., Lit.)

*Sons of John Peterson Stewart & Frances Dungy of Powhatan Co.VA/White Co.TN/Gallia Co. OH

****

Note: Macedonia Church at Burlington, Ohio, in Lawrence County, the first Black Baptist Church west of the Appalachian Mountains, was meeting by 1807-1813. Union Baptist Church was organized in 1819 and joined Macedonia Church to form the first Providence Association of the Anti-slavery Missionary Baptist Church. In 1834 the Association was renamed the Providence Regular Missionary Baptist Church Association.

Between 1838 and 1853, the first Black Baptist Church in Michigan was organized at the Chain Lake Church in Calvin Township, Cass County, MI. About 1855, many families associated with the Union Church of Lawrence and Gallia counties of southern Ohio began moving to Cass County, Michigan. Some of the organizers of Chain Lake

Church were named as families from Lawrence and Gallia counties Ohio, and many are buried at Chain Lake Cemetery.

Lawrence County, OH, was the Ohio River crossing for most of these families. Their first contacts between 1820 and 1850 were often members of the Macedonia Church. Those church members either settled the families around Burlington or sent them north to other church members with the Union Church at the northern edge of Lawrence County. If the settlers did not remain around Union Church in the Poke Patch community, they traveled further north through several counties in central Ohio. Highland County near Hillsboro had an enthusiastic community with members from the Ward manumission and members of the Stewart/Cocker families of the Poke Patch area. The trip to freedom continued to Cass County, MI, and Canada, with many stops on the way.

Figure A75 – Civil War Soldiers Michigan

CIVIL WAR SOLIDERS 102nd MI with Lawrence/Gallia Connections
*sons of Richard & Barbary Creasy Stewart

Co B	Co B		Co C
Brown, John	Dungie, John	*Stewart, James M.	Artis, George
Brown, Stuart	Seaton, Joseph	*Stewart, John J.	Calloway, Creed
Coker, James	*Stewart, Geo. W.	Stewart, John T.	Stewart, John E.
Coker, Michael	d 20 Nov 1863	*Stewart, Littleberry	*Stewart, Richd. M.
			d 7 Jan 1865

Chain Lake Cemetery – Cass County, Michigan
Connection to Lawrence County, Ohio or Cabell County, West Virginia

GCOH = Gallia Co. OH 1850
PWGC = Powhatan Co. VA, White Co. TN, Gallia Co. OH, Cass Co. MI
CCWV = Cabell Co. WV 1849 manumission

Brown, Henry – 1835 ---- GCOH -#2198 s/Jesse
Coker, John C.- 1812-1897 - GCOH #2191 – (P)WGC
     w/Mary (Richman) 1810- (her father Uriah died in 1858 in Calvin (?) Chain Lake. #2209 GCOH)
Dungey, Nancy w/Richard – 1800---   GCOH #2204
     h/Richard 1795—
Halestock, Eli – (b 1848 Cabell) CCWV s/Alex & Peggy Sanders Halestock
     Elisha (probably sis Eliza b 1850)
     Elizabeth (sis 1854)
Mathews, Pleasants 1807-1856 – GCOH #2200
     w/Susannah _________ 1816—
Radford, John 1798-1889 – m/Cynthia Sanders CCWV
     Cynthia should be there- b 1812 still living 1880 Cass (Porter Twp name Radd)
Sanders, Adre =Ada b1763 VA d 1850 Cass CCWV
Sanders, Arthur -s/Calvin CCWV
Sanders, Carrie – da/Calvin CCWV
Sanders, Calvin – CCWV s/Levi & Jane
Sanders, Daniel – 1809-1953 CCWV s/Zebedee
Sanders, Elihu – CCWV s/Levi & Jane
Sanders, Gertrude (Brown) - CCWV w/Calvin
Sanders, Jacob B. -1817-1855 CCWV s/Solomon
Sanders, Jane – 1825-1870 CCWV da/Charlotte – w/Levi

Sanders, Laura – 1847-1921 CCWV w/Elijah
Sanders, Levi – 1825-1879 CCWV m/Jane – s/Solomon
Sanders, Martha – 1858-1878 da/Montique CCWV
Sanders, Peter - 1821 aft 1880 CCWV
Sanders, Phyllis - 1804-1859 CCWV 1st w/Solomon, Sr.
Sanders, Rolley B. - s/Jason-s/Solomon CCWV
Sanders, Sebede = Zebedee 1762-1850 CCWV
Sanders, Solomon - 1773-1863 CCWV
Sanders, Woodford - 1839-1887 CCWV s/Solomon
Seaton, William – 1834 ----- GCOH #2218 s/Gilbert & Matilda
Stewart, Amanda M.________ w/ Wm. A. GCOH #2201
Stewart, Barbara (Creasy) – 1800-1875 w/Richard W. PWGC
Stewart, Elizabeth (Harris) 1844 ---- w/John
Stewart, G. W. 1837--   s/Richard GCOH 2219 or 1842 s/ Richard W. GCOH 2190
Stewart, Isaac (Perry) 1821-1894 (p)WGC (Gallia 1840)
Stewart, James M.   1828--- s/Richard GCOH #2219
Stewart, John E. (probably) 1830-1861 s/Richard GCOH #2219
Stewart, John J. -1845-1864 s/John J. GCOH #2208
Stewart, John J. – 1818-1892 GCOH #2208 -----------ADD
Stewart, Marinda (Dungey) w/Isaac Perry – 1820-1877
Stewart, Martha _____   w/Little Berry (Gallia 1840) - PWGC
Stewart, Mary (Dungey) w/William -1795-1882 -PWGC
Stewart, Richard M.-1833- 1865 GCOH #2216 (Civil War)
Stewart, R. W. (Richard W.) 1818-1884 PWGC (GCOH #2190) w/Barbara

Bibliography

African Americans in Southern Ohio – www.anglefire.com

American Baptist Collection, "African-American Baptist Annual Reports: Ohio," "Regular Baptist Churches of Color: 1837." Samuel Colgate Historical Collection. American Baptist Historical Society: www.ABHSarchives.org

Atlas of Lawrence County, Ohio. (Hardesty 1882 – Lake 1887). Reproduction - Lawrence County, Ohio. Historical Society, 1985. (Hardesty Personal History Department.) (Lake – Township Maps.)

Boase, Paul H. "Slavery and the Ohio Circuit Rider." Ohio History Quarterly LXIV 1955: pp195-205.

Bonine Research Library: "The Stewart Family Papers." Vandalia, Michigan. www.urscc,org

Bossard Memorial Library, Gallipolis, Ohio: Repository of James Sands Articles.

Chain Lake Cemetery, Calvin Township, Cass County, Michigan. Members contributions. www.cassmichigangen@yahoo.com

Fain, Cicero M., III: *Black Huntington – An Appalachian Story.* University of Illinois, 2019.

Federal Census of Agriculture of the United States 1850 & 1860, Gallia & Lawrence Counties, OH.

Federal Census of Population of the United States 1820 through 1900 – Gallia, Jackson, and Lawrence Counties, Ohio, 1850 and 1860 – Cass County, Michigan, 1820 and 1830 – White County, Tennessee.

Ferguson, Thomas E.: *Ohio Lands, A Short History.* Ohio Auditor of State. Columbus, OH, 1987.

Gallia County, OH, Deeds Vol. 1 – 6 1803-1819. Family Search: film 009700695.

Gallia County, OH. Marriages 1803-1825. Bossard Memorial Library.

Gallia County Historical Society: "Index to Early Gallia County Marriages."

Griffith, Alva H. *Register of Free Negroes* (Ward will - Pittsylvania County, VA). Heritage Books, 2007.

Hayes, John – personal interview – 17 Apr 2022 – the family lived at Getaway 1830-2022.

Ingles, Wayne B., *Symmes Creek.* Franklin Printing Co., Zanesville, OH: 1967. – Roads.

Iron Furnaces – www.oldindustry.org/OH_HTML/OH/_Buckeye.html - www.oldeforester.com

Jones, Dennis R.: *Gallia County, Ohio Residents 1800-1825.* "Chattel Lists 1812-1818, Land Tax Lists 1806-1811, Wolf & Panther Scalp Lists 1806-1816, 1800 & 1820 Census. Gallia County Genealogical Society, 1997.

Keels, Lee. Pictures and personal information about Union Baptist Church. Personal Interview June 2021.

Kouns, Sharon: *Folklore and More – Lawrence County, OH.* 2020.

Ironton Register/Lawrence County history – http://lawrencecountyohio.com

Lawrence County, OH. Deeds 1818 – 1880. Recorder's online site: www.lawrencecountyohrecorder.org

Madison Co. VA - Twyman will and other court documents, Madison, VA. Court House.

Miller, Jr. Warren E. *North Carolina's Free People of Color 1715-1885*: LSU: 2020.

Ohio Historical Society: Special Enumeration of Negroes, 1863. Columbus, OH.

Ohio Memories: www.ohiomemory.org/ditital/collection/siebert/search

150 Anniversary Program of the Providence Association of the Missionary Regular Baptist Church. (From the Collection of Wilma Fox.) – (also held by Gallia County Historical Society.)

Pratt, Edward – personal interview 2 Apr 2022 – family residents of Getaway area 1830 -2022.

Sands, James. See newspaper articles below.

Warfield, Reverend B., Jr., *History of Chain Lake Baptist Church-1838-1948.* Printed: Chain Lake Church.

Washington, Booker T. *Two Generations under Freedom.* Outlook Magazine: Vol. 73 #6-pp293-306. 7 Feb 1903 NY. (Weekly 1870-1953)

White County, TN: Wills, Probate, Inventory, and Settlement. Sparta, TN. 1810 – 1826.

www.freeafricanamericans.com

www.urscc.org Bonine, Mary Ann: "Note Books." Bonine Research Library, Vandalia, Michigan

www.urscc.org Underground Railroad Society of Cass County (Michigan)

Cassopolis Vigilant – history and information about Cass County, Michigan: Cassopolis, MI
        Sanders' manumission, Stewart Family, Chain Lake Church
Cincinnati Commercial -Cincinnati, OH – newspaper
        17 Jan 1870 – "A Story About Iron Furnaces."
Dowagiac Daily News: Underground railroad stories. Dowagiac, Michigan.
Gallipolis Tribune (see Sunday Times Sentinel)
Herald-Advertiser – Huntington, WV – Sunday newspaper
        7 Jul 1929 – " 'Underground Railway' in Quaker Bottom was Active in Slavery Era," R. C.
Hall
        2 Sep 1934 – "Mount Pisgah Church is Proctorville Landmark," R.C. Hall
        27 Feb 1938 – "One Time Slave Who Made Good," R. C. Hall
        24 Jul 1938 –"Getaway Ohio Possesses an Odd History" R.C. Hall
Ironton Democrat – Ironton, OH - newspaper
        11 Nov 1875 - "Some History of the Burlington Academy" – Obituary – Rev. G.C. Beaman
Ironton Journal - Ironton, OH - newspaper
        19 Jul 1871 – Death of Mrs. Matilda Johnson (manumitted Ward- mother of Gabe)
Ironton Register - Ironton, OH – newspaper
        19 Feb 1857 – "Oak Ridge Furnace."
        21 Mar 1863 – "Colored People in Union Township: Rome Township: Burlington."
         1 Jun 1865 – "Iron Furnaces."
        20 Aug 1868 – "Macedonia Association."
        22 Feb 1872 – James Ditcher, a successful underground conductor' married
        31 Oct 1878 – "An Underground Railroad Conductor Interviewed" – James Ditcher
         9 Apr 1886 – Mrs. Lynch – a Black Citizen obituary (Rosetta Bryant m Phil Lynch 1835)
        18 Aug 1887 – Abner Johnson – Obituary (brother to 'Gabe') Ward - manumitted 1827
         8 Sep 1887 - "Talk with Charles Wilgus - How they lived in those days." no author.
        28 Feb 1888 – Jonathan Cradic age 72 (manumitted Ward s/Lewis & Winnie Craddock) minister
         1 Jun 1888 - Philip Lynch obituary (b 1812 - manumitted Ward – UGRR conductor)
        21 Jun 1888 -" Origin of Local names" no author
        28 Jun 1888 - James Ditcher – Obituary (GAR) b 1823
        11 Oct 1888 – Abner Holt – Obituary – manumitted 1856
        21 Nov 1889 – "Dedication of New Church at Macedonia Hill."
        22 Mar 1894 – Calvin Sanders – Obituary (Cabell Co. Sanders to Cass Co. MI back to Law. Co.)
        11 Jul 1895 – "Reminiscence of Burlington, Events, and Persons at the County's former Capital."
         6 Aug 1895 – "General Muster, Hotel Incidents & c."
        15 Aug 1895 – "Some Reminiscence" – H. Imes, Imes, IA
        12 Sep 1895 – "The Circus and Incidents thereof" – John G. Wilson (s/Stephen Wilson)
         5 Mar 1896 – "Old Times – The Exodus of the 37 Blacks from VA to Burlington in 1849."
        21 May 1896 – "Who Killed Andrew Boggs of Burlington, Ohio" by John. G. Wilson
        27 Aug 1896 – obituary Ed Harris - Black worked at Belfont Furnace.
        12 Nov 1896 - "Slave Days" (Garland manumission- 1852) – Obituary - Lewis Brooks, Sr.
        20 Jul 1899 – Gabriel Johnson – Obituary – manumitted 1827
        13 Feb 1902 – Lavina Ditcher – Obituary – (wife of James Ditcher)
Jackson Standard – Jackson, OH - newspaper
        14 Mar 1867 & 8 Aug 1878 "Old Baptist Association," by editor Davis Mackley.
        Ragland Manumission
Scioto Gazette - Chillicothe, OH - newspaper
        1810 - Reward. Ben 17 - TW brand on the cheek. Return to Thomas Ward, Cabell Co. VA.
Scott, Christian: "Jefferson Scott- A slave who walked from North Carolina to Ohio and Freedom,"

Gallia County Historical Society: Vol. 17, No.1, page 1, Spring 1992.
Stewart, Roma Jones: The Migration of a Free People – Cass County's Black Settlers from North
    Carolina." *Michigan History*, Jan./Feb. 1987, pp. 34-38.
Sunday Times Sentinel – Gallipolis, OH – newspaper – (Gallipolis Tribune)
    3 Feb 1985 – "Poke Patch on Gallia route for runaway slaves in '40s" – James Sands
    26 Feb 1989 – "A Black Pioneer" – James Sands
    26 Feb 1995 – Underground railroad tracked through Gallia County" – James Sands
    9 Feb 1997 – "The Road to Freedom" – James Sands
    23 Feb 1997 – "The Important Role of Gallia Furnace in the Underground Railroad" – Jas. Sands
    20 Nov 1997 – "Poke Patch underground railroad station; slaveowners hired spies
        to stop runaways". James Sands
Wayne County News – Wayne County, WV – 'Out of the Past' by Byron T. Morris
    "25 Nov 1835 - Lucy – manumitted by Burwell Spurlock"

Index

About the Author

➢ Born during WWII and raised in the Appalachian region of America.

➢ Living in Ohio near the Ohio River.

➢ Educated at Marshall University with an AB in Education and a MS in Geography.

➢ A teacher with experience from kindergarten music to college geography.

➢ A historical geographer who has compiled and written 50 regional information books.

➢ A creator of numerous informational maps.

➢ A speaker at state, regional and national conferences on Genealogy.

➢ An author of a six volume historical trails series about America's migration trails.

➢ An author of *Cabell County's Empire of Freedom - The Manumission of Sampson Sanders' Slaves*

➢ A contributor and instructor for the Marshall University Dr. Carter G. Woodson Lyceum and Institute of Black History